MONEY MANAGEMENT

M. HERBERT FREEMAN, Ph.D.
Professor Emeritus of Business
Montclair State College

DAVID K. GRAF, Ph.D.
Northern Illinois University

Under the general editorship of
LEONARD B. KRUK
formerly with Montclair State College

MONEY MANAGEMENT

A Guide to Saving, Spending, and Investing

BOBBS-MERRILL EDUCATIONAL PUBLISHING · Indianapolis

The Bobbs-Merrill Company, Inc.
4300 West 62nd Street
Indianapolis, Indiana 46268

First Edition
Second Printing 1981
Interior Design by Sally Lifland
Cover Design by Richard Listenberger

Library of Congress Cataloging in Publication Data

Freeman, Max Herbert, 1907–
    Money Management

    Includes index.
    1. Finance, Personal.   I. Graf, David, joint
author.
II. Title.
HG179.F73   332.024   80–11335
ISBN 0–672–97181–X

CONTENTS

PREFACE

Managing money can become more of an art and less of a juggling act with the important commodity of information. Inflation, changes in family patterns, and the growing role of women in the work force have all contributed to a new interest in personal finance. *Money Management* was written to guide interested consumers to more efficient personal financial planning. With one eye on the marketplace and the other on the economy, the authors have compiled a text that can serve as a plan of action when taken as a whole or as an individual topic guide when taken chapter by chapter.

Chapter 1 introduces the budget, and the following chapters add depth to the budgeting categories. Chapter 9 covers all basic forms of insurance except auto insurance, which is included in the transportation chapter, and homeowner's insurance, which is discussed in the housing chapter. A topic new to the personal finance/consumer economics text —consumer complaints—is dealt with in considerable detail in Chapter 12, which explores both third-party agencies and the legal system. Taxation, the summary of the calendar year, also forms the capstone for *Money Management*. Two optional chapters at the end of the text—one on basic economic understandings and one on the now critical subject of inflation —provide a conceptual framework for those interested in economic theory.

Each of the chapters is followed by questions—some open ended some based directly on the book. Our thanks go to Les Dlabay for developing the provocative personal experience projects also found at the end of each chapter.

M.H.F.
D.G.

1

MANAGING
MONEY

· *UNDERSTANDING THE ECONOMIC PICTURE*
· *DRAWING UP A BUDGET*
· *ESTIMATING NET WORTH*
· *WRITING A WILL*

Individuals have different values, wants, needs, goals, and even backgrounds to consider when planning the financial management of their personal affairs. However, a knowledge of the experiences of others and an awareness of economic trends can be most helpful in the development of an individual program. It is in this spirit that this chapter considers where we as consumers currently stand and what tools are available to help us in managing our financial responsibilities.

THE ECONOMIC PICTURE

The life of the American consumer has been undergoing some dramatic changes since the early 1960s. A few fundamental economic and social developments have radically altered consumer needs, and both consumers and the marketplace are currently in the process of adjusting to these new realities.

The biggest problem plaguing most consumers is inflation, which is now eating up most salary increases. For example, in 1978 a $5,000 raise for an individual earning $50,000 actually resulted in a real wage decrease when increases in Social Security, income taxes, and cost of living were taken into consideration.

Prices and wages are not the only victims of inflation—the value of savings and retirement plans is also in jeopardy, for most traditional types of investments, such as savings, savings bonds, and certificates of deposit, earn at or below the 6-percent inflation level after income tax is taken into account. It is no wonder, therefore, that inflation is called a hidden tax.

A second difficult problem faced by consumers is that of increased medical costs. According to *Business Week,* between 1950 and 1977,

- hospital charges skyrocketed from $3.7 billion to $65.6 billion
- doctors' fees leaped from $2.7 billion to $32.2 billion
- total expenses for health soared from $12 billion to $162.6 billion, a figure that is expected to double by 1983
- total health costs as a percent of GNP were nearly double the 4.5-percent rate of 1950.

With current rates of growth, health care costs could approach 10 percent of GNP by 1983.[1]

A third problem is that of energy. Energy costs continue to rise year after year. Trends point to smaller homes, smaller cars (but not necessarily fewer of them), and higher prices. And with businesses moving in increasing numbers to suburban areas, the need for gasoline is becoming ever greater.

A fourth problem relates to the growth of the single life style. In 1979 there were nearly 49 million single persons in America. Many singles are heads of households—in 1978 14 percent of all heads of households between the ages of twenty-five and thirty-four were women without husbands present. Another large segment of the singles population consists of individuals living alone. In a recent year, the more than 15½ million people who lived alone accounted for 21 percent of all households in the country. Many of these solitary individuals are widows. In the past, a widow would have expected to move in with her children, but today the widowed woman has fewer children on whom to depend and is also far more independent. A third large group of singles is made up of those individuals who have chosen cohabitation over marriage. In 1977, cohabitating individuals made up 2.5 percent of all households.

All of these single households must cope with a marketplace geared to serving traditional families. Although a law was passed recently (the Equal Credit Opportunity Act) that made it easier for women to buy housing and other large-ticket items, women still have problems with credit and other aspects of financial planning. And cohabitating couples have to deal with a widespread prejudice in favor of married couples in

[1]"Unhealthy Costs of Health," *Business Week,* September 4, 1978, p. 59.

areas of insurance, child custody and child visitation rights, tenant rights, medical benefits, and estates. In some states cohabitation itself is still a violation of the law.

A FINANCIAL PLAN

To cope effectively with all these problems, the modern consumer must engage in careful money management. Financial mistakes are often made by intelligent people who simply have not taken the time to straighten out their own personal finances. And young consumers start off with two strikes against them: inexperience in the business world and very limited finances.

A Budget

One of the most helpful financial planning records an individual or a family can have is a financial budget. A financial budget is a plan for using estimated income to make estimated expenditures during a certain period of time. The period may be a week, two weeks, a month, three months, six months, or a year.

According to the 1974 General Mills Family Report, one out of two families indicated that they maintained some kind of a budget.[2] Further probing revealed, however, that only 12 percent actually drew up any kind of formal or structured budget.

Why aren't people more interested in formal budgets? Much of the problem lies in the misunderstanding of what a budget should be. To many people, budgeting is like dieting. They feel that in order to follow the rules they must cut back on spending until it hurts. Some start off by slashing essential categories, such as spending for food. But peanut butter and turkey sandwiches for every meal grows old fast. Other consumers eliminate all spending for recreation and entertainment, with the notion that they can get along without them. But budgeting to survive rather than to really live is a mistake. Most people can only fool themselves for a short time. Then the budget fails with a crash.

Yet other consumers make tight little budgets that look quite plausible on paper, but the budgeter has neglected to consider birthday and holiday gifts, social visits, or the possibility of emergencies.

[2]Yankelovich, Skelly and White study, "General Mills American Family Report for 1974–75."

Steps in Preparing a Budget.   The first step in preparing a budget is to determine long-range, intermediate-range, and short-range goals.

Most people have long-range goals that cannot be accomplished for many years. These goals may include a pleasant retirement, a good education for children, or a substantial savings program.

Intermediate-range goals may include such mundane but important items as a new furnace or roof or an exotic vacation a year or more from now.

Short-range goals will actually be the most important determinants of the annual budget. They include expenditures for recreation and entertainment, gifts, and contributions.

Since the budget deals with future income, the second step is to derive an accurate assessment of income. Income may come from many sources:

- wages (including employer supplemental unemployment benefits), salaries, bonuses, commissions, fees and tips
- dividends
- earnings (interest from savings and loan associations, mutual savings banks, credit unions, etc.)
- interest on bank deposits, bonds, notes
- interest on U.S. Savings bonds.
- profits from businesses and professions
- share of profits from partnerships and small business corporations
- pensions and annuities
- profits from the sale or exchange of real estate, securities, or other property
- rents and royalties
- share of estate or trust income
- alimony, separate maintenance, or support payments received from a spouse or a former spouse.

Gross income is the amount an individual earns. The amount that remains after taxes is called *net income* or *disposable income*. Disposable income should be realistically estimated, and it should be listed by the month it is scheduled to arrive.

The third step is to use past financial records to prepare a list of your current fixed and variable expenses. *Fixed expenses* are obligations that must be paid at a certain time. Examples of fixed expenses are rent to a landlord; mortgage payments to a savings bank; automobile loan payments to a finance company; premiums to an insurance company. *Variable expenses* may occur each week or month, but they vary in amount. Expenditures for food, transportation, and clothing may be a part of an individual's spending pattern, but the dollar amounts will not be the same

Item	Jan.	Feb.	Dec.	Total
Total money income				
Major fixed expenses: Taxes: Federal				
State				
Property				
Auto				
Rent or mortgage payment				
Insurance: Medical (including prepaid care)				
Life				
Property				
Auto				
Debt payments: Auto				
Other				
Savings for: Emergency fund				
Flexible expenses: Food and beverages				
Utilities and maintenance (household supplies and services)				
Furnishings and equipment				
Clothing				
Personal care				
Auto upkeep, gas, oil				
Fares, tolls, other				
Medical care (not prepaid or reimbursed)				
Recreation and education				
Gifts and contributions				
Total				

FIGURE 1-1. Sample budget. (U.S. Department of Agriculture, "A Guide to Budgeting for the Young Couple," *Home and Garden Bulletin, No. 98, July 1977, p. 7.)*

each month. The sample budget in Figure 1-1 illustrates some categories of fixed and variable expenses.

Notice that a special category is created for savings so that it becomes an obligation to save something for the future. There is no easy answer to the problems of inflation and economic uncertainty. One thing is certain, however—automatic savings are essential to meet established goals.

When past spending patterns have been monitored and determined, it is time to prepare a plan to allocate future disposable income. This may be difficult at first, because it is one thing to allocate monthly payments for taxes, insurance, and other annual fixed payments, but it is quite another to provide enough at the outset to cover months that have already passed but must be included in the totals. For example, $1,200 for insurance may easily be divided by twelve months in order to show that $100 must be set aside per month. However, not all of the various premiums will be paid on the same date. The auto insurance may have been paid six months ago, the life insurance eight months ago, and the disability insurance last month. In order for you to have enough money to pay the premiums when they are due, some catching up will be necessary at first. For example, during the months before you make your next payment, you must accumulate extra amounts equal to half of the auto insurance premium, three-quarters of the life insurance premium, and one-twelfth of the disability insurance premium.

The new budget must also allow a certain amount for emergencies (see Spending Rules below). In addition, to avoid the necessity of recording every penny of spending, it is wise to allocate to each family member a small allowance which need not be accounted for.

The next step is to determine and allocate the discretionary income. *Discretionary income* is the amount of disposable income (if any) that remains after the fixed and variable expenses have been paid. This discretionary amount is really the only money an individual is free to spend according to individual goals. The problem for many consumers today is that disposable income takes all of the funds available, leaving little or no discretionary income. Consumers faced with this problem tend to overuse their credit cards and installment credit. The careful budgeter will always have some discretionary income, which he or she will allocate according to the goals developed in step 1.

A record book in which to record projected and actual income and expenses may be purchased in any stationery store, or one may be prepared from material on hand. If the budget is for an entire household, the person with the best flair for details should handle the budgeting. The decisions, however, should be made jointly by the group.

Items will have to be adjusted periodically to reflect expenses that were unforeseen or not estimated correctly from past spending patterns.

And at the end of a predetermined time, the whole budget should be evaluated to again analyze how the money is being spent. Revision may be in order at this point to reallocate funds for greater efficiency or satisfaction. When a satisfactory, effective plan has been created, all that remains is to follow it and periodically evaluate and revise it.

Spending Rules.   Some basic "spending rules" may be helpful in setting maximums in various categories of budgeting. The rules are generalizations, of course, and as such do not always fit every financial situation. Each must be weighed in the light of your own values, spending habits, and needs.

1. For better financial security, an individual should set aside six months' salary for emergencies. This emergency money should be placed in liquid investments (those that can be converted easily to cash) with low risks. A good argument can be made for keeping a smaller emergency fund—the six-month rule best applies to someone whose job is uncertain and who would not be covered by unemployment insurance should a layoff occur. The six-month rule is also applicable to an individual who has little employer-paid or private health and disability insurance.

2. A consumer's short-term borrowing (one year or less) should not exceed 20 percent of monthly income. This rule is among the most common tools in adjusting consumer spending for those in credit-related debt. The 20-percent figure may actually be too high for individuals whose incomes are uncertain or highly seasonal. Any layoff or loss of a large percentage of income could drastically affect a person who spends at the 20-percent level, especially since most of this type of short-term purchasing is for items that depreciate rapidly (appliances, clothing, auto accessories). The 20-percent rule may actually be too low for individuals who pay for almost everything with credit cards but who pay the entire bill each month. In some localities, it is possible to charge everything from groceries to speeding tickets on credit cards— they have become an almost total substitute for cash.

3. Life insurance coverage is at its optimum when premiums account for 10 percent of income. The rule does not apply, however, to those with need, other sources of income, investments, or anticipated inheritance.

4. In periods of rapid inflation, one effective way for a home buyer to keep up with the cost of living is to get a mortgage for the greatest possible amount for the longest period of time. A small amount will leverage (make more powerful) a larger purchase. While the payments will seem high at first, inflation and wage

increases will ease the pressure as the years pass. In a period of recession, however, the higher payments could become more troublesome—especially if income decreases. In addition, some consumers may not want to have the worry or anxiety caused by high mortgage payments or may prefer to invest in other ways.

The rules described above may be helpful when establishing spending patterns, but they do not reflect all financial situations. It is always wise to have one eye on the rules and the other on individual spending.

Another method of estimating your spending needs is to look at government data on how others are spending their money. The U.S. Department of Commerce estimates "average" spending by consumers each year. In 1978 the typical American spent 20 percent of income on food, 15.5 percent on housing, 6.4 percent on utilities, 10.3 percent on health care, 14 percent on transportation, and 6.7 percent on recreation. The remainder of the money went for personal items, home expenses other than utilities, charity, and education.

Net Worth Statement

Just as the stockholders of a corporation or the owners of a small business assess profit and net worth, the individual can and should compute personal net worth. Net worth is the difference between assets (what is owned) and liabilities (what is owed). A net worth statement is also called a balance sheet, and net worth is also called capital.

There are several reasons for developing a net worth statement. First, a home and its contents generally increase in value each year, and an annual estimate of net worth will ensure that you keep an adequate amount of homeowner's insurance in force. Second, a net worth statement is also helpful to have available to show creditors when you are obtaining financing. Finally, a net worth statement provides a comparison of family financial health from year to year. It can be a satisfying feeling to watch net worth increase from year to year because of a strong program of money management. Conversely, a sharp decrease in net worth may be an indication that debts are too high.

Figure 1-2 shows how to go about establishing a statement of net worth.

A Will

One last touch to cap a financial management plan is a will. Any person who has property should have a will, and yet authorities say that 60

BALANCE SHEET

ASSETS

Cash in checking accounts _____
Cash in savings accounts _____
Savings certificates _____
U.S. savings bonds _____
Cash value of life insurance _____
Market value of house or apartment _____
Market value of other real estate _____
Surrender value of annuities _____
Pension equity _____
Market value of securities
   stocks _____
   bonds _____
   mutual fund shares _____
   other _____
Current value of durable posessions _____
   automobiles _____
   household furnishings, household
   appliances, & equipment
   furs and jewelry _____
   collectibles (accounts receivable) _____
   recreation & hobby equipment _____
Loans receivable (notes receivable) _____
Interest in a business _____
Other assets _____
   Total assets _____

LIABILITIES

Current bills outstanding _____
Installment debts _____
Balance due on mortgages _____
Personal loans _____
Taxes due _____
Other debts _____
   Total liabilities _____

SUMMARY

Assets _____
Liabilities – _____
Net worth or capital _____

FIGURE 1-2. A Net Worth Statement.

percent of all Americans die without one.[3] Why does this happen? Some find the idea of planning for one's death abhorent. Others feel that a will is costly and difficult to have drawn. Actually, the cost is not necessarily

[3]George Coughlin, "A Will Is a Way to Avoid Trouble," *Parade,* October 22, 1978, p. 12.

high—a typical lawyer's fee for a simple will ranges from $50 to $100. The task need not be difficult, either. It is not necessary to make an itemized statement of your assets or a detailed disposition statement. You need only leave general instructions as to how any possessions and property should be distributed upon your death.

A person who dies without a will is said to have died *intestate*. The person's assets will be distributed according to the laws of the state in which the deceased lived.

Wills should be prepared by an attorney who is experienced in estate planning. Every adult member of a family should have a will prepared by this person. One need not wait until after marriage to draw one up, for as your assets grow and life situation changes, it is an easy matter to have a will updated. The will should be kept where it is readily available—*not in a safe-deposit box.* Copies of the will can be left with a banker or an attorney. If the will is changed, it should be done with the aid of an attorney.

Many people feel that joint ownership or tenancy in common is as effective as a will. Joint tenancy creates joint ownership in real or personal property between two or more people so that if one of them dies, the deceased's interest in the property terminates and the interest automatically passes to the surviving joint tenant or tenants. Tenancy in common also creates mutual ownership in property; however, the common property passes to heirs or beneficiaries—not to a co-tenant or co-tenants.

While there are advantages to the joint tenancy concept, it is not an all-purpose way of avoiding probate, as many have claimed. Individuals cannot escape estate-tax liability through the use of joint ownership arrangements; matter of fact, creation of joint interests can result in income-tax liability. In addition to tax drawbacks, other problems can crop up. For example, giving complete title to a spouse or other beneficiary who is inexperienced in managing financial affairs or property may be financially unsound. Also, joint ownership is quite inflexible. Better flexibility may be provided through wills and trusts. For example, if a couple died in an auto accident without a will but with property in joint tenancy, the property would pass to the one to die last and then to that spouse's relatives. With a will property could be divided as each person wanted.

FINANCIAL ADVICE

The amount of money a typical American family will have to manage in a lifetime is no small sum. *U.S. News & World Report,* in a January 23, 1978, article, estimated that a typical family of four will earn $744,000. They used 1976 real dollars and assumed that the husband is twenty-four and the wife twenty-one when they marry, they have two children, and the husband dies first at age seventy-one. Largest items on the spending side were food ($113,000), housing (159,000),[4] transportation ($101,000), and taxes.

The size of these figures gives some indication of just how important effective money management can be. Therefore the rest of this text will focus on ways to use your limited resources to best advantage in all areas of consumer spending, from food shopping to securities investments.

Other sources of outside help include magazines, newspapers, and other mass media, which offer timely advice to consumers who are trying to remain current in their planning. Magazines such as *Business Week, Money, Changing Times,* and *Consumer Reports;* daily newspapers such as the *Wall Street Journal;* and television programs such as "Consumer Survival Kit" and "Wall Street Week" are all useful for the progressive money manager.

Finally, a source of outside help that is becoming more visible today is the firms made up of individuals who call themselves financial planners, consultants, counselors, or financial advisors. They may actually be divided into two groups. The advice-only firms belong to the Association of Independent Financial Advisors. They charge a fee based on an individual's income and do not actually engage in the sale of securities, insurance, or bank instruments. However, they will usually only accept as clients individuals with incomes of over $50,000 a year. The other group (a much larger one) belongs to the International Association of Financial Planners. While many of these advisors are knowledgeable in varying fields, they are most often licensed to sell mutual fund shares, securities, real estate, and insurance.

Whether they receive it free or pay for it on the installment plan, Americans are searching for more financial advice. The combination of general inflation, high medical costs, high energy costs, and the complexities of personal life is making people ever more aware of the importance of financial planning.

QUESTIONS FOR DISCUSSION

1. What recent economic occurrences have strained typical family budgets?
2. What types of legal and financial problems face unmarried couples who choose to live together rather than marry?

---

[4]This does not include the purchase price of a house, which is considered an investment.

3. Why might a time budget be as important as a financial budget?
4. What is the difference between disposable and discretionary income? Which figure should you look at when deciding whether or not to purchase a new household appliance?
5. What factors might influence the determination of a proper size for a family emergency cash fund?
6. What are the advantages of having a net worth statement?
7. Classify the following items as assets or liabilities: dishwasher, home mortgage, cash, credit-card bill. How is net worth determined once assets and liabilities are known?
8. What situations might necessitate a change in a will?

PERSONAL EXPERIENCE PROJECTS

1. Read financial planning articles in magazines such as *Changing Times, Everybody's Money* (which you can obtain from your local credit union), and *Money*. Note specific suggestions that could help you improve your financial situation.
2. Conduct a survey to determine differences among families of various sizes in spending patterns and financial goals.
3. Survey consumer attitudes toward spending for hobbies, sports, and other leisure-time activities. Determine the influence of inflation, marital status, and family size on these expenditures.
4. Interview various consumers about methods for coping with financial emergencies. Determine what items are reduced first when people are forced to make budget cutbacks.
5. Prepare a report on ways of reducing living expenses. Examples could include joining a health maintenance organization (HMO) to reduce medical expenses and lowering home temperature to reduce heating costs.
6. Write a summary of your life style. Include such factors as family income, living quarters, eating habits and tastes, hobbies, and recreation. Also comment, if you wish, on what changes you would like to make in your life style.
7. Interview married and single consumers to determine differences in their spending patterns and financial goals.
8. Survey various consumers' budgeting practices. Obtain information on the type of financial records maintained, percentage of income spent on various items, and opinions regarding budgeting.
9. Keep track of your income and expenses for a month. Then analyze your financial records to determine ways you could save more money, and ways friends and advertising influence your spending.

Finally, use this information to prepare a budget that would be appropriate for you.

10. Prepare a statement of net worth for you or your family. Be sure to consider all items of value (assets) and all amounts owed to others (liabilities). Determine ways you could improve your net worth.

2
BANKING SERVICES

Banking industry studies have indicated that over the next several years the strongest potential for earning growth for banks will come from the consumer segment of the market. With this information in mind, many banking institutions, especially in metropolitan areas, are introducing and promoting a wide variety of special plans for loans, savings accounts, and checking accounts. Only through knowledgeable shopping can the consumer determine which of these plans will best serve his or her needs.

Many ads promote a package plan in which a customer pays $4 per month for "free" checking, "free" traveler's checks, "free" credit cards, and a "free" safe-deposit box. This offer is often "bought" by individuals who write few checks, seldom travel, can qualify for credit cards on their own, and have little to place in a safe-deposit box. They purchase this plan without assessing their needs and thus overbuy.

Other consumers who do have assets fail to make proper use of them. When he died in 1977, Elvis Presley had a balance of over $1,000,000 in his checking account, and much less in his savings accounts.

Still other individuals spend more in overdraft fees than in charges for their checking account itself.

Even those who diligently compare the costs and benefits of various banking services are confused by the new offerings of credit unions (share drafts) and of savings banks and savings and loans (NOW accounts). Commercial banks further add to the confusion with dozens of special types of accounts, including a new type, effective November 1, 1978, which allows banks to make automatic transfers from special savings accounts to checking accounts. A January 1975 article in *Consumer Reports* stated that the cost of these various types of accounts can run from zero to almost $50 per year.

The first portion of this chapter is devoted to helping you determine which of the many banking choices available would be best for you. Then, to help you prepare for the future, a second section describes and analyzes the new electronic funds transfer system. Finally, the last section explains the relationship of the business of banking to the economic system.

TYPES OF BANKING INSTITUTIONS

Full Service Banks

Full service banks, also called commercial banks, are corporations chartered by either the state or the federal government. As corporations they are owned by stockholders and are operated to make a profit. If a bank has a trust department, the word "trust" is used in its name. Deposits in nearly all commercial banks are insured by the Federal Deposit Insurance Corporation (FDIC). Recently the ceiling on insurance coverage of each account held in a different legal ownership capacity in one bank was increased to $100,000. There are about 14,000 full service banks in the fifty states.

Savings Banks

Mutual savings banks, as the name implies, are organized on a nonprofit basis and specialize in savings. They are owned by their depositors rather than by stockholders and are administered by trustees. After all expenses are paid, a large part of the earnings goes to the depositors as interest on their deposits. Some of the earnings are used as additional reserves to increase the protection of the depositors.

Some savings banks are supervised by state banking authorities and subject only to state regulations. Most savings banks, however, are supervised by the Federal Home Loan Bank, in which case their deposits are insured by the Federal Deposit Insurance Corporation up to a maximum of $100,000 for each account held in a different legal ownership capacity in that bank.

There are about 500 mutual banks in eighteen states.

Savings and Loan Associations

Savings and loan associations are also known as building and loan associations, cooperative banks, savings associations, and homestead associations. They are located in all fifty states, as well as in Washington, D.C., Guam, and Puerto Rico. They were originally founded in order to use the savings of depositors to make loans to prospective buyers or owners of homes for their purchase, construction, repair, or refinancing. Such loans are supported by first mortgages to assure their repayment. More than half of the home mortgages in this country are still financed by savings and loan institutions. The profits on the interest paid by the borrowers are distributed to the shareholders.

Most savings and loan associations are mutual corporations with the depositors as part owners. Shareholders elect a board of directors to help with the management of the association.

Savings and loan associations are chartered by either the federal or the state government. The federal associations are members of the Federal Home Loan Bank (FHLB), with their deposits insured by the Federal Savings and Loan Insurance Corporation (FSLIC). Many states also require their chartered savings and loan associations to be members of the Federal Home Loan Bank System and the Federal Savings and Loan Insurance Corporation. The FSLIC insures accounts in their organization up to a maximum of $100,000 for each account held in a different legal ownership capacity in that bank. This is the same protection given by the FDIC to depositors in the banks they insure.

One group of savings and loans called "Moms and Pops" is made up of small institutions that keep part-time hours, use volunteer help, and, since they are not regulated by the federal government, pay higher rates of interest. "Pennsylvania claims the largest contingent of uninsured, part-time S & L's, with 139 holding assets calculated in 1977 at $243 million. New Jersey has 40; Ohio has 12 uninsured S & L's, but the Ohio variety operates full-time in their own offices."[1] The major drawback of these small institutions is their lack of insurance on deposits. States are beginning to move toward offering this insurance, however.

Credit Unions

A credit union is classified as a cooperative—an association of people with a common bond. The common bond may be union membership, place

[1]Deborah A. Randolph, "For Some, S & L's Back-Room Dealings Are a Way of Life," *Wall Street Journal*, April 10, 1979, p. 1.

of employment, professional association, place of residence, or some other commonality. A cooperative member-user of a credit union is a shareholder rather than a depositor and as such has one vote regardless of the balance in his or her account.

All credit unions are either federally or state chartered. The federal credit unions are supervised by the National Credit Union Administration (NCUA), an independent agency which also insures the deposits in all federal credit unions. State credit unions that apply and meet its standards may also buy NCUA insurance, which provides a maximum of $100,000 coverage on a single shareholder.

Overlap in Services

At one time particular institutions were responsible for specific segments of the financial business. Traditionally, savings institutions financed the housing industry by reinvesting long-term savings in home mortgages. The savings banks and savings and loan associations grew because the commercial banks were not providing the necessary funds for the increased numbers of home buyers. The commercial banks, on the other hand, elected to concentrate on short-term lending, both to business and to consumers. Frequently the commercial banks and the savings institutions would work in tandem. The commercial bank would provide the builder with short-term funding (eighteen months or less), and the savings and loan or savings bank would fund the twenty-five- or thirty-year mortgage.

In recent years, though, distinctions in the lending market have become blurred. Savings institutions have been given the power to increase their short-term loans, and commercial banks have lengthened lending periods and increased the amounts that can be borrowed by businesses and individuals.

Credit unions have made some of the most startling gains in the financial sector. Originally organized to offer low-cost loans to factory workers in order to protect them from loan sharks, credit unions have exploded far beyond their initial purpose. There are now 42,000,000 saver-members. During the past ten years the total assets of commercial banks have risen 147 percent, savings and loans 193 percent, and credit unions 281 percent. Credit unions now have deposits in excess of $63 billion. In the past year, credit unions provided approximately 20 percent of all installment loans extended to consumers. Much of this gain can be attributed to the volunteer labor, the free or low-cost office space, and the tax-exempt status the credit union holds as a nonprofit organization—low overhead allows the credit union to lend money to members at rates below those of their competitors. Their low lending rates, combined with the fact that they grant simple-interest loans rather than the more costly add-on loans offered by most commercial banks and all auto finance companies, have made credit unions a particularly popular source of auto loans.

To further complicate the lending market, some states, such as Illinois, have given state-chartered credit unions the power to offer home mortgages for up to twenty-nine years. Federal credit unions may make mortgage loans of up to thirty years, although few of them are large enough to do so.

The credit union has also been given more latitude in the savings area. A commercial bank may pay a top rate of 5¼ percent. The savings bank and the savings and loan association top is 5½ percent. United Air Lines Employees Credit Union, one of the nation's largest, was paying 9 percent on savings in 1979. Thus credit unions enjoy more stability and fewer fluctuations in savings accounts. In recent years, money flowed out of commercial banks and savings institutions, but credit union members tended to keep their share accounts intact. The higher credit union rate satisfied its members, while depositors in other institutions shopped around for higher interest rates.

Auxiliary banking services are becoming quite competitive in all four institutions. All of them may offer the sale and redemption of U.S. savings bonds, traveler's checks, and money orders. The number of additional financial services available varies with the individual institutions. Savings banks may, for example, sell low-cost life insurance in states where the law permits it, such as New York. Most credit unions offer life insurance on deposits; the limit varies from $1,000 to $5,000. Thus if a member has a savings balance of $1,000 when he or she dies, the beneficiary could receive $2,000. Commercial banks often offer trust and credit-card services to their customers.

CHECKING ACCOUNTS

Checking accounts are the most popular banking service after savings accounts. (Savings accounts will be discussed in detail in Chapter 3.) A checking account allows one to pay bills and other financial obligations without handling excessive amounts of cash, and provides a permanent record of every transaction. It is also a convenient and safe way of banking funds that must remain easily accessible.

Selecting a Checking Account

Not too many years ago, commercial banks had a monopoly on checking accounts. Savings institutions were permitted to pay an extra ¼ percent on savings accounts, while commercial banks could offer checking accounts to their customers. But recently savings institutions, and even credit unions, have begun to capture some of the checking account business. In response to this competition, commercial banks are offering a great variety of plans for the banking customer. They are tempting consumers with no-charge checking accounts, special service packages, and even free financial advice on a wide variety of subjects.

Types of Accounts.   What are some checking account plans that are common today, and what do they cost?

Free Checking.   Free checking is promised in many bank advertisements to encourage consumers to open an account. What is free checking? At its best, free checking means no monthly service fee, no minimum balance, and no charge for printed checks. In other words, no strings attached. The free checks in this type of account have blank spaces for check numbers to be filled in by the customer. They usually contain a printed name line but no address. The customer who wants scenery, symbols, and other frills on a check will have to pay for them. In some college communities checking accounts are offered free to college students by small or medium-sized banks as part of a public relations program.

Minimum Balance Account.   Under the minimum balance system a customer may write an unlimited number of checks with no charge, provided a minimum monthly balance is maintained. This amount varies with each bank; usually the biggest banks require larger minimum balances than the smaller banks.

If a customer's account drops below the minimum balance during the month, the bank will charge either a flat fee for the month or a variable penalty. Some banks on the penalty system penalize the customer for every check written during the month if the minimum balance is not maintained, while others compute the charge on the basis of the average balance for the month.

In any case, this type of account is often advertised as a "free" account. This is not exactly true. The customer should consider the opportunity cost—what he or she would gain if the minimum balance were placed in a savings account to earn interest. If the customer writes very few checks, this type of account may not be a good deal. Also, if the customer has a difficult time maintaining the minimum balance, the cost of the account may run from $24 to $48 per year.

Special Checking.   Special checking is suitable for persons who write only a few checks per month. Banks generally charge a flat fee ranging from 25¢ to $1 per month, and then from 10¢ to 15¢ for each check written during the month. Who can be called a "light" check writer? A light check writer is one who writes fewer than fifteen checks a month. (An average check writer issues about twenty checks per month, and a heavy writer issues at least twenty-five checks per month.)

Package Plan.   Most package plans usually include a checking account with personalized checks; a rent-free safe-deposit box; free traveler's checks, cashier's checks, and money orders; and in some cases reduced rates on loans. Some package plans also include incidental services which are ordinarily available free of charge to any qualified consumer, such as bank credit cards, check-guarantee cards, and overdraft protection in the form of loans for checks drawn in excess of the balance in the checking account.

These plans cost anywhere from $2 to $4 per month. Are they worth it? Again, the consumer has to look at basic needs. How much does the individual travel? Are traveler's checks part of a free service in that savings institution? Are the safe-deposit boxes available on demand, or are they only available if the institution just happens to have one free? If the bank offers a reduced annual percentage rate of interest (APR) on loans, is it truly lower than the rates in competing banks? If it is lower, does the individual expect to borrow money frequently? After you eliminate the already free services and omit the ones not likely to be used often, does the $24 to $48 cost per year still represent a bargain? Investigate before buying.

Overdraft Account.   The overdraft privilege is available in many banks either separately or as part of a package account. The customer is given a predetermined credit limit, up to which point the bank will pay on checks even when the checking account is overdrawn. The amount of the overdraft is automatically converted to a loan. The cost of such a loan usually ranges from 12 percent to 18 percent per year.

The contract the customer signs to open such an overdraft account may be rather involved. Many people assume that they pay interest only on the amount of the overdraft, but this is not always true. Some banks charge interest on a minimum amount of $50 or $100, even if the amount of the overdraft is only $1. All higher amounts are also increased to multiples of a stated figure, such as $50 or $100. Customers also tend to assume that (1) interest will be charged by the bank for only the exact number of days the loan is used, and (2) when the customer deposits enough money to cover the overdraft the deposit automatically cancels the loan. Actually, the overdraft provision of many contracts calls for the initiation of a loan payable in installments on specific dates (or when the customer specifically comes in to pay the amount in full). Always read the "legalese" in any contract carefully before signing.

NOW Accounts.   Savings institutions across the country are beginning to offer the NOW account (negotiable order of withdrawal), which is actually an interest-bearing checking account. The NOW account depositor must maintain a certain minimum balance at all times. The amount varies, but it is usually $500 or more. The rate of interest paid (5 percent maximum) is usually below the regular savings bank rate (5¼ percent maximum). Thus the interest earned from a NOW account may be far less than the interest income earned by keeping a regular savings account and a regular checking account, even if the depositor pays a certain amount for checks drawn on the checking account.

Share Accounts.   Credit unions have entered the interest-earning-checking-account competition with share drafts, which are similar to NOW accounts. "Share drafts aren't a household word yet, but the idea is catching on," says Fred Ringenburg of ICU Services, the credit union organization that designed and markets the program. "About 70 credit unions a month are going on share drafts. And we expect half the nation's largest credit unions will offer them by 1981."[2] If that prediction is accurate, more than 20 million member-savers will be utilizing the service by 1981.

In order to institute share draft accounts, a credit union has to utilize an existing check-clearing medium, such as that of a commercial bank, or invest in such a system itself. Since the banking industry in general has not looked favorably on cooperative ventures and setting up a new system is an expensive process, the future of share draft accounts is currently in some doubt.

However, recently some of the larger banks have come to the aid of share draft customers. "The banks, who clear share drafts through the Federal Reserve system for fees of 2.8¢ to 4.55¢ per, now have enough volume to make it profitable," says Elinor Upton, vice-president at Chase Manhattan Bank, the nation's largest share-draft-clearing bank. "They want to keep it," she says.[3] But forty other large banks are still supporting any legislation that would curb share drafts.

Convenience.   Are account costs the only criteria in the selection of a banking institution? For most people, the biggest single factor in deciding where to bank is convenience. Hours are extremely important to working people. Low fees help little if the customer cannot get to the bank when it is open. Are there enough tellers during a rush period? What is the quality of services? It pays to ask questions at various banks before opening an account. An efficient bank will have someone who can readily describe the principal services and costs. Being shunted from one person to another or getting incomplete or unsatisfactory answers to questions may be a harbinger of the shape of things to come.

[2]"Share Drafts a New Way to Bank," *Everybody's Money,* Spring 1979, p. 4.
[3]"A Blitz on Behalf of Credit Unions," *Business Week,* July 16, 1979, p. 40.

Other Banking Services.   Banks offer various services. You may want to inquire about the existence or cost of one or more of the following services before selecting a bank.

Correspondent Privileges.   The banking system is a network, and almost all banks have correspondent relationships with other banks. Under this system they process each other's checks, lend each other money, and exchange information and services. If you move to a new city where your bank has correspondent relationships, your banker can introduce you by phone or letter and attest to your credit reputation, etc. This action may encourage the new bank to accept out-of-town checks in case of a cash shortage or an emergency, or to help with other financial problems. Many banks welcome new-resident customers with programs that range from city tours to short-term interest-free loans.

Automatic Transfers.   In addition to automatically transferring money from a savings account to a checking account when you overdraw your account, many banks will automatically invest your money in mutual funds, stock, or U.S. savings bonds if you authorize them to do so.

Simplified Bank Statements.   Some banks offer unscrambled bank statements on which checks are listed in the order in which they were written. This makes it easier for customers to balance the bank statement at the end of the month.

Stop-Payment Orders.   All banks will stop payment on a check issued by a depositor when instructed to do so. There is a charge for this service, however.

Handling Bad Checks.   Banks generally charge for each check written for which adequate funds are not available for payment. The charge varies from bank to bank.

Decorative Checks and Checkbooks.   Checks and checkbook covers are sometimes free if ordered in solid colors; however, when you want special colors, textures, or dimensions there is almost always a charge for them.

Truncation.   Credit unions have pioneered a system called truncation, which is rapidly becoming popular with other financial institutions as well. Truncation is a word that the banking industry uses to refer to the practice of not returning canceled checks to the checking account customer after payment has been made. The Federal Reserve Board expects 60 billion checks to be written during 1985 (almost double the 1978 figure of 32 billion). Since the processing cost runs between 25¢ and $2 per check, billions could be saved each year by inhibiting the flow of paper.

Rather than return canceled checks to customers, the financial institution microfilms and stores them. Approximately 40,000 checks can be stored on a cassette tape four inches in diameter. When a customer wants a photocopy of a particular check, the institution can recall the check from the microfilm in a matter of seconds. Since the IRS is nearing the point where they will accept photocopies of checks, the process of truncation will surely grow in popularity. Retrieval will most likely be free for the first five to ten checks; there will probably be a small charge on subsequent checks.

Phone Payment of Bills. Some financial institutions are now offering a telephone bill-paying service. The consumer simply telephones the necessary details to a bank offering this service, and the bank will withdraw money from an interest-bearing account to pay the bills. There is a small charge for this service, but the consumer benefits by a reduction in check writing and in postage bills. A depositor with a touch-tone phone can punch the numbers necessary to pay bills. This service may or may not benefit an individual, depending on the service charges and on the number of bills paid per month.

Using a Checking Account

Once you have chosen a bank and a banking program, opening a checking account is a simple matter. Signature cards are merely prepared and signed by the person or persons authorized to write checks on the account.

A deposit must then be made before any check can be written. If checks are deposited, they must be properly endorsed with the name of the depositor. A sufficient amount of time specified by each bank must elapse after checks have been deposited before you can write checks against that money.

Writing Checks. Before writing any check, you must ensure that the balance in the account is adequate to pay it, and then record the amount on the stub or the check register. This will prevent you from overdrawing on your account.

Checks must be written in ink or on a typewriter. The date must be the current date—a check written on April 20 should not be dated April 26. Checks may be dated on Sundays or legal holidays.

The name of the payee (the person to whom the check will be paid) must be written in full. It is not wise to write checks payable to "Cash" or "Bearer," for if such checks are lost, they can be cashed by the finder.

The amount of the check in figures should be written as close to the dollar sign as possible. The amount in words should start at the left, and any blank space should be filled in. Otherwise the check can be "kited" (increased by a forger). Finally, the signature must agree with the signature on the signature card.

A change in the amount of a check makes it unusable, so if you make a mistake, you mark the check "void" or "canceled" and write a new one.

If payment on a check must be stopped, the bank must be notified immediately and the necessary bank forms prepared and submitted to the bank.

Reconciling a Checking Account with the Bank Statement. The bank sends each depositor a monthly statement of checking account transactions, together with all the canceled checks paid by the bank that month. The statement shows all the activity in the account during the month:

1. beginning balance
2. deposits and the dates made
3. checks and the dates paid
4. service charges, if any
5. total deposits
6. total payments
7. new balance at end of month.

The depositor checks the checkbook balance against the bank statement (reconciliation) balance through the following steps:

1. Arrange the canceled checks in numerical order or by date of issue.
2. Compare the canceled check with the stub or the check register to be sure that the amounts agree, placing a large check mark on the stubs as you go. Make a list of the numbers and amounts of checks that have not yet been paid by the bank. Record the total amount of the unpaid checks on the bank statement in the reconciliation box.
3. Subtract bank service charges from the checkbook balance.
4. Subtract the total of the outstanding checks (see step 2 above) from the new bank balance on the bank statement.
5. Add to the bank balance any deposits shown in the checkbook but not on the bank statement (deposits in transit).
6. Compare balances; the corrected checkbook balance and the corrected bank statement balance must agree.
7. Record this bank reconciliation in the checkbook. To do this usually requires recording the bank charges and subtracting them from your checkbook balance (see step 3 above). Be sure to change your checkbook balance if the bank reconciliation statement turns up an error.
8. File the canceled checks for future reference. The Internal Revenue Service requires that they be kept for three years to support income tax reports. For legal purposes they are usually kept for six years.

Most banks provide reconciliation worksheets on their monthly statements. The equation below illustrates the process most of these worksheets follow in helping you reconcile your checkbook.

Balance on bank statement	Checkbook balance
+New deposits	−Service charges by the bank
−Outstanding checks	New checkbook balance
Adjusted balance	

BANKING IN THE FUTURE

During the 1960s it was predicted that the banking system would "drown in a sea of checks." To prevent such a crisis, the banking industry began moving toward a nationwide electronic funds transfer (EFT) system. This system may replace the familiar check with a plastic "debit" card. The debit card would be inserted into electronic terminals in every retail outlet and maybe in homes and offices as well. It would eliminate or radically reduce the need for people to go to a bank in order to carry on routine transactions. The debit card would be used for purchases, deposits, withdrawals, payment of bills, and even borrowing money. The current credit card is used to defer the payment of a purchase until twenty to thirty days after the receipt of the bill. The debit card, on the other hand, would be used to immediately withdraw money from a bank account. If the balance were to fall below zero, the deficit would be automatically converted into a customer loan.

Operational Features

The EFT system is not yet a complete reality today, as some had envisioned it would be. Parts of it, however, operate in many everyday banking activities.

Automated Teller Machines.   Thousands of automated teller machines are now in operation. They dispense cash, receive deposits, and show balances in the accounts handled. The machines are frequently outside bank walls, in airports, or in central business sections. They are really small branch banks (see Figure 2-1).

Point-of-Sales Machines.   Another 11,000 machines, called point-of-sale machines, are at work in retail stores, providing the simplest form of electronic banking available today. The necessary guarantee card is no more than a simple identification device. When it is inserted into a

FIGURE 2-1. An Automated Teller Machine. (Photo courtesy of Docutel Corporation.)

store computer terminal, the bank computer tells the operator whether there is enough money in a cardholder's account for the check to clear. The cardholder may also use the card to verify his or her current bank balance.

Direct-Deposit Programs.   In many areas payroll and pension checks are deposited through an electronic payment system. The Social Security Direct Deposit Program was launched in 1976 to allow Social Security benefits to be deposited electronically. The program eliminates the need for recipients to stand in line and prevents checks from becoming lost or stolen. In 1980 the federal government expects to be paying 40 percent of its salaries, Social Security, and other benefits electronically. Many very large corporations now pay their employees in this manner also.

Banking by Phone. Another way the EFT system has been used by consumers is through the banking-by-phone method of paying bills described previously. Customers with a touch-tone phone can dial the computer directly and then punch the numbers of the bills to be paid by the financial institution.

Opposition to EFT

Consumer Resistance. The greatest problem with the EFT is consumer resistance. It is estimated that in 1980 only about 15 percent of the payments normally made by check will be processed by EFT. Even when fully developed, the system will probably never replace more than 70 percent of paper-based fund transfers. Why does the individual consumer mistrust the system and the "consumer movement" oppose many aspects of the EFT?

Many consumers are reluctant to lose the "float" they now enjoy on credit cards. They rely on using their money during the extra days between the time they make the purchase and the time they pay the credit card bill.

Many consumers like to use checks for paying bills because they serve as a permanent record of payment; customers often keep their canceled checks at least three years. EFT does not guarantee such a record to the banking customer.

Consumers fear a greater invasion of their privacy as more and more data become available in a national EFT computer network. Such a system would surely allow stores and banks greater access to the buying habits of specific consumers, destroying the relative anonymity a cash customer enjoys.

Retailer Resistance. Retailers are also concerned about the EFT system. They are worried that the debit card will abolish the loyalty that store credit cards have created, thus taking away their most affluent and best-paying customers.

The nation's two largest bank cards, Mastercharge and Visa, are already moving toward debit cards that provide automatic money payment from customers' bank accounts. Visa has tested cards that can be used as either credit or debit cards, and Mastercharge has a new debit card that can be used for both purposes. These cards are cash equivalents, and they can be used anywhere. Where sponsoring banks permit overdraft privileges to depositors, cards even permit their holders to spend more than is in their accounts. Some retailers have already conceded that the bank cards will prevail in the credit-card market. J. C. Penney became the first national merchant (aside from some discount chains) to offer Visa customers the opportunity to charge at their stores. Sears Roebuck and Company and Montgomery Ward stores are also experimenting on a smaller scale with accepting national bank cards.

U.S. Postal System Resistance.   Another group that has severe doubts about the EFT system is the U.S. Postal System. J. T. Ellington, Jr., Senior Assistant Postmaster General, told a federal commission that nearly half of postal service revenue now comes from delivering bills and remittances in payment of them. "Electronic payments would bypass the postal system and it would divert valuable mail and revenues from a postal system already beset by financial problems," Ellington told the National Commission on Electric Funds Transfers.

Banking Industry Resistance.   It currently costs banks about 30¢ to process a check. The EFT system could cut this cost dramatically if it operated extensively throughout the United States. However, the initial capital outlay required is enormous—up to $50,000 to install a single automated machine and up to $3,000 for each point-of-sale terminal. Most of the small banks feel that such costs would make it difficult for them to stay in business. The only solution would be the creation of a national nonprofit or government-operated EFT system.

STRUCTURE AND REGULATION OF COMMERCIAL BANKING

The average consumer perceives the bank in a narrow sense only. Bogged down with daily business and personal activities, the consumer thinks of the banking industry in terms of making deposits, balancing the checkbook, obtaining an occasional loan, and making payments on it. The effect of banking on consumers is actually much greater than most of them realize.

The banking system creates money by making the unspent and deposited income of savers available to investors. These investors pay others, many of whom redeposit the money. The redeposited money is in turn loaned out again, and so on. Such lending and relending of money can give a small original deposit dramatic power.

Because the banking system wields power of this magnitude, it is heavily regulated. The United States really has a dual banking system. A new bank may seek to operate under either a federal or a state charter. These charters place the bank under the regulations of one of three federal agencies, one of the fifty states, or a combination of both.

Federal Regulation

The Comptroller of the Currency. The Comptroller of the Currency is an official of the U.S. Department of the Treasury. The Comptroller is responsible for regulating national banks and also for issuing and redeeming Federal Reserve notes (paper money). The most controversial of the Comptroller's responsibilities is that of deciding whether new banks that apply for membership should be chartered as national banks. Great care must be taken to see that too many charters are not granted, for this would lead to failures, or too few, for this would result in lack of competition.

The Federal Reserve System. The Federal Reserve Act of 1913 required all federally chartered banks to join the Federal Reserve System. State-chartered banks who met the requirements were given the option to join. About 39 percent of all U.S. banks are currently members of the Federal Reserve System. The remaining banks are under state charters and are not, therefore, required to become members of the Federal Reserve System.

While the individual member banks are concerned with making a profit, the Federal Reserve System is devoted to increasing and decreasing the nation's stock of money to promote the nation's economic goals. The broad policy formulated in an attempt to attain economic goals—such as full employment, stability, and growth—is called *monetary policy.* The Federal Reserve monetary policy decisions are made by a group of twelve. The group includes seven board members and five of the presidents of the twelve regional Federal Reserve Banks.

The Federal Reserve Board utilizes three principal techniques to realize its goals:

1. Raising and lowering the interest (discount) rate it charges member banks for borrowing from it.
2. Regulating the amount of money the commercial banks must set aside to meet the demands on checking and savings accounts. This reserved amount of money may not be used for loans.
3. Buying and selling government securities through the Federal Reserve's open-market operation.

The least-used tool is the reserve requirement. Since most banks tend to be "loaned up" to the maximum limit, it would be an extremely harsh measure for the Fed to require an increased amount of reserves. This would mean that the member banks would have to recall or discount loans to meet the new reserve requirement. Discounting means that the member bank would take some of its customers' interest-earning loans to the central bank and sell them at a lower rate than it would have earned had it held them until they matured. The difference in the rate the member bank would have earned and the amount the Federal Reserve Bank will pay is the cost of discounting the interest-bearing paper.

The tool most often used by the central bank is open-market operations. The Federal Reserve Board feeds its money supply into the economy by buying or selling bonds and notes issued by the U.S. Treasury. These are *not* U.S. savings bonds; they are government securities usually held as investments by banks and corporations, who earn interest on them. The Federal Reserve has an agent in New York who, on general orders issued in Washington, secretly buys and sells these bonds and notes. When the New York agent buys treasury bonds and notes from the market (usually banks), the Federal Reserve gets the previously sold paper from the banks and the banks get money from the Federal Reserve. The banks now hold money that may be loaned out, rather than the paper they previously were using as an investment. As it is loaned out over and over again, the original amount of money has a multiple economic effect.

When it wants to tighten up the money supply, the Open-Market Committee does just the opposite. It sells the interest-earning bonds and notes to banks in exchange for money that is then no longer free to be used as loans.

To make these decisions, the Federal Reserve Board watches a number of financial indicators. The most important indicators are the basic money supply (cash plus checking accounts) and the interest rates that banks charge each other for loans.

During recent years a substantial number of banks in all parts of the nation have withdrawn from the Federal Reserve System. In 1960, 46 percent of U.S. banks were members of the Federal Reserve, compared to 39 percent recently. The percentage of total deposits held by member banks has declined from 80.1 percent in 1970 to 71 percent in 1978. As a result, at least one-fourth of the commercial-bank deposits and more than three-fifths of all banks are outside the Federal Reserve System.

In order to determine why so many banks have recently withdrawn from or chosen to remain outside the Federal Reserve System, a nationwide study was conducted. The study surveyed 250 randomly selected banks that had withdrawn from the Federal Reserve System during the 1965–74 period. Table 2-1 contains the findings of the survey, which suggest that the Federal Reserve Board may need to make fundamental revisions in its reserve requirements to bring them closer to state requirements. If the state requirement is lower, the bank has an obvious incentive to withdraw from the Federal Reserve—the chance to increase profits by making more loans. Critics of the Federal Reserve System reserve requirement regulations say that without revision of this requirement, the long-run future of the Federal Reserve System is in doubt.

The FDIC. In 1933 the Federal Deposit Insurance Corporation (FDIC) was formed to protect bank depositors and promote sound banking practices. About 98 percent of all commercial banks and 69 percent of all mutual savings banks are insured by the FDIC. Since 1933, the FDIC has dispersed $1.5 billion to depositors in banks that failed. The FDIC can either pay off accounts or try to get other banks to take over an insolvent bank. Most often the FDIC is successful in finding a takeover candidate. For example, in 1973, when the U.S. National Bank of San Diego failed, its accounts were immediately assumed by the Crocker National Bank.

TABLE 2-1. Four Most Important Disadvantages of Federal Reserve Membership As Reported by Banks Leaving the System (percentage of total responses)

Disadvantages of Membership	Most Important	Next Most	Third Most	Fourth Most
(1) Federal Reserve requirements	90.4%	3.8%	2.2%	0.0%
(2) Similar services provided by correspondents	3.8	49.0	23.9	11.1
(3) High capital requirements	3.8	15.1	15.2	5.6
(4) Required Federal Reserve stock subscription	1.9	17.0	21.7	27.8
(5) Nonmember bank access to Fed services	0.0	5.7	23.9	30.6
(6) Strict Fed examinations	0.0	0.0	2.2	5.6
(7) Employees cannot work for another bank	0.0	5.7	2.2	8.3
(8) Archaic regulations	0.0	3.8	8.7	11.1
TOTALS	100.0%	100.0%	100.0%	100.0%

Source: Professor Rose, *The Bankers Magazine*, Winter 1976, p. 47.

Only federal banks are required to participate, but most state-chartered banks choose to do so as well.

State Regulation

State banks that either choose not to join the Federal Reserve System or do not qualify to do so are regulated by state banking laws. State banking laws were created primarily to prevent bank failures, a goal they have been pursuing principally through limitation of competition. However, many feel that more competition would be healthy for the banking industry.

One issue in the question of competition versus control is the practice of branch banking. In branch banking a single bank operates more than one banking office. Each state decides whether branching of state-chartered banks will be legal in that state. Today twenty states allow branch banking, while thirty either limit or prohibit it.

Proponents of such a system point to economies of scale in being larger. They also say that branch banking is safer than unit banking because funds from one branch may "bail out" another branch in a depressed area. The practice would also enable a bank to open a branch in an area where it would not pay to have a main bank. In states that do not allow branch banking, many low-income areas are not being served by banks. Also, funds to meet the needs of depositors are more readily available and customer services often less costly in a branch banking system.

Opponents of branch banking have four major arguments. First, they point out the tendency toward monopoly control by a few large banks under the branching system. Second, the unit bankers say that branches do not necessarily reduce prices or provide better service to customers. Third, the opponents of branching feel that the correspondent bank arrangement already provides the smaller banks with the benefit of a smooth flow of money. Finally, opponents argue that bigness means impersonal attention and indifference to the needs of the community and its customers.

Competition in banking will continue to be an issue in the banking community. Movements are now underway to alter the McFadden Act, which restricts a bank to doing business only within its state boundaries. "If the McFadden Act is repealed, out-of-state branches are likely to blossom into national banking networks. The US could end up with thousands fewer banks than the 14,000 commercial banks now in existence," says Stephen T. McLin, a Bank of America official.[4] The educated

[4]Richard F. Janssen, "Expanding US Banks Hope Law Will Allow National Competition," *Wall Street Journal*, June 21, 1979.

consumer should participate in making banking decisions when they become issues for legislative action.

QUESTIONS FOR DISCUSSION

1. What type of loan is most commonly made by a savings and loan company?
2. Why can credit unions often afford to charge a lower rate than other financial institutions for member loans?
3. What are the hidden costs in a minimum-balance checking account?
4. What terms in an overdraft checking account agreement should you investigate before signing?
5. What are the savings and loans', savings banks', and credit unions' alternatives to checking accounts?
6. Why do credit unions offer share drafts to their members?
7. What are the steps in reconciling a checking account with the bank statement?
8. What is the advantage of electronic funds transfer?
9. Contrast a debit card and a credit card.
10. Why do some retailers resist the debit-card concept?
11. Why do some small banks think they would find it difficult to compete under the electronic funds transfer system?
12. What are the advantages of being a state bank? A federal bank?
13. Name the three principal techniques used by the Federal Reserve System to regulate the money supply.
14. Why is the number of Federal Reserve member banks decreasing?
15. What are the advantages and disadvantages of branch banking?

PERSONAL EXPERIENCE PROJECTS

1. Conduct a survey of "free" checking accounts. Determine the hidden costs and the restrictions placed on consumers. Obtain information regarding the cost of other services, such as printing checks, stopping payment on checks, and making overdrafts.
2. Contact local credit unions to determine the availability of share drafts. Contact savings and loan associations that offer NOW accounts. Compare both to conventional checking accounts in light of cost and convenience.
3. Survey advertisements for "free" gifts that may be obtained when savings deposits are made. Look for restrictions imposed on consum-

ers or lower interest rates offered in order to allow for the "free" gifts.

4. Find out the costs of overdraft checking accounts. Then contact banks that offer automatic transfer of funds from savings to checking to protect consumers from overdraft. Compare these two methods for cost and convenience.

5. Contact the Federal Reserve System, Office of Consumer Affairs, Washington, DC 20551, to obtain information regarding common complaints of consumers about banks. Compare the information obtained with banking complaints of local consumers.

6. Discuss with other consumers the possibility of a cashless, checkless business system. Consider the various advantages and disadvantages for businesses and consumers.

7. Contact local bank officials regarding the use of debit cards in your area. Obtain information on the measures that are being taken to protect consumers in the areas of lost or stolen cards, release of confidential financial information, and consumer redress for defective purchases.

8. Compare several contracts for overdraft checking accounts. What are the costs, what is the minimum amount that may be borrowed, and what are the terms of repayment?

9. Survey ten persons who have checking accounts to find out what techniques they have found helpful in maintaining and reconciling the checkbook.

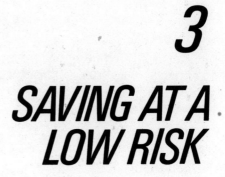

3

*SAVING AT A
LOW RISK*

· *CHOOSING A SAVINGS ACCOUNT*
· *BUYING BONDS*
· *INVESTING IN TREASURY INSTRUMENTS*
· *PURCHASING T-CERTIFICATES*

Savings are the unspent, unconsumed part of income. If the unspent funds are just put into a box or drawer they are only hoarded; they will not create additional wealth. However, if they are invested in some financial institution that puts them to work, they can create more wealth. In return for the loan of the unspent income, the individual receives a financial reward in the form of interest or dividends.

WHY SAVE?

If we asked ten people why they were saving their money, we would get ten or even twenty different answers. These answers can be grouped into long-range and short-range objectives. Short-range goals include buying cars, big-ticket appliances, homes; taking vacation trips; saving for emergencies; protecting a current life style from the ravages of inflation. Long-range goals encompass ensuring a comfortable retirement, starting or buying into a business, preparing for children's college education, achieving general financial security, and estate-planning for children and grandchildren.

The first step in beginning a savings program is to determine your goals. Once you have identified your goals, you must choose a method of saving. You may want to set aside a certain percentage of your income or a certain dollar figure each month, or you may elect to let the exact amount of your savings vary from month to month (but be sure you set something aside each month).

The amount you save will depend on several variables. Statistics show that the ability to save increases as income increases. It should also come as no surprise that when income is regular and dependable, savings are easier to accumulate. In addition, the economic condition of the country often influences savings: when money is uncertain, people tend to try to put more aside. Personal economic conditions also influence savings—the age of the individual, the number of necessities of life already acquired, changes in life style.

Regardless of your situation, however, it is extremely important that you start now, with a realistic amount that will not cause you to be left with unpaid bills or financial headaches. Even small amounts eventually accumulate into substantial ones.

For example, a consumer deciding to put aside 52¢ an hour for a normal eight-hour day and a seven-day week would accumulate $125 a month or $1,500 a year. Table 3-1 shows the amounts that would be accumulated if the consumer deposited the $1,500 at the beginning of each year at 7½ percent (or 7.9 percent effective yield) for just ten years.

TABLE 3-1. Ten Years' Savings at 7½ Percent

Age of Depositor	Available at Age 65
0–10	$1,528,290
10–20	714,482
20–30	334,023
30–40	156,157
40–50	73,004
50–60	34,129
60–65 (5 years only)	9,476

It is obviously most profitable to begin a savings program early in life. Over half the value is lost with each ten years one waits to start saving. On the other hand, if a saver deposits the $1,500 annually for more than ten years, the total amount saved does, of course, increase. For example, if an individual deposited $1,500 at 7½ percent at the beginning of each year from age twenty to age sixty-five, the yield would be $606,789.

WHERE TO SAVE

Chapter 2 on Banking presented the various types of financial institutions that exist in this country. All of them have savings departments, some with many types of savings accounts.

Commercial Banks

Commercial banks welcome savings-account depositors with "commercials" in all the advertising media. Since these banks are located in all sections of every city and suburban community in all the fifty states, every person who wishes to save can readily do so, either in person or by mail.

The maximum rates of interest paid to savings depositors have been limited by U.S. Government Regulation Q. Commercial banks have been restricted to paying one-quarter of a percentage point less interest than savings institutions are permitted, and they frequently calculate interest on a less liberal basis than the savings institutions.

Savings Banks

Generally called mutual savings banks, special savings banks serving the needs of consumers who wish to deposit their savings are now in their second century of operation.

The maximum interest rates paid by the savings banks are also controlled by U.S. Government Regulation Q. The maximum interest rates are usually one-quarter of a percentage point more than those the commercial banks and trust companies are permitted to pay. The savings banks also frequently calculate dividends on a more liberal basis than the commercial banks. Many of them compound continuously on a day-of-deposit-to-day-of-withdrawal basis.

Frequently, they also offer many of the same services that the commercial banks provide their depositors, such as free checking accounts and traveler's checks.

Savings and Loan Associations

The interest rates paid by savings and loan associations on passbook or statement accounts are the same as those paid by the savings banks for similar accounts. Both groups have been permitted by U.S. Government Regulation Q to pay one-quarter of a percentage point more interest than the commercial banks may pay. On special time or certificate-of-deposit accounts issued for six or more years, the savings and loan associations generally pay one-quarter (unless the rate exceeds 9 percent) of a percentage point more interest than some savings banks and all commercial banks. They generally pay the highest legal interest rate, and they usually compound interest continuously.

Savings and loan companies and mutual savings banks are also known as *thrift institutions*. The term thrift institutions or thrifts will be used to encompass both organizations throughout the remainder of this chapter.

Credit Unions

Credit unions generally pay higher dividend or interest rates to their members than other savings institutions pay their depositors. Some credit unions pay much less—it all depends on their income and expenses. A credit union will not promise a particular rate in advance, as would a bank or savings and loan. The savings rate that will be paid is announced at the end of a quarter, when all expenses and income have been calculated. Most credit unions may be relied upon, however, to pay the same or occasionally a higher rate than in past quarters, depending on the economy.

New powers given to federal credit unions will soon allow them to pay somewhat higher rates on longer-term savings deposits than on their now familiar quarterly accounts. This power will place the credit union in competition with other savings institutions for the certificates-of-deposit market.

TYPES OF ACCOUNTS

Most savings institutions offer at least two kinds of accounts.

Regular Accounts

In regular accounts, deposits and withdrawals are recorded either in a passbook or on quarterly statements. Money can be deposited or the balance on deposit can be withdrawn at any time, and interest is paid regularly at stated rates (discussed below). In some banks and thrift institutions there are technical time limitations of thirty or sixty days' notice for withdrawals, but these are seldom enforced.

Special Accounts

In recent years, many banks, many thrift institutions, and some credit unions have developed special accounts with higher interest rates to attract more consumer savings. To receive the higher interest rates the consumer must agree in advance to leave the money for at least a specified period of time. This can range from ninety days to six or more years.

The time-account interest rates range from 5½ to 8 percent, depending on the length of the period and current federal regulations. Minimum deposits of various amounts are required for the different time periods. Time accounts are also called certificate-of-deposit accounts.

These special accounts carry two penalties if the depositor withdraws the money before the end of the stated time. First, the special higher interest rate is reduced to the regular interest rate paid by the institution; and second, interest for ninety days is lost. This penalty forfeit is an important factor to consider before opening a special account.

INTEREST RATES

All savings institutions pay interest at stated rates. The 1979 rates at commercial banks and thrifts ranged from as low as 2 percent to as high as 8 percent, depending on the location of the bank or thrift, competition, type of account, and U.S. government banking regulations. As was mentioned previously, the federal government has set limitations on the maximum amount of interest that can be paid by certain banks and thrifts for certain types of accounts.

This stated interest rate is an important factor in determining the yield or the income received from savings, but it is by no means the only one. The income from the same amount of money, earning the same stated rate of interest, may vary by as much as 170 percent, depending on which of the fifty or more methods of computing interest is used.

Stated Interest Rates

First let us see how stated interest rates affect earnings. One way to demonstrate the importance of stated interest rates is through use of the *Rule of 72s*. The consumer can readily use this simple calculation to learn how long it will take for money saved and deposited to double itself.

For example, suppose that a person is considering a savings plan that pays 6-percent compound interest with a possible deposit of $1,000. When will the $1,000 become $2,000? Just divide the 6 into 72: 6/72 = 12. This shows that the $1,000 will become $2,000 in twelve years if no withdrawals are made.

Now let us assume that another savings plan offers 8-percent compound interest. When the 8 is divided into 72 (8/72 = 9) we see that it will take only nine years, rather than twelve years, for the $1,000 to become $2,000. This formula provides a simple and rapid method of comparing the return on different interest rates.

The wise consumer will shop around for the best rate. Investigate before saving!

Methods of Compounding Interest

Interest is computed at different times by various institutions (see Table 3-2). Interest may be computed continuously, daily, monthly, quarterly, semiannually, or annually.

TABLE 3-2. Interest Earned on a $1,000 Deposit Saved for One Year at 6-Percent Interest

Method of compounding	Interest earned
annually	$60.00
semiannually (every 6 mos.)	$60.90
quarterly (every 3 mos.)	$61.36
monthly	$61.68
daily	$61.83

Assume a consumer deposits a total of $1,000 at the beginning of a year. At the end of the year, if the interest rate is 5 percent, simple interest, $50.00 (1000 × .05) will be credited to the account. *Simple interest* is interest earned only on the amount deposited and not on previously accumulated interest.

Compound interest is interest earned not only on the amount deposited but also on the interest accumulated. Now suppose a consumer deposits $1,000 in January in a bank that compounds semiannually (twice a year). At the end of June, the bank will credit the consumer's account with $25 interest, computed by multiplying the $1,000 by ½ of the 5 percent (2½ percent) for the half year the money has been on deposit. $1,000 × .025 = $25. At the end of December, the bank will compute the interest on $1,025 for a half year. $1,025 × .025 = $25.63. The total for the year is $50.63, while at simple interest it was only $50.00. If the interest were compounded on a quarterly basis, it would be higher. If compounded on a monthly basis, it would be even more. And if compounded on a daily basis, it would be much higher.

Still higher is the interest one receives if interest is *compounded continuously*. In this method, interest is compounded by computer from minute to minute, seven days a week. It results in the highest return at any rate of interest. It is especially productive in a six-year, 7.75-percent time certificate. After six years, the effective yield is over 10 percent. Many savings institutions are using this method.

Methods of Calculating Interest

The stated rate of interest and method of compounding are not the only considerations in shopping for savings. A study at the University of Kansas showed that when a certain sum of money was saved at 6 percent with quarterly compounding and crediting of interest, the final sums varied by as much as 68 percent, depending on which of the four most popular methods of calculating interest was used. A total of $4,000 was invested over a three-month period, with an initial deposit of $1,000 at the beginning of January. There were three withdrawals totaling $2,000 in March.

Low Balance. With the low balance method, the interest yield was only $44.93, because the lowest balance was the initial $1,000. The high balance of $4,000 by early March did not even enter into computation. Unfortunately, many commercial banks (30 percent) still use this method of computing interest, according to the American Banking Association.

FIFO. With the first-in, first-out (FIFO) method, the March withdrawals of $2,000 were deducted from the first deposits of $2,000 in January. This meant that interest was lost right from January, although the withdrawals were not made until March. The interest yield was only $52.44. Again, unfortunately, many commercial banks (about 16 percent) still use this method.

LIFO. With the last-in, first-out (LIFO) method, the March withdrawals of $2,000 were deducted from the most recent deposits in February and mid-January. This more sensible operation yielded $58.44 interest. This method is used by about 5 percent of the commercial banks.

Day-of-Deposit to Day-of-Withdrawal. Under the day-of-deposit-to-day-of-withdrawal system, interest is paid for the actual number of days the money remains in the account. This daily interest from the day of deposit to the day of withdrawal is the best buy of the four for the consumer saver; this method yielded $75.30. According to the American Bankers Association, about half of the commercial banks and the insured savings and loans use this liberal method. No figures are available for the savings banks.

The variation from $44.93 to $75.30 makes it very obvious that calculating methods deserve careful investigation by all consumer savers. Investigate before saving!

Average Balance.   One final method that the study did not include is that of average balance. In this method, the average balance is determined for each account. One way to do this is to add the opening and closing balances for the period and divide by two. For example:

Opening balance $ 800.00
Closing balance   1,000.00
$$2\,\overline{)1{,}800.00} = \$900.00 \text{ Average balance}$$

Another way is to add the ending daily balances and divide the total by the number of business days in the month. For example:

Total daily balances $3960
Business days $22 = \$180$ Average daily balance

The interest is then calculated on the average balance.

Method of Recording Interest

The calculation of interest is one process; compounding is another. A third important step is recording the interest in the depositor's account. Compounding and recording are not always simultaneous. Some banks and thrifts compound on a daily basis but credit depositors' accounts on a quarterly basis. Thus, if a depositor closes the account before the quarter ends, the interest is not recorded in the account. Investigate before saving!

Grace and Dead Days

Some financial institutions give as many as ten grace days a month. This means that money deposited by the tenth of a month starts earning interest from the first of the month. And some banks still pay interest for the full month on money withdrawn from an account as early as three days before the end of a month. These three days are called dead days in the banking business. Grace days and dead days increase the actual or effective yield of a savings account over the stated interest rate.

Other Cost Variations and Limitations

Excess Withdrawals. Some commercial banks limit the number of withdrawals that can be made from a savings account during a certain period (to two or three usually). They charge for any withdrawals beyond the limit.

Premature Closing. Some banks charge a fee if a depositor closes a new account in the first month or first quarter after the account is opened.

Minimum Balance. Many banks will not pay interest if a depositor does not maintain a certain minimum balance.

Closing Balance. A considerable number of banks will not pay any interest unless a specified balance is left in the account until the end of a quarter. Thus a depositor would lose the interest for a whole quarter on a $10,000 account if it were closed even one day before the quarter ended.

Inactive Accounts. In some states, accounts that have been inactive (no deposits or withdrawals) for five years are turned over to the state banking department and interest payments may be stopped.

All of these special rules decrease or even eliminate the amount of interest earned in a given period. Automatically, then, they decrease the effective yield of income on the stated interest rate. Investigate before saving!

U.S. GOVERNMENT SAVINGS BONDS

The U.S. government was very successful in helping to finance the two world wars through the sale of U.S. government war bonds. After World War II, the government brought out U.S. government savings bonds, which also became very popular with low- and middle-income consumers. Low-salary employees bought the smaller denominations of these bonds by the billions through payroll deduction plans.

Types of Bonds

The bonds now come in two series—series EE and series HH. These series are replacing the old series E and series H, which are being phased out.

Series EE Bonds. As of January 2, 1980, the EE bonds are being issued in denominations of $50 (cost $25); $75 (cost $37.50); $100 (cost $50); $200 (cost $100); $500 (cost $250); $1,000 (cost $500); and $10,000 (cost $5,000). All the bonds mature in eleven years and nine months. Thus, for example, the bond for which the buyer pays $25 will have a maturity value of $50 eleven years and nine months from the issue date.

All the bonds earn interest at the average rate of 7 percent, compounded semiannually. The bonds can be redeemed anytime after six months after date of purchase, but the interest rate at six months is less than 7 percent; it increases gradually, reaching 7 percent only at the eleven-year mark. They can be redeemed at almost any financial institution that is an authorized federal paying agency. The bonds, as obligations of the U.S. government, are the safest investment any saver can make. They are even safer than cash, for if the bonds are lost or stolen duplicate bonds can be obtained. The limit of purchase in any year is $15,000 maturity value per person. All the bonds carry an automatic ten-year extension privilege at the same interest rate.

Series HH Bonds. Series HH bonds differ from series EE bonds in that the buyer pays the full maturity value for them at the time of purchase, and every six months receives the interest earned. The bonds come in denominations of $500, $1,000, and $5,000. The interest rate is 6.5 percent right from the start, but an interest penalty is imposed if the bonds are redeemed before the ten-year maturing period ends. The limit of purchase in any year is $20,000 per person, and purchase limits are upheld through the listing of Social Security numbers, which buyers of either type of savings bond must provide.

Advantages

As already indicated, U.S. government bonds offer a very high degree of safety, a reasonable yield, and the possibility of early redemption. In addition, savings bonds have several other advantages.

The income from U.S. savings bonds is free from state and local income or personal property taxes. Thus, where there are state and local income or personal property taxes, the actual yield is even higher than 6 percent. Interestingly enough, bond interest income is not exempt from federal taxes.

Another advantage of Series EE bonds is that the income tax can be deferred. The holder of the bonds is given the option of declaring the annual income every year or waiting until the bonds are cashed in and then declaring the total income for the whole period in that year. If the former option is exercised, however, it must be continued on an annual basis.

A third considerable tax advantage of savings bonds is that a parent can buy savings bonds in a child's name, with the parent as a beneficiary but not a co-owner. The yearly income can then be listed on the child's income tax. Unless the income is more than the child's minimum exemption, no tax will be due. Thus, when the bonds are cashed in to meet college or other needs, all the interest that has accumulated will be free from federal income tax as well as from state and local income and property taxes.

Both EE and HH bonds may be registered in any one of three ways. First, they may, of course, be registered in the name of any person. Second, they may be listed in the name of any two persons as co-owners. This means that either of the two owners can cash the bonds by endorsement without the approval of the other. In case of the death of one of the owners, the survivor becomes the sole owner. Third, the bonds can be registered in the name of one person and one beneficiary. These bonds are then payable to the beneficiary on the death of the owner. The beneficiary need only provide proof of the death of the owner. The beneficiary may then keep the bonds until maturity or ask for new bonds designating him or her as owner.

Banks and all other authorized financial institutions sell or cash U.S. savings bonds free of charge at any time. To buy or sell them is a very simple operation. All you need in order to buy them is the necessary cash and your Social Security number. All you need in order to redeem them is possession of the bonds and identification proving that you are the registered owner or designated beneficiary. It is above all this simplicity, plus the safety and the reasonable yield, that has made so many millions of Americans the owners of many, many billions of dollars' worth of U.S. government savings bonds.

TREASURY INSTRUMENTS AND MONEY-MARKET CERTIFICATES

Millions of Americans have found that double-digit inflation has made U.S. treasury instruments a very attractive investment. The three most common of these high-yield investments are described below, along with a related offering of banks and thrift institutions.

Treasury Bills

The U.S. Treasury sells Treasury bills (T-bills) every week. The maturity periods for these savings vehicles are three, six, and nine months, with three and six months being most common. The minimum denomination for T-bills is $10,000. They may be purchased directly from Federal Reserve banks, or indirectly from stock brokerage firms, banks, or thrift institutions. When purchasing directly from the Federal Reserve bank, an individual must make an offer that includes the rate of return he or she is willing to accept in exchange for lending money to the Treasury. This can be tricky—it requires a thorough knowledge of the rate of T-bills sold during the previous week and of the current market conditions, two factors which will determine the rate of this week's sales. Therefore, individual investors generally make what is known as a noncompetitive tender (offer), which means that the rate of return should be an average of the highest and lowest offers that were made by institutional and other large investors. Purchasing through a brokerage firm is easier; however, brokerage firms do charge $25 for a $10,000 T-bill.

Since the owner's name is not printed on the face of the bills, it is important that care be taken in storing them.

Treasury Notes

Treasury notes usually mature in two to ten years. The lowest denomination is $1,000, but most are for $5,000. They may be purchased from the same sources as T-bills.

Treasury Bonds

Treasury bonds are long-term securities. They mature after ten years or more. The minimum denomination for Treasury bonds is $1,000. Treasury bonds are not sold on any set schedule by the Treasury—they are sold as the government needs money.

T-Rate Certificates

Banks and thrift institutions are allowed to sell six-month certificates at rates based on the current market price of T-bills. Interest earned on these $10,000-minimum certificates may be paid monthly, quarterly, or at maturity (six months), depending on the account and the institution.

The Federal Reserve has also granted banks and thrifts permission to offer a four-year certificate-of-deposit with a maximum interest rate 1 percentage point (1½ percentage points for banks) below that paid on Treasury instruments with a similar maturity date. There is no minimum investment associated with this instrument.

Compared with T-bills, T-certificates have two drawbacks:

1. While interest earned on Treasury instruments is exempt from state income tax in some states, such as New York, interest earned on the bank or thrift T-certificates is generally taxable.
2. Cashing in a T-certificate will result in a sizeable penalty, while a T-bill may be sold on the open market much as a share of stock or a corporation bond would be.

The savings accounts and other investments presented in this chapter represent relatively safe and liquid ways of investing small or large amounts of unspent income. (*Liquidity* refers to the ease with which one can change from cash to savings and savings back to cash without loss of value.) Some savings possibilities that are not as safe or as liquid as those presented in this chapter will be discussed in Chapter 10 on Investing in Securities.

QUESTIONS FOR DISCUSSION

1. What is the difference between a passbook account and a statement account?
2. What would you suggest that an individual look for in selecting a savings account?
3. How can the Rule of 72s assist the saver?
4. Why is the day-of-deposit-to-day-of-withdrawal method of calculating interest the most beneficial to the savings account customer?
5. How do grace periods and dead days work to the depositor's advantage?
6. How does a Series EE bond differ from a Series HH bond? Why might a buyer choose one or the other?
7. How can a savings bond's effective rate be higher than the issued rate?
8. Define liquidity. Should all savings and investments be liquid?

PERSONAL EXPERIENCE PROJECTS

1. Conduct a survey of consumers' attitudes toward saving. Determine the amounts various individuals attempt to save, reasons for saving, places they save, and recent uses of savings.
2. Conduct a survey of the methods used at different saving institutions to calculate interest (low balance, FIFO, etc.). Also obtain

information on frequency of interest compounding and recording, grace days, early withdrawal penalties.

3. Collect advertisements from banks and other savings institutions that offer "free" gifts for making a new or additional deposit. Contact the Federal Home Loan Bank Board, 1700 G Street, N.W., Washington, DC 20052, and the Comptroller of the Currency, Washington, DC 20219, for information on government restrictions regarding savings premiums.

4. Conduct a survey of consumer preferences in savings institutions. Determine the main factor that influences the choice of a place to save—convenience, safety, service, interest rate, frequency of interest payment, gifts, etc.

5. Compare savings interest rates at various financial institutions: a commercial bank, a savings and loan association, a mutual savings bank, and a credit union. Discuss reasons for the differences in rates.

6. Discuss with a bank official and business owners the influence local consumer saving has on economic growth. Obtain information from the bank on government restrictions regarding the percentage of savings that may be used for making loans.

7. Conduct a survey of savings plans available at a commercial bank. Compare time restrictions, liquidity, safety, interest rates, yields, and minimum deposits.

8. Compare the insurance coverage of various savings institutions. Obtain information on amount of coverage and restrictions from the Federal Deposit Insurance Corporation, Office of Bank Customer Affairs, 550 17th Street, N.W., Washington, DC 20429; the National Credit Union Administration, 2025 M Street, N.W., Washington, DC 20056; and the Federal Savings and Loan Insurance Corporation, 320 First Street, N.W., Washington, DC 20052.

9. Interview a banker or other employee of a financial institution where U.S. savings bonds are sold. Obtain information on current interest rates, time restrictions, and advantages of this form of saving.

4
CONSUMER CREDIT

Chances are you have charge accounts in certain local stores. And when you buy gasoline at a service station, you probably charge it with a credit card. In these simple and common transactions you are using consumer credit: buying and using the goods or services first, and paying for them later. The same principle applies when you borrow money from a bank to pay tuition, or from a finance company to pay for a car. Consumer credit operates on trust—the department store, gasoline company, hardware store, bank, or finance company trusts you to pay back what you owe.

Is consumer credit a necessity or a convenience, a blessing or a curse?

Bill Brown is fifty years old. He prides himself on the fact that he has always paid cash for everything he has ever bought. His motto is "If you can't pay cash, don't buy it!" Suddenly Bill runs into a medical problem he can't handle with cash. His wife is ill, and the doctors cannot determine just what is wrong. She may need extensive surgery. Since he does not have enough cash to pay for the medical expenses already incurred, Bill decides that for the first time in his life he will have to borrow money. In this case consumer credit is a necessity.

Dan White is thirty-one years old. When he and Sally were married, they furnished their whole apartment with new furniture. To do this, they took out a large loan. Over the next few years Dan and Sally found it easy to get credit cards—and even easier to find uses for them. One day Dan decided to clean up their debts by taking out a consolidation loan. Their many bills were combined into one loan payment. The new, smaller payment, although it was extended over a longer period, was much easier to pay than all the old bills. It also gave Dan and Sally more money to spend. That is when Dan saw the car of his dreams. He had no down payment, but he had to have it. Dan borrowed the down payment from a small loan company and financed the rest through a dealer plan. He knew he was getting ripped off, but he wanted the car. Last week when Dan came home from work Sally had some special news—they were going to be parents. Since Dan and Sally do not have a maternity benefit clause in their health insurance plan, they know they will have to borrow more money.

What will happen to Bill Brown and Dan White? The two situations describe extremes in the case of consumer credit. Both individuals will be frustrated in their efforts to obtain a loan.

Bill Brown will be surprised to learn that he is not considered a good risk; lenders will want to look at his credit history, and they will not like what they see. They will have little evidence that he can cope with credit because he has never used credit. He may not get his loan, although it is certainly needed. This is a sad and unfair aspect of consumer credit.

Dan has, of course, a different problem. He and Sally have abused credit. They are about at the end of the rope in their ability to repay. It's too bad that the cutoff has to come at such a poor time, but there is little chance that Dan will get his loan.

At the end of 1979, there was over $1 trillion worth of American consumer credit on the books, largely in the form of credit-card spending, personal loans, and mortgages. Used wisely, credit has allowed millions of people to enjoy needed items immediately. Had they been obliged to save until they had cash to pay for the items, inflation might have prevented them from ever buying some of them. On the other hand, many others splurged in what seemed to be an easy way to get everything they had always wanted. Did they always enjoy splurging? Often this led to fussing, fuming, and fighting over money; pressure from bill collectors; irreparable damage to credit reputations; and even bankruptcy.

This chapter deals with how wise consumers intelligently plan for and use their powerful consumer ability to buy now and pay later.

BUILDING A PERSONAL CREDIT HISTORY

Before stores, banks, loan companies, and credit unions will be willing to trust you, they will want to ask questions about your financial background.

These institutions can tell by the answers to certain questions whether you are a good credit risk—they have learned from past experience what types of people will probably use credit responsibly and what types should probably not be trusted.

When you apply for a credit card, installment loan, or personal loan, the store or lending agency will probably ask for the following information:

1. occupation
2. present and past employers
3. present salary
4. length of time with present employer
5. home address and length of time at that address
6. marital status
7. present and past creditors
8. Social Security number.

The store or lending agency will then verify your past credit history with a credit bureau. Merchants and lenders get credit reputation reports from credit bureaus on more than a hundred million customers every year. Over one million of these persons are denied credit on the basis of something undesirable found in a credit report.

Almost every community has a credit bureau. Some are very small; but regardless of size, all credit bureaus cooperate, so a person's credit file can almost always be obtained. Suppose a department store in Minneapolis finds from a credit-card application that the applicant's last address was in Atlanta. It is a simple matter for this store to have the Minneapolis credit bureau see that the records are transferred from Atlanta. Even a prospective employer in a new location can obtain an applicant's credit record.

The bureaus watch the newspapers for notices of court actions, arrests, bankruptcies, tax claims, and legal judgments. All this information is filed and then distributed to subscribers for a small fee. For a larger fee, credit bureaus will also check with banks and employers and investigate public records in the courthouse and city hall.

This seems like a lot of personal information to be kept on file for the benefit of stores and lending agencies. What happens if they receive some incorrect information? Or what if undesirable information about a person with the same name as yours is placed in your file by mistake? This could be very damaging.

The Fair Credit Reporting Act was legislated to protect consumers from the consequences of just such mistakes. Under this act you have the right to:

1. Be told the name and address of the consumer reporting agency responsible for preparing a consumer report that was used to deny you credit, insurance, or employment or to increase the cost of credit or insurance.

2. Be told by a consumer reporting agency the nature, substance, and sources (except investigative-type sources) of information (except medical) collected about you.

3. Obtain all information to which you are entitled free of charge when you have been denied credit, insurance, or employment within thirty days of your request. Otherwise the reporting agency is permitted to charge a reasonable fee (usually from $3 to $8) for giving you the information.

4. Be told who has received a consumer report on you within the preceding six months or within the preceding two years if the report was furnished for employment purposes.

5. Have incomplete or incorrect information reinvestigated, unless the request is frivolous, and, if the information is found to be inaccurate or cannot be verified, to have such information removed from your file.

6. Have the agency notify those you name (at no cost to you) who have previously received the incorrect or incomplete information that this information has been deleted from your file.

7. Have your version of a dispute placed in the file and included in future consumer reports.

8. Exclude adverse information after seven years. One major exception is bankruptcy, which may be reported for fourteen years.

The Fair Credit Reporting Act does not give you the right, when you visit a credit bureau, to receive a copy of your file or to physically handle it. Because of a loophole in the Fair Credit Reporting Act, the bureau agent may merely read you the data. However, most credit bureaus will let you handle your file, and many will even make a copy for you. The credit bureau in your community can be located by consulting the yellow pages of your telephone book under such headings as "Credit," "Credit rating," or "Reporting agencies."

A credit reputation report does not always help the store or lending agency in making a decision to grant credit. Young people often do not have a credit reputation because they have never applied for credit. Older women may experience the same problem if they have always relied on their husbands' reputations instead of establishing credit in their own right. Women's groups are now succeeding in changing this situation with new regulations forcing credit-card companies to report credit in both names if the consumer desires.

How does a consumer establish a good credit reputation? The chances of getting credit are greatly improved if a person:

- Owns property.
- Has rented in the neighborhood for some time and has a good record of paying rent and utility bills.
- Has a regular job or has worked while attending college.
- Does not have any other debts.
- Has a savings account and makes regular deposits.
- Has borrowed money from a bank or other financial institution and has repaid the loan promptly.
- Has a charge account and has paid the bills promptly.

The theory most often used in granting credit is sometimes referred to as *the three C's of credit.* The three C's of credit are being measured in the typical credit-card application in Figure 4-1.

The first C is character. Character is reflected by the way a person has paid bills in the past. Character also includes one's reputation in the community and may be determined by referring to personal references.

The second C is capital. Capital refers to how much the individual is worth. The credit guarantor wants to know what property or money outside of regular income could be used to repay the debt.

The third C is capacity. Capacity answers the questions "Can you afford to pay the debt with what you are presently making?" and "What are your earning prospects for the future?"

The three C's are all important when the credit grantor must decide whether or not to take a chance on an individual; however, a person without credit experience (character) may still be granted credit on the basis of capital and capacity until a solid credit reputation can be established.

Many credit grantors are now using some form of numerical rating system for personal-loan and credit-card applications. A number of the numerical rating systems have been designed for decision making based on computer programs. The score card illustrated in Figure 4-2 is an example of a rating system.

In building the scoring system the following factors are considered:

1. *Stability.* How long has it been since the applicant changed residence or position? Does the applicant have a phone? Does the applicant own a home or property?
2. *Occupation.* Professionals usually get the highest scores. Unskilled workers rate very low.

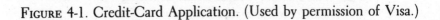

FIGURE 4-1. Credit-Card Application. (Used by permission of Visa.)

3. *Income.* This factor is actually more useful in setting credit limits than in predicting good credit risks, but it is fed into the score.
4. *Financial history.* Past credit record is one of the most important considerations and may overbalance all other factors.

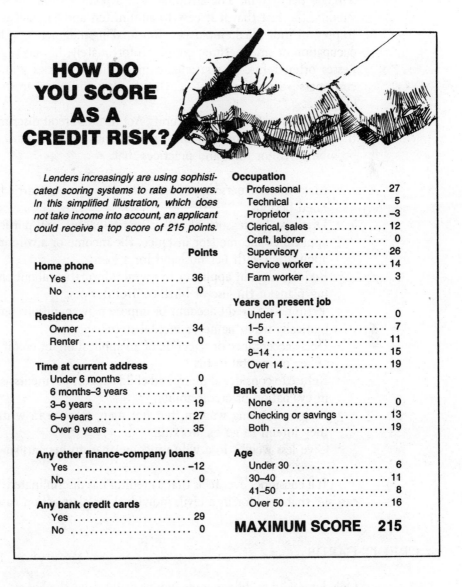

HOW DO YOU SCORE AS A CREDIT RISK?

Lenders increasingly are using sophisticated scoring systems to rate borrowers. In this simplified illustration, which does not take income into account, an applicant could receive a top score of 215 points.

	Points
Home phone	
Yes	36
No	0
Residence	
Owner	34
Renter	0
Time at current address	
Under 6 months	0
6 months–3 years	11
3–6 years	19
6–9 years	27
Over 9 years	35
Any other finance-company loans	
Yes	–12
No	0
Any bank credit cards	
Yes	29
No	0

Occupation	
Professional	27
Technical	5
Proprietor	–3
Clerical, sales	12
Craft, laborer	0
Supervisory	26
Service worker	14
Farm worker	3
Years on present job	
Under 1	0
1–5	7
5–8	11
8–14	15
Over 14	19
Bank accounts	
None	0
Checking or savings	13
Both	19
Age	
Under 30	6
30–40	11
41–50	8
Over 50	16

MAXIMUM SCORE   215

FIGURE 4-2. A Credit Rating System. (Reprinted from *U.S. News & World Report,* August 22, 1977, p. 65. Copyright 1977 U.S. News & World Report, Inc.)

Age was formerly considered, but the Equal Credit Opportunity Act has made this factor virtually useless as a basis for credit scores.

Point scoring may vary from city to city because of regional differences in incomes and occupations. One chain organization finds that it must construct a special system for each of its outlets, at a cost of about $50,000 per system. The advantages of a point system are its statistical validity, the fact that it is easy to administer, and the fact that it helps to prevent individual employees from making judgments on the basis of occupation or sex or ethnic group. Unfortunately, however, ghetto businesses often refuse to participate in credit businesses and bury their customers' records in the store, thus forcing customers to stay with the old stores.

The Equal Credit Opportunity Act forbids credit discrimination on the basis of race, color, religion, national origin, sex, or marital status. It prohibits creditor rules and practices that:

- Make married persons more creditworthy than unmarried or separated persons.
- Disallow, for reasons of sex or marital status, any portion of an applicant's income (for instance, the income of a wife in a joint application with her husband for a loan).
- Require a credit applicant to reveal information about childbearing plans or the use of birth-control devices.
- Terminate a credit account or impose new conditions on it automatically when name or marital status changes.
- Delay acceptance or rejection of an application for credit because of sex or marital status.
- Refuse to consider alimony and child-support payments as income in evaluation of credit ability.
- Require working women, but not men, to state in writing that they intend to go on working.
- Give less weight to a wife's income than to her husband's.

If a consumer ever feels that a creditor has discriminated, the person can sue that creditor in a civil, individual, or class action case.

CREDIT CARDS

Only high- and middle-income groups could enjoy the benefit and convenience of charge accounts and credit cards up to the end of World War II. In the last thirty years, however, the credit card has become a very important factor in the tremendous increase in consumer credit.

Advantages and Disadvantages

Can credit cards be a bargain? It all depends on how the cards are used. A typical group of cardholders gave the following reasons why they use credit cards:

It beats carrying cash. I have heard of too many people being mugged or robbed and thus out the cash. At least with credit cards you can stop the cards from being used if they're lost or stolen—and not lose so much.

There are times when items come up on sale and I'm caught short of cash in my account. I can simply use the card, have the item for immediate use, and then pay when I have the money.

It's easier to write out just one check at the end of the month instead of a lot of little checks. Sometimes it's even hard to get a check accepted, or if it is, there's too much red tape before the sales clerk will take it.

I like it for recordkeeping reasons. I always keep my slips and at the end of the month can check them off against my bill. I have a good record for tax purposes, and it helps me manage a recordkeeping system more efficiently.

If I'm dissatisfied with an item I can get a refund on my credit card, whereas if I had paid cash the chances are the store would not have given me a cash refund. Also, if the business refuses to settle my complaint, it is an easy matter to stop payment on the disputed item while I work on satisfying my complaint.

I use my credit card strictly as a substitute for cash. That way I get to use the store's money and goods for up to one month without paying even a penny more than in a cash deal.

It's almost impossible to rent a car without a credit card. It ensures that you won't get stranded, and it allows you to buy airline tickets and make reservations by phone.

There is another side of the coin to these advantages, however.

First, while it is generally true that carrying credit cards is safer than carrying cash, there may still be some liability on the part of the cardholder. The card issuer (store, bank, or oil company) can collect up to $50 if not notified of the loss of the card before unauthorized use of the card. The Truth-in-Lending Law, which set this upper limit, requires that the card issuer tell the cardholder how and where to report all losses.

The Electronic Fund Transfer Act, which went into effect August 1, 1979, limits a consumer's loss on a lost or stolen debit card to $50 if he or she reports the loss of the debit card within two days of learning of the loss. The liability increases to $500 if the two-day limit has passed and the financial institution can prove that the card would not have been misused if the consumer had reported the loss.

Second, possible advantages of simple and convenient bookkeeping can become costly disadvantages to a cardholder who simply pays bills without checking for mistakes. For example, when Ellen traveled extensively during the summer, she charged her gasoline at each stop. She did not keep receipts. When she received her statement for payment, she simply wrote a check for the full amount and mailed it. If she had checked carefully, she would have noticed that one dishonest service station had raised her bill from $6.75 to $16.75. Even if she had noticed the change, she could not have done anything about it without her original receipt to prove the discrepancy.

Finally, credit cards do ultimately cost their holders. In some cases the individual cardholder pays a yearly fee; in other cases, where the direct cost of the credit operation is paid for entirely by the businesses using it, the customer pays more indirectly. Stores that use Visa and Mastercharge, for example, are charged between 1.7 and 4.5 percent (based on the volume of credit-card sales) on the merchandise bought by people holding these cards. This charge on credit-card purchases is made by the sponsoring bank in return for immediate cash paid to the merchant by the bank. The credit-card company then collects the debt. However, the merchant who accepts these cards passes the costs on to all the customers—cash and credit purchasers alike.

The Fair Credit Billing Act of 1975 makes it legal for a store to grant a discount to a customer who pays cash rather than use a credit card. However, the store is not required to do so—and few do.

Credit cards also cost their holders more simply because the holders are tempted to buy more when they can defer the payment until later. It is this fact that makes it generally profitable for stores to accept credit cards. It is not unusual for people to consider a trip to the shopping mall a recreational activity. This "something to do" usually costs money, especially for the shopper who is short of cash but has the "plastic" instead.

Finally, the most commonly discussed cost of credit-card use is the charge on unpaid balances. Fewer than half of all cardholders pay their entire balance each month. The business or bank collects a revolving charge on the unpaid portion. The amount of the charge depends on the maximum rate allowed by the state.

It is quite obvious from this discussion of the advantages and disadvantages of credit-card use that the old expression still holds true: "For nothing you get nothing."

Credit-Card Agreements

The terms of the credit agreement are set forth on the back of most credit-card bills. Besides the annual percentage rate, there are some other points that deserve attention.

Charges. One is the method the credit-card company uses to compute charges. Most credit cards are revolving in nature. The customer who charges has three alternatives when the bill is received:

1. Pay in full.
2. Pay the minimum amount on the statement.
3. Pay a sum in excess of the minimum payment but below payment in full.

If the holder of a bank card pays the bill for the current month's purchases in full, he or she normally does not have to pay any charge. (See discussion later of one short-lived exception.)

If, however, the cardholder elects either the second or third alternative, he or she will pay a charge on the unpaid balance. There are various methods used by credit-card plans to compute these charges. To explain and define them let us use an example.

Herman Rogers receives his bill on July 30. According to his agreement, he has twenty-eight days in which to pay the full amount, the minimum balance, or some amount in between. The credit-card agreement states that there will be a charge of 1 percent a month (12-percent APR) on unpaid balances. His bill is $200. On August 15, Herman pays $50 on the bill. On August 20, Herman charges a $75 item.

Adjusted Balance Method. If the credit-card charges are computed using the adjusted balance method, Herman will have a bill of $225 on August 30 and a carrying charge of $1.50. The charge (assuming a month of thirty days) is computed as follows:

$200   Balance at the beginning of month
 − 50   Payment on the fifteenth
 150   New balance for charge purposes
× .01
$1.50   Carrying charge

Notice that Herman's new purchase has nothing to do with the charge for this month. Herman pays a carrying charge only on what is owed on the last day of the month.

According to the previous balance method, Herman's carrying charge for the past month will be $2.00. This charge is computed as follows:

$200 Beginning balance
× .01
$2.00

Notice that no consideration is given to the payment on the fifteenth or to the new purchase on the twentieth. The method is quite commonly used by department stores.

Average Daily Method. The average daily method is utilized by credit-card companies in two forms.

The basic method does not take into account charges for new purchases. An average is simply determined from the exact balance of noncurrent charges on each day of the month, and the carrying charge is based on that average. Using this method, Herman's carrying charge will be $1.75. To compute the charge:

$200 Beginning balance
−50 Payment on the fifteenth
$150 New balance

$200 × 15 days = $3000
150 × 15 days = $2250
          30          $5250

$175 Average daily balance
30 days)$5250
3000
2250
2100
150
150

$175 Average daily balance
× .01
$1.75 Charge

Obviously, it is advantageous to the consumer to make the payment as early in the month as possible in order to bring down the average balance. This method is used by many department stores.

A variation on the average daily balance is used by bank credit cards such as Visa and Mastercharge. Under this variation, new purchases are considered in the average daily balance. Herman's charge under this system will be $2.00.

$200 Beginning balance
−50 Payment on the fifteenth
$150
+ 75 New purchase on the twentieth
$225 New balance

To compute the charge:

$$\begin{array}{rcl}
\$200 \times 15 \text{ days} & = & \$3000 \\
150 \times 5 \text{ days} & = & \$ 750 \\
225 \times \underline{10} \text{ days} & = & \underline{\$2250} \\
30 & & \$6000
\end{array}$$

$$\begin{array}{r}
\$200 \text{ Average daily balance} \\
30 \text{ days})\overline{\$6000}
\end{array}$$

$$\begin{array}{r}
\$200 \\
\underline{\times .01} \\
\$2.00
\end{array}$$

To avoid charges on new purchases, the customer must pay the bill in full each month.

Some banks have gone one step further in attempting to collect more interest. One such bank, Citibank, the nation's second largest bank, decided in 1976 to levy a 50¢-a-month service fee on its Mastercharge customers who did not incur interest charges because they paid their bills promptly. Since this provision was not set forth in the original applications, a Long Island lawyer, Richard Ostor, immediately sued to get his 50¢ back. He won in both the lower court and the Appeals Courts. While 50¢ does not sound like much, over 300,000 other customers were affected during the twenty-month period Citibank charged the fees, so the estimated take was $1 to $2 million.

Acceleration Clause. A second clause on most credit agreements that merits your attention is the acceleration clause. The acceleration clause reads "In case of default in payment or other breach thereof, your entire outstanding balance will then become due and payable." However, businesses generally will not enforce this option unless your minimum payment is long overdue.

Limitations. After the application has been approved, you will receive your credit card. Read it carefully. There are different cards for different purposes. Some cards are good for only one store or certain types of purchases within a store. Many cards have credit limits, which depend on capacity, capital, and character. Some general-purpose cards for use in many stores charge membership fees. Bank cards generally do not charge a membership fee but do set credit lines for cardholders. They also allow their cardholders to borrow money on the card at a specified APR. This rate is charged from the day you borrow, however—you do not have thirty interest-free days.

Billing Errors—Fair Credit Billing Act

There may be times when you have a question about your credit balance. In the past, many people became frustrated trying to discuss this situation with computers. The Fair Credit Billing Act of 1975 affords the consumer billing protection in a number of ways. Following are your rights as set out in the 1976 pamphlet "Fair Credit Billing," by the Board of Governors of the Federal Reserve System.

BILLING ERROR

You may challenge either the purchase or the price of an item that appears on your billing statement. The law defines an error as any charge:

· Not made either by you or by someone authorized to use your account.
· Poorly identified, for a different amount or on a different date than is shown on the statement.
· Something which you did not accept on delivery or which was not delivered according to agreement.

Billing errors also include:

· Failure to credit your account properly.
· Computational or accounting mistakes.
· Failure to mail your statement to your current address, provided you notified the creditor of your address change at least 10 days before the billing period ended.

A request for additional information or an explanation about a questionable item is also considered a billing error.

IN CASE OF ERROR

If you think your bill is wrong or want more information about it, follow these steps:

1. Notify the creditor in writing within 60 days after the bill was mailed. Be sure to include: your name and account number; a statement that you believe the bill contains an error and an explanation of why you believe there is an error; the suspected amount of the error.
2. While you are waiting for an answer, you do not have to pay the amount in question (the "disputed amount") or any minimum payments or finance charges that apply to it. But you are still obligated to pay all parts of the bill that are not in dispute.
3. The creditor must acknowledge your letter within 30 days, unless your bill is corrected before that. Within two billing periods—but in no case more than 90 days—either your account must be corrected or you must be told why the creditor believes the bill is correct.
4. If the creditor made a mistake, you do not pay any finance charges on the disputed amount. Your account must be corrected for either the full amount in dispute, or for a part of that amount along with an explanation of what you still owe. You then have the time usually given on your type of account to pay any balance. If no error is found, the creditor must promptly send you a statement of what you owe. In this case, the creditor may include any finance charges that accumulated and any minimum payments you missed while you were questioning the bill.
5. If you still are not satisfied, you should notify the creditor within the time you have to pay your bill. However, the creditor has now fulfilled his legal obligation (except for the requirements that follow regarding your credit rating).

YOUR CREDIT RATING

Once you have written about a possible error, the creditor may not give out information to other creditors or credit bureaus or threaten to damage your credit rating. Until your letter is answered, the creditor also may not take any collection action on the disputed amount, or restrict your account because of the dispute. A creditor can, however, apply the disputed amount against your credit limit.

But, after the bill has been explained—and if you still disagree in writing within the time allowed for payment and do not pay—the creditor can report you as delinquent on your account and begin collection proceedings. If this is done, the creditor must also report that you challenge your bill, and you must be provided in writing the name and address of each person to whom your credit information has been given. When the matter is settled, the creditor must report the outcome to each person who received information about you.

DEFECTIVE MERCHANDISE OR SERVICES

The law now provides that you may withhold payment of any balance due on defective merchandise or services purchased with a credit card, provided you have made a good faith effort to return the goods or resolve the problem with the merchant from whom you made the purchase.

If the store that honored the credit card was not also the issuer of the card, two limitations apply to this right:

· The original amount of the purchase must have exceeded $50; and
· The sale must have taken place in your state or within 100 miles of your current address.

In the case of defective merchandise or services, a legal action may result to determine the validity of your claim.

PENALTIES AND OTHER PROVISIONS

The law provides that any creditor who fails to comply with these rules applying to billing errors and credit ratings automatically forfeits the amount of the item in question and any finance charges on it, up to a total of $50, even if no error occurred. You as an individual may also sue for actual damages plus twice the amount of any finance charges, in any case not less than $100 or more than $1,000. Class action suits are also permitted.

The law also includes requirements for prompt reporting and crediting of payments or return of merchandise. In addition, it provides that credit card issuers may not prohibit stores which honor their cards from offering discounts to customers who pay in cash or by check.

TO FIND OUT MORE

Creditors must provide you a complete statement of your Fair Credit Billing rights when you first open an account and at least twice annually (or send a shorter version with each billing). If you have any further questions about Fair Credit Billing, you may write to any Federal Reserve Bank or to the Board of Governors of the Federal Reserve System, Washington, D.C. 20551. If your question is about a particular creditor, you may want to address it to the attention of the appropriate enforcement agency.

INSTALLMENT CREDIT

A revolving credit-card account, a personal loan, and a charge account at a store are all examples of noninstallment credit. There are, however, many types of consumer credit based on installment contracts.

A credit transaction is classified as installment if the customer assumes a schedule of fixed payments until the item is fully paid. The credit card–holder and charge-account customer need not conform to fixed payments, and the personal loan only involves one payment at the end of the loan period rather than installments.

The following are examples of installment credit.

1. Consumer A has signed an agreement to pay a retail store for a refrigerator over a ninety-day period in three equal payments with no interest.
2. Consumer B has signed an agreement to pay a door-to-door salesperson's company for a set of encyclopedias over a two-year period.
3. Consumer C has gone to a local bank and obtained an automobile loan which will be paid over a thirty-six-month period.

The refrigerator and encyclopedia transactions may be examples of conditional sales contracts. The automobile loan is an example of a secured sales contract.

PROSPECTIVE BORROWERS

Determine a down payment and monthly payment you can afford.
List possible sources of financing.
Gather loan information.
Compare APRs.
Read the chosen contract carefully.

In a secured loan, the collateral (or security) is often the item purchased, such as the automobile. If the purchaser defaults (fails to pay the installments), the lender may in most states repossess and resell the item to recover the unpaid remainder of the loan. In the case of conditional sales contracts (refrigerator and encyclopedia transactions), the title does not pass to the purchaser until the item is fully paid. Therefore, the seller has the right to have the item returned for resale. Many state legislatures are taking a closer look at these contracts. Too often the individual is urged to sign the contracts even if he or she cannot afford to pay for the item, because the sellers know they can simply repossess and then sell the item again.

While the conditional sales contract and the secured sales contract are technically different, their legal effect is much the same. The lender or seller will use the proceeds from a default sale to complete the payments due. If the sale nets a greater amount than the loan balance (extremely rare), the purchaser who defaulted will be given the difference. If the sale price is less (usually the case), the purchaser who defaulted will still have more to pay. It is for this reason that most lenders or sellers require a down payment at the time of purchase. Without this initial down payment, the sellers could lose a great deal in the case of a repossession sale.

Instead of using a purchase as collateral, the borrower may use an existing savings account or other assets as security for a loan. Many lending institutions will offer lower APRs to borrowers who will leave a savings account with them until their loan has been paid. But a question comes up here as to whether a person should borrow at all if he or she has savings. Why not use the savings and then resave on a payment schedule the same way you would have had to pay the loan?

Depending on individual circumstances, you have a wide range of options in purchasing goods and services with credit. The options may include a cash installment loan, an agreement with the retail establishment, or any of the three examples of noninstallment credit. The cash loan may be borrowed from a variety of sources. Besides the obvious sources, such as banks, consumer finance companies, savings and loan associations, and credit unions, there are some other equally good sources of installment credit, such as an insurance policy. If you have a policy that is building a cash value, it may be an economical and convenient source of credit. The main disadvantage of a loan on a policy is that it reduces the insurance protection by the amount of the loan.

With so many sources available, it is wise to shop around for the best possible loan. A look at one particular case should help to clarify the procedure and considerations in installment-loan shopping.

Consider the case of Janice Breen. Janice has finally found just the car she wants. The sticker price is $4,392.11, but she is able to close the deal at $3,800.

Down Payment and Loan Period

Janice's first step now is to determine her best down payment, for it is extremely difficult to compare credit installment payments if you do not know exactly how much you want to borrow. After a careful review of her financial situation, Janice decides that the largest down payment she can afford without using up too much of her savings is $800.

Janice then secures figures on estimated monthly payments on a $3,000 loan over various loan periods. She determines that with her current take-home income, she can afford the payments on a thirty-six-month loan. A look at her budget shows that she will still be able to save each month.

She decides on the thirty-six-month loan rather than a longer one because she wants the car paid off as soon as possible for two reasons. First, deferring the price over any added months would make the total sum larger. Second, the new car might not be as much of a thrill after three years and making payments could become depressing.

Installment Loan Sources

After having spent valuable time finding the "best deal," Janice is not about to make the mistake of taking the first offer of a loan, so she makes a list of possible sources for an automobile loan.

For a $3,000 loan she cannot use the consumer finance company, because in her state they are not permitted to make a full loan of $3,000. She also finds that a noninstallment loan is normally not available for automobile purchases. Still, there is a sizeable list of possibilities, because she can afford a car and she is a good credit risk:

1. *Local Banks.* All banks do not charge the same rate for automobile loans.
2. *Credit Union.* Only the credit union where she is a member can be included in the comparison.
3. *Insurance Companies.* Many insurance companies make automobile loans in addition to selling automobile insurance.
4. *Automobile Dealer's Plan.* Often an automobile dealership will offer a plan. Some dealership plans are sponsored by the manufacturer, such as General Motors; others may operate through a local bank. In the case of a bank-sponsored loan, it is wise to go to the bank yourself. Often the rate is cheaper at the bank because the dealership adds a charge for its services.

Gathering Information

The stage is now set for comparison. Janice will want to determine monthly payments, finance charges, deferred payments (total amount of money she will pay), and annual percentage rates of the various lenders. In most cases it will not be necessary for her to actually go in person to the lenders; she can obtain the information from a loan officer over the telephone. The loan officer will ask for the sticker price, actual price, down payment, and length and amount of desired loan. It is very helpful to use a chart such as Table 4-1 to record this information.

TABLE 4-1. Gathering Loan Information

Lenders	Monthly Payment	Dollar Value of Charges	Deferred Price	APR Rate
Bank A				
Bank B				
Credit Union				
Ins. Co. A				
Ins. Co. B				
Auto Dealer				

Evaluating Options—the APR

The key to all consumer-credit costs is the APR, or annual percentage rate. In the past, borrowers had no way of knowing how much it cost to borrow a certain amount of money for a certain period of time. Today borrowers are more fortunate. The Truth-in-Lending Law requires that all lenders tell the prospective borrower the "true interest rate" of the loan.

What is a true interest rate? Suppose that a person borrows $100 for a year at 6-percent interest. At the end of the year the individual pays back $106. The true interest rate and annual percentage rate is 6 percent. But suppose the consumer borrows $100 to be paid back in monthly installments. Is the true interest rate and annual percentage rate still 6 percent? No! It is almost twice that rate, because the full $100 is used for only the first month. If the monthly installment is $10, in the second month of the loan only $90 is being used. Each month a smaller amount of money is being used. Thus the true annual percentage rate is actually over 11 percent.

Janice must make sure the actual APR is quoted rather than some other type of interest rate or a figure per $100 borrowed. This is important in order to make an accurate comparison.

Once she has made comparisons, she will proceed to the lender with the lowest APR to check out the entire contract.

Reading the Contract

In this final step, the main question to be answered is "Do I understand the contract?" Janice will read it carefully to make sure she knows:

1. The exact APR. It must be displayed in easy-to-read numbers.
2. Exactly how many payments she will make.
3. Exactly how much money will be due in each payment. She will need to make sure the payments are the same size. Some contracts have a *balloon clause* which provides for one large payment at the end of the contract. This makes the other payments seem smaller, but it may be difficult to repay or refinance the final large payment.
4. Exactly when each payment is due. Are there late days or a grace period so that she is not penalized for failing to pay on the exact date?
5. Exactly how much all the payments add up to in terms of dollars (the deferred price).
6. Exactly what happens if she fails to pay off the loan. There are a variety of recourses available to lenders, such as extra charges or even repossession, and they should be stated in the contract.
7. Exactly whom she will be paying. This applies mainly to a situation where one is financing a purchase through a seller. For example, if you purchase an automobile by signing an installment contract with the auto dealer it is possible for them to sell that contract for cash instead of waiting for your payments. The company that buys the contract replaces the original seller as holder of the contract, and payments are made to the new holder. This new holder is referred to as a *holder-in-due-course.*

   It used to be difficult for buyers to stop payment on a purchase if the merchandise had been misrepresented by a seller who in turn had sold the contract to a third party. But effective May 1976, the Federal Trade Commission (FTC) adopted a rule regarding holder-in-due-course transactions. The rule states that sales contracts must contain a notice preserving the buyer's right to stop payment in the case of defective material that the seller refuses to repair or replace.

It is illegal for the seller to include a clause that would waive (give up) the buyer's right to stop payment. The FTC regulation does not apply if Janice buys the car from the dealer and then goes out and obtains a loan from a financial institution under a separate contract. It only applies where one buys and finances directly from the seller, who in turn sells the contract to a third party.

Besides automobile sales, the most common types of transactions involving the holder-in-due-course are purchases of furniture and appliances, home improvements, freezer or food plans, and courses of training and instruction.

8. Exactly what, if anything, the salesperson or manager promises to do. All promises should be in writing on the contract, for verbal agreements are very difficult to prove.

9. Whether there is a penalty for early payment in full. Most installment contracts state that prepayments will be covered by the Rule of 78s (sometimes called the actuarial or sum-of-the-digits method). Under this system, most of the interest is taken by the lender during the first months (over half is taken in the first four months of a one-year loan), leaving you with very little advantage if you pay early. Also, since you then have not had the use of the money during the entire agreed-upon period, the APR actually exceeds the agreed-upon amount. So even if you pay back a one-year installment loan in six months, the lender receives nearly all of his or her profit. Most credit unions grant loans using simple interest calculated on the unpaid balance. Therefore, the borrower pays interest on money only for the length of time it is borrowed. However, if Janice does not plan to pay her loan off early, then the size of the APR is more important than the prepayment conditions.

10. Whether or not she is paying an additional fee for credit life insurance, a life-insurance policy that leaves an amount equal to the loan to the store in the event the borrower should die. Credit life insurance premiums may not be included in the loan without the borrower's specific permission in writing on a loan application. The buyer should definitely attempt to negotiate credit life insurance out of the contract in states where it is legal to include it, for, as a 1979 study in *Consumer Reports* shows, credit life insurance is no bargain:

For most borrowers, who are getting short-term loans, the cost of credit life doesn't seem dramatic. That $99.17 charge for credit life on a car loan is spread over 36 payments.

Who could complain about an extra charge of $2.75 a month? Almost nobody does. Yet, in fact, credit insurance is ludicrously overpriced.

If you bought insurance under the terms described above you'd be paying the equivalent of about $13.86 per $1000 of term life-insurance coverage per year. In the conventional insurance market, a 35-year-old can easily buy a $100,000 term life-insurance policy for about $3.50 per $1000 of coverage. In other words, credit life insurance, in this example, costs almost four times as much per unit as conventional term insurance.[1]

A typical installment contract disclosure form is shown in Figure 4-3.

DISCLOSURE STATEMENT

1. Proceeds	$3850.00
2. Other Charges	———
3. Amount Financed (1 & 2)	$3850.00
4. Finance Charge	$ 606.08
Service Charge ———	
Interest $606.08	
5. Total of Payments	$4456.08
6. Annual Percentage Rate	$ 9.73%

Total of payments is payable in __36__ monthly installments of __$123.78__ starting on __2-05-78__ and continuing on the 5th day of each month until the final installment payment on 1-05-81.

DELINQUENCY CHARGE
"Late Charges" (5¢ per $1.00, maximum $5.00) will be payable on any installment more than 10 days in arrears.

FIGURE 4-3. Installment Contract Disclosure Statement

[1] "Credit Insurance: The Quiet Overcharge," *Consumer Reports,* July 1979, p. 415.

FINANCIAL DISASTER

Why do so many consumers have financial problems? There are many reasons why individuals fall into debt. Some people misjudge the economy and their job's relationship to it. Personal misfortune may wreck the best kept budget, particularly if insurance is inadequate. Most often, however, overspending is the major cause of credit difficulty. Failure to accurately take into account expenses, overuse of credit, and inability to purchase credit wisely all may lead to financial disaster. Whatever the cause, the solution requires proper handling of creditors and seeking of financial relief.

Handling Creditors

After thirty days with an unpaid bill, most firms will send a dunning letter. This letter asks for payment in a very polite manner. Subsequent letters may contain progressively firmer language, until the business finds it necessary either to utilize the legal means at its disposal in order to collect the debt or to turn it over to a collection agency. If you have difficulty in paying a bill, the best policy is to notify the business and explain the problem. If the loss of a job or other unforeseen circumstances have made it impossible for you to meet your payments, get in touch with your creditors and tell them this. Often you can work out a satisfactory arrangement.

Getting behind on payments can cause severe emotional strain, especially if accounts are turned over to collection agencies. Some collection agencies have in the past used unethical methods to collect overdue bills. Recently, however, a Fair Debt Collection Practices Act went into effect. This act protects consumers from:

- abusive language
- threats of violence
- harassing phone calls at all hours of the day or night
- publication of "show lists" naming defaulting debtors
- misleading or false representation by collection agents (a collector's posing as a person taking a financial survey or as a repairperson in order to get into your home to shame you into paying
- efforts to collect from the wrong person
- attempts to collect twice on the same debt
- collection suits filed in far-off locations.

Businesses that violate the Act may be liable for fines of up to $500,000 or 1 percent of their net worth. The Act is enforced by the Federal Trade Commission.

Obtaining Financial Relief

What can you do to overcome serious financial problems?

Credit Counseling. You can get help in setting up a budget or working out your debt difficulties from an expert at one of the 167 credit counseling services around the United States. Usually these services are free. To find a service near you, write the National Foundation for Consumer Credit, 1819 H Street, Washington, DC 20006.

Consolidation Loans. A consolidation loan lumps all your outstanding debts into one loan, and you then make one payment a month. Unfortunately, however, the total cost of such a loan may be higher than that of the individual loans in the end. It could also cause you to overextend yourself further if you use the money freed up through a longer, smaller-payment loan to obtain more credit.

Bankruptcy. The Federal Bankruptcy Statute provides for two types of bankruptcy for individuals.

The first is full bankruptcy. Filing of the court action costs $60, and a bankruptcy attorney generally charges between $150 and $400. Husbands and wives must file separately.

Under full bankruptcy, most of the bankrupt's assets are sold to pay as much of the debt as possible. The bankrupt is then absolved (cleared) of most of the rest of the debt.

A new federal law exempts the following property:

- up to $7,500 in equity in a home and burial plot
- your interest, up to $1,200, in a motor vehicle
- your interest, up to $200 for any single item, in household goods and furnishings, clothes, appliances, books, animals, crops, and musical instruments
- up to $500 worth of jewelry
- any other property worth up to $400, plus any unused part of the $7,500 homestead exemption
- up to $750 worth of implements, books, or tools of trade
- any professionally prescribed health aids.

States may enact different standards, in which case the debtor may then select the law he or she wishes to follow.

Conversely, some debts that may not be canceled under bankruptcy include mortgages, alimony, and child support. If the bankrupt deliberately agrees at the time of bankruptcy to retain certain debts to unpaid creditors, the agreement is binding if the court agrees it is in the bankrupt's best interest to enter into such an agreement.

A person may not go bankrupt again for six years, and credit bureaus may keep a record of bankruptcy on their files for fourteen years.

The second type of bankruptcy is called Chapter 13 bankruptcy, or the wage earner plan. Chapter 13 of the Federal Bankruptcy Statutes provides the individual the opportunity to repay debts according to a court-supervised schedule of payments. The typical term of repayments is three years. The court will appoint someone to supervise a debtor- or lawyer-filed financial plan after its approval by the court. The advantage of such a plan over a consolidation loan is that the cost is less, and the advantage over full bankruptcy is that the bankruptcy does not appear on the individual's credit record. Not every debtor would find this program applicable, however. Creditors whose debts amount to two-thirds or more of their annual salary would have little chance of paying them off even with a Chapter 13 plan. The moral of this chapter is "Live within your financial means."

Is bankruptcy a cleansing of foul debts or a disgrace? One lawyer says, "Personal bankruptcy is something like contracting a venereal disease —socially acceptable but nothing to brag about!"[2] In some cases, where individuals have been encouraged from every side to borrow and buy or buy and borrow, blame for the bankruptcy must be shared by business and the consumer. In other cases, where individuals are merely taking advantage of the system, society pays the bill for one person's personal benefit.

But in either situation it is the individual who is likely to feel the ill effects eventually, for a bankruptcy on the credit record generally means a sure turndown of any future loan application—and that one may be for the most important loan in the person's life.

QUESTIONS FOR DISCUSSION

1. What is meant by the statement "the credit bureau doesn't grant credit, it only keeps the records"?

[2]Mark Sufrin, "Bankruptcy and the New State of Grace," *Chicago Tribune Magazine,* December 3, 1978.

2. Why is it important for women to apply for credit in their own names?
3. How has the introduction of point scoring systems made the granting of credit a fairer process? How have the systems benefited the businesses that use them?
4. What are the advantages of credit cards to the consumer? To business?
5. What is meant by the "float" in consumer credit cards?
6. Which of the methods of calculating credit-card interest is the most expensive to the cardholder? How can knowledge of carrying-charge computation methods be useful to the cardholder?
7. If you have a problem with merchandise you bought with a bank credit card, what are your rights if the merchant refuses to assist you with your problem?
8. What have the Fair Credit Reporting Act, the Equal Credit Opportunity Act, the Fair Credit Billing Act, the Fair Debt Collection Practices Act, and the Truth-in-Lending Law done for the consumer in the area of credit protection?
9. What is a secured loan?
10. What is the difference between having title to an item and having possession of an item?
11. What is the difference between deferred price and selling price? What difference may this make to the credit buyer?
12. What elements are considered in computing the annual percentage rate?
13. What should you look for in an installment contract before signing?
14. Define holder-in-due-course. When is a holder-in-due-course situation created?
15. What choices are open to a person who is deeply in debt?
16. What are the dangers in consolidating consumer credit debts?

PERSONAL EXPERIENCE PROJECTS

1. Conduct a survey of consumers' use of credit. Obtain information on the frequency of credit use, the types of purchases made on credit, the types of credit used, and opinions on advantages and disadvantages of using credit.
2. Discuss with a local department store credit manager or a credit-card company employee the various factors that make an individual a good credit risk.
3. Compare the interest rates and methods of interest computation for various credit cards and charge accounts. You can obtain this infor-

mation from credit-card applications and other cost-disclosure material provided by the store or credit-card company.

4. Interview local store managers who accept credit cards. Inquire as to costs of the service, benefits to the business, and problems encountered. Find out if the merchant offers a discount to customers who pay cash, as allowed by the Fair Credit Billing Act.

5. Obtain a copy of a credit report on yourself or a member of your family. Analyze the information on the report for completeness and correctness. Attempt to determine the sources of the information in your credit rating. Write to the Federal Trade Commission, Pennsylvania Avenue at Sixth Street, N.W., Washington, DC 20580, for further information on the Fair Credit Reporting Act.

6. Contact various banks to determine the types of loans and credit plans available. Obtain information on their lending policies, interest rates, and other costs or restrictions.

7. Visit a consumer finance company to discuss their lending policies, reasons people borrow from them, the maximum interest rates they may charge, and the extent to which consumers borrow for debt consolidation.

8. Discuss the strengths and weaknesses of the Truth-in-Lending Law with various credit managers, consumers, and legal aid employees. (Refer to "Attack on Truth-in-Lending," *Consumer Reports,* October 1977, p. 608 for background information.)

9. Contact a local credit union to obtain information on their lending policies. Also discuss bankruptcy and its alternatives with one of the credit union's financial counselors.

10. Interview a credit manager or credit collection agency employee on problems he or she encounters and the rights of consumers who are delinquent with credit payments.

5

CONSUMERISM— THE ART AND THE STRUGGLE

In recent years, the term "consumerism" has become a common household word. The definition of consumerism, however, is still somewhat unclear. A Sentry Insurance Company study conducted by the Harris pollsters revealed that consumerism means different things to different groups (see Table 5-1). In this chapter we shall adopt the most popular definition—consuming/buying/purchasing/using things—and suggest some methods of accomplishing these goals economically and effectively in the face of several substantial challenges.

The first of these challenges is the changing marketplace. Changes in consumer tastes and needs are forcing business to offer new and different buying possibilities about which the consumer must be fully informed in order to obtain the most satisfaction from his or her purchases.

Second is the advertising industry. Advertising can help a consumer to make buying decisions, but does it? In a sophisticated marketplace where choices are extensive and difficult to make, clever advertising by psychologically oriented marketing people can mislead the unwary consumer.

Third is the quantity of product information available today. A consumer must have accurate and complete information in order to function effectively in the modern American marketplace. The average consumer finds a glaring lack of product information in some areas and an

TABLE 5-1. The Meaning of "Consumerism"
What does the word "consumerism" mean to you? Does it mean anything else?

(Sample size:)	Total Public (706) %	Consumer Activist (216) %	Government Consumer Affairs (85) %	Non-Insurance Regulator (31) %	Insurance Regulator (32) %	Senior Business Manager (98) %	Business Consumer Affairs (52) %
1. Consuming/buying/ purchasing/using things	37	24	18	19	9	12	12
2. Organizations/groups/ lobbyists protecting, advocating, fighting for public's/consumers' rights	14	29	36	39	38	41	37
3. Growing awareness of needs of consumers and what they buy	8	23	18	23	31	13	25
4. Organizations/groups/ consumers trying to get best value for their money	6	15	7	19	9	11	21
5. Buying power of consumers, control over buying (boycott)	5	1	—	3	3	—	—
6. Organizations/groups concerned about keeping prices down/regulating prices	5	2	1	—	—	1	2
7. Organizations/groups/ consumers fighting to get better quality products	4	6	4	—	3	7	6
8. Organizations/groups are ineffective/not accomplishing anything; a waste of time	2	—	—	—	—	1	—
9. Organizations/groups trying to get laws passed to help public and consumers	2	—	—	3	—	—	—
10. Ralph Nader's movement	2	—	—	—	3	3	—
11. Tries to protect public from unsafe products and food	1	2	6	3	3	4	4
12. Consumers fighting big business monopolies	1	3	—	—	—	2	2
13. Consumers being duped/ coerced/brain washed into buying products not needed	1	—	—	—	—	—	—
14. Labeling laws/new regulations to protect consumer	1	1	—	—	—	—	—
15. Movement/balance/equal bargaining between buyer and seller	—	10	14	13	3	9	10
16. Educating/informing/ advising consumers	—	12	9	3	—	—	6
17. Involvement of public in decision-making processes of government and business that affect them	—	5	5	3	3	3	—
18. Efforts of producers to correct inequities and show concern for public	—	—	6	6	—	2	4
19. Any other answer	9	3	3	—	16	4	8
20. Nothing, doesn't mean anything to me	4	—	—	—	—	—	—
Don't know	23	—	—	—	—	—	—

"Consumerism at the Crossroads—A National Opinion Research Survey of Public, Activist, Business, and Regulator Attitudes Toward the Consumer Movement," conducted for Sentry Insurance by Louis Harris & Associates, Inc., and Marketing Science Institute, a nonprofit research organization associated with the Harvard Business School. Used by permission.

almost unlimited mass of information in others. He or she must learn to seek out and sort through information efficiently in order to properly evaluate a particular buying situation.

Finally, at the end of the chapter, some carefully prepared and tested buymanship guidelines will be presented. It will be up to you as an intelligent consumer to evaluate these guidelines and select those that suit your particular needs in a specific situation.

THE CHANGING MARKETPLACE

In Chapter 1 we discussed the dramatic changes taking place in the life of the American consumer in response to new realities such as inflation and the rise in single-family households. These developments have had a profound effect on numerous aspects of the marketplace, in food and other industries.

The Food Industry

What kind of changes are taking place in the food industry?

Grocery Stores.   Inflation has increased energy, labor, and tax expenses. At the same time, the trend is for consumers to spend more food money on eating away from home. Since grocery store chain profits have traditionally been considerably less than a cent on a dollar of sales, many food stores are in serious distress. Under pressure to hold sales volume and profits, they are changing the face of the traditional supermarket.

The No-Frills Store.   One chain has as its major attraction rock-bottom prices. This chain and stores that follow its approach advertise little, supply no bags, and accept no checks. The no-frills store is generally only half to a third the physical size of the typical supermarket and carries only a fraction of the 8,000 items carried by the average supermarket. It often sells no refrigerated foods and may not even mark the prices on the individual items.

The Plush Superstore.   Ralph's in Los Angeles and Byerly Foods in Minneapolis have adopted the opposite approach. They offer more and better grades of meat, a full assortment of ethnic foods, and a first-class atmosphere in which to show them off. These stores take seriously a survey by *Progressive Grocer* which showed that price rated only fifth with consumers after cleanliness, clear price marking, good products, and freshness dating. Behind price ranked accurate and pleasant checkers, well-stocked shelves, and a good meat department.

The All-Purpose Store.   The supermarket of the past averaged 22,000 to

25,000 square feet. Many of the new stores range from 30,000 to 55,000 square feet. Even smaller stores are installing new sections to attract more customers. The new space is used for fast-food restaurants, liquor, or non-food items ranging from small appliances to motor oil. Grocers are gambling that consumers will want to "combination shop" for various needs in a supermarket. In addition, nonfood items yield a larger profit margin for the stores than do food items.

The Automated-Checkout Store. The advent of automated stores is beginning to change the looks of the checkout counter in some supermarkets. Figure 5-1 illustrates the universal product code found on more than 75 percent of packages in food stores. The code includes ten digits. The first five identify the manufacturer; the second five identify the line item. Each product and variation of the product has a unique universal product code.

The checkout cashier uses an optical scanner in the form of either a wand or a window to read the code and print the amount on a cash register tape for the customer. A few years ago only about 500 stores in the U.S. had such scanners, but the number has been increasing rapidly. The scanners are generally found only in large stores, however, for the cost is approximately $100,000 for eight checkout scanners. The scanners increase the accuracy and speed of cashier checkout and packing. They also provide automatic inventory updating and other data at a very low cost.

The Generic Products Store. Stores across the country are adding a line of generic products. These generic products are usually "standard grade," a lower U.S. government rating than fancy or choice. The standard grade, however, is considered to be as nutritionally wholesome as the higher grades. Generic products are available in only a limited number of package sizes, and they are advertised less to reduce promotional expense. The canned foods have less sugar in the syrups; the paper items have less fragrance; and the soft drinks are often available only in "regular top" cans rather than in the popular "pop top" cans.

A Chicago food chain that was an early leader in generic lines now

FIGURE 5-1. The Universal Product Code

"We're not going in. Mama says she's just window shopping!"

Reprinted, courtesy of the *Chicago Tribune*.

has eighty-eight such products. It estimates that consumers can realize a 10- to 35-percent saving over the cost of national brands. A study by *Consumer Reports* in its June 1978 issue showed that, in one chain, the no-name food basket cost $8.76, the private-label basket cost $10.75, and the brand-name basket cost $12.34.

The Independent Grocery Store.   The formation of the Independent Grocers' Alliance (IGA) has been a tremendous help to the independent grocers in their battle to survive. The organization closely resembles a cooperative with independent grocers as its members. There are no licensing agreements, and the wholesaling operations are independently owned. Wholesalers selected by the board of directors merely have charter agreements with the IGA. This gives them exclusive rights to enroll the more than 3,350 IGA retailers and to sell nationally recognized products in those stores in specified geographical areas. This bulk buying by thousands of independents has allowed them to compete most effectively with the chain operators.

The Consumer Food Cooperatives.   There are more than 40,000 co-ops in the United States, a large number of which are engaged in the sale of food. Any individual, group, or firm can apply for a nonprofit corporation or cooperative charter.

Ten to fifteen families is said to be the best number for a small food co-op. The group usually deposits a modest amount of money with the co-op for working capital, and the co-op is on its way. Co-ops must first set up goals. Members should all have a voice in deciding on the types and quality of food bought. Then ordering, pickup, packaging, and record-keeping tasks are delegated. Co-ops must be sure to set up a reserve fund so that buying at cost does not run them into a deficit. This can occur if unexpected expenses arise or if active volunteers get tired of playing the role of middleperson in order to save money.

In addition to the financial saving, another advantage of the co-op is the sense of fellowship members gain from working together. The Cooperative League of the USA, 1828 L Street, N.W., Suite 1100, Washington, DC 20036, is a good source of information for persons who want to organize a buying cooperative.

Restaurants. At the same time that the grocers moan about the consumer dollars that are slipping away toward the restaurant, the restaurant owners are seeking new ways to increase their flow of dollars.

Theme Restaurants. Atmosphere has become important in luring more patrons. Successful themes for restaurant sites include railroad stations, warehouses and factories, airports, bank vaults, and even monasteries.

Fast-Food Chains. The fast-food chains do not offer much in the way of atmosphere, but they use low prices and efficiency as their lure. The U.S. government estimates that in a recent year the twenty largest fast-food chains grossed over $16 billion. This represents a gain of $6 billion and 18,000 outlets in a two-year period.

The problem for the consumer appears to be in the nutritional value of the food offered by these restaurants. To keep food and labor costs down, chains are increasingly relying on centrally prepared and frozen entrees, which are thawed and then boiled in a pouch or heated in a microwave oven before being served to customers. Food prepared via these fast-food techniques does not have the nutritional value of the freshly prepared food that diners in a quality restaurant expect to be served.

Other Products and Services

Discount Clothing. The food industry is not the only one in which discount shopping has become widespread. According to Iris Ellis of Jacksonville, Florida, author of a guide to factory outlets, there are now 8,000 outlets in the U.S., compared with 1,000 five years ago. The largest center of factory-owned outlets is in Reading, Pennsylvania, where more than a million shoppers spent an estimated $115 million in a recent year.

Many manufacturers are secretive about their outlet operations because they fear they may antagonize the sellers of their regular merchandise. Most outlet merchandise is marked "irregular." Irregular clothing may contain obvious flaws, flaws barely visible to the eye, or, in some cases, no flaws at all.

There are, in addition to the possibility of flaws, certain other drawbacks to factory outlets. In many cases, the factory has removed the labels from the items. In numerous stores, the fitting rooms are not very private —if they exist at all. Many outlets refuse to cash checks or accept credit cards, and they do not perform alterations.

But inflation, lower net income, and a desire for good quality at low prices have set the stage for an increase in the popularity of factory clothing outlets. For many consumers they have become a regular source of family clothing.

Increase in Customer Services.   Many major retailers are dramatically increasing the number of services they offer to consumers. Some marketing consultants predict that one-fifth of all department-store revenue may come from services in the near future. This will be an increase of 6 to 7 percent over recent-year service income. More emphasis is being place on restaurants, health services (including dentists), beauty shops, do-it-yourself courses, and even alterations of women's clothing, an unheard-of service in the past. The major retailer hopes to make the department store a one-stop shopping center.

Shopping by Mail.   Retailers have begun to inundate consumers with catalogs. Catalogs are expensive to produce ($1 to $2.50 per catalog), but producing them is still cheaper than building new stores or adding new floor space to existing stores. Retailers have found that the catalog is an effective market-testing device and that it has a more lasting impact than does a media advertisement. Some retailers list all their goods in one book; others mail specialized-merchandise catalogs at various times of the year. This form of shopping, which many consumers welcome, has given rise to a new set of guidelines and laws designed to protect consumers who shop by mail.

When ordering by mail, keep in mind the following guidelines:

· Buy by mail only if you cannot get comparable quality and price locally. There are two reasons for this rule. First, it is always best to examine a product before you buy it. Second, if you buy a product and it is not satisfactory, you will probably get faster and more personal attention locally.
· Deal only with reputable organizations. If in doubt, ask a local consumer organization or a Better Business Bureau.

- Find out what warranties are offered. For example, can you return the goods for a refund of the full amount of the sale?
- Order the product well before you need it. You may have to wait as much as a month for delivery of a mail order.
- Never send cash with a mail order. Use a check or money order.
- Examine the order carefully as soon as it arrives. Return it at once if it has been damaged or is not satisfactory.

To help the mail-order shopper, the Federal Trade Commission (FTC) has passed the following regulations:

- If the company expects a delay in sending you the merchandise, they must notify you of this delay and provide you with a free means of replying to them (for example, a postage-paid postcard). The company should, if possible, tell you when they expect to ship the merchandise.
- When the company notifies you of the delay, you have several options, depending upon the length of the delay. If the delay is thirty days or less, you may (1) cancel your order and get your money back, (2) agree to accept the new shipping date, or (3) choose not to answer. If you don't answer, the company may assume you agree to accept the new shipping date.
- If the delay is more than thirty days, you *must* give your express consent to the delay. Otherwise, the company must return your money at the end of the first thirty days of the delay. Even if you agree to wait longer, you may still cancel your order at any time.
- If the original payment was made on a credit card—such as Visa or Mastercharge—the refund must be credited to the account within one billing period. If the buyer paid by check or money order, the refund must be by cash, check, or money order, and it must be sent within seven business days. It is not legal to offer credit or coupons good on another product instead of a refund.

Some kinds of mail-order services are not affected by this law. Magazine subscriptions, photo-finishing services, and nursery products (because they have to be shipped during certain seasons) are examples of those exempted.

Mail-order shopping can result in good-quality merchandise at a reasonable price. But investigate *before* you send your money.

These are a few of the many innovations in retailing that have emerged in the effort to meet the needs of working couples, single households, and money-conscious inflation fighters. There seem to be two extremes developing successfully at the same time. One trend is toward lower prices for the money-conscious consumer. The other is toward convenience at higher cost for the time-conscious consumer. Both require the reevaluation of shopping techniques.

ADVERTISING

Researchers know a great deal about consumers. The charge-account customer, the check-cashing customer, and the coupon-clipping customer are all subjects of marketing research. Marketers know, for example, that consumers

- like things that glitter
- generally move to the right when shopping
- enjoy products that appear to be on sale, especially if the goods have been marked down
- like gadgets, trim, or options on the things they buy
- like to think of themselves as original in their tastes and opinions
- enjoy looking at merchandise and advertisements in their natural surroundings
- generally want things because their neighbors have them.

Marketing researchers have accumulated this information by relying less on what consumers say about what they do and why they do it and more on laboratory research involving sophisticated techniques. They are using psychiatric group-therapy techniques to uncover the reasons people buy the products they do in spite of only imagined differences. They are observing the steps a consumer goes through in choosing products, even down to eye movements.

Marketing and advertising studies have even been made of what sex-related thoughts occur to the average adult male under age thirty, between thirty and sixty, and after age sixty. It appears that a growing share of the $6.5 billion spent in a recent year on TV advertising was devoted to sex-related advertising.

Advertising Under Fire

Recently consumer-oriented researchers have begun to turn the tables on the advertising industry with studies designed to educate consumers about advertising and the ideas it promotes.

Is Television Advertising Informative?   Alan Resnik and Bruce Stern, Assistant Professors of Marketing at Portland State University, Portland, Oregon, conducted a study to see how much television advertising was informative.[1] Their evaluative criteria are listed in Table 5-2. Based on 378 network commercials, their study revealed that more evening advertising (60.3 percent) than afternoon (41.3 percent) or morning (46 percent) was informational. The researchers felt that the advertising they observed painted a "gloomy picture" in that only half the sample advertisements met the liberal criteria of useful information. Advertisements for food, personal care, and laundry- and household-related products were the least informative of those surveyed.

Is Price a Good Indicator of Quality? Although advertisers would have you think so, high cost is actually often a result of the prestige ad campaign designed to sell the product. Studies have shown that high prices may actually indicate low quality in items such as soap, cosmetics, toilet articles, clothing, and convenience foods. This is particularly true in the case of suntan lotions, frozen pizzas, and children's clothing.

Are Advertisements Reliable? The 1977 Sentry Insurance Company study asked the question "How much, if any, TV advertising do you think

TABLE 5-2. Evaluation Criteria for
Identifying Informational Advertising

---

1. Price or Value
2. Quality
3. Performance
4. Components or Contents
5. Availability
6. Special Offers
7. Tastes
8. Packaging or Shape
9. Guarantees or Warranties
10. Safety
11. Nutrition
12. Independent Research
13. Company-Sponsored Research
14. New Ideas

Source: "An Analysis of Marketing Content in Television Advertising," *Journal of Marketing,* January 1977.

---

[1]"An Analysis of Information Content in Television Advertising," *Journal of Marketing,* January 1977, p. 52.

is seriously misleading—all of it, most, some, not very much, or none at all?" Table 5-3 shows the results when the public, consumer activists, and business managers were polled. The business manager was the most positive of the three. The consumer activist and the public were less than enthusiastic about the honesty of product advertising.

Improving Advertising

Consumer groups have long urged manufacturers to make their advertising more informative. Despite their efforts and those of the federal government, too many advertising campaigns are still of little informative value. Some are actually fraudulent or dangerous. You can help to improve advertising—first, by refusing to be taken in by misleading advertisements, and second, by complaining about unfair advertising.

How to Detect Misleading Advertisements. How can a consumer screen a truthful and informative ad from a deceptive and vague one? Part of the solution is in the language. Watch for weasel words such as "helps to," "up to," "can be," "like," "as much as," "the look of," "refreshes," "fortified," "virtually." Look for useless words such as "super," "fantastic," "never," "better," "improved," "better than ever," "introductory offer," "free," "act now," "order right away," "special," and "comparable value." Be on the lookout for superlatives of any kind. Watch for unfinished claims such as "You can be sure if it's a Gremel." Ask yourself, "Sure

TABLE 5-3. How Much, if Any, TV Advertising Do You Think Is Seriously Misleading?

	Total Public	Consumer Activist	Business Manager
All of it	9%	7%	—
Most	37	60	12%
Some	39	30	55
Not very much	11	2	32
None at all	2	*	1
Not sure	3	*	—

*Less than 0.5%.
"Consumerism at the Crossroads—A National Opinion Research Survey of Public, Activist, Business, and Regulator Attitudes Toward the Consumer Movement," conducted for Sentry Insurance by Louis Harris & Associates, Inc., and Marketing Science Institute, a nonprofit research organization associated with the Harvard Business School. Used by permission.

of what?" Be wary of vague claims such as "Hotchah tastes good like a soda should."

How to Complain About an Ad.   The Council of Better Business Bureaus, National Advertising Division, 845 Third Avenue, New York, NY 10022, is the primary consumer complaint bureau for national advertising. Advertisements are investigated when complaints are received from consumers or other advertisers. The Council's authority to engage in this practice was upheld by a Colorado court when challenged by irate business organizations on the basis of restraint of trade. So if you have a complaint about a national ad, write to the BBB.

If the BBB's actions do not satisfy you, then contact the Federal Trade Commission (FTC), which has the authority to determine and enforce truth and fairness of advertising. When the FTC becomes aware of a violation, it must first notify the advertiser that the law is being violated. Often a case is settled either before a complaint is issued or before the completion of FTC hearings. The commission and the alleged offender agree to a consent order, which generally states that the respondent, while neither admitting nor denying violation of any law, will discontinue certain practices.

If no consent order is agreed upon, the advertiser has thirty days to show why a cease-and-desist order should not be issued. If the advertiser does not produce convincing evidence, the cease-and-desist order is issued. The order may be appealed in court within sixty days. A case in court may have any of these results:

- out-of-court settlement
- a finding that no violation occurred
- a finding that a violation did occur, in which case the practice is stopped and refunds, fines, or remedial advertising may be required.

The Commission itself has no criminal powers—no authority to imprison or to fine. If one of its final cease-and-desist orders is violated, however, it may, acting through the Justice Department, seek civil penalties of up to $10,000 a day for each violation. The FTC may sue in court for up to three years after the violation occurs or up to one year after the cease-and-desist order has been issued.

In the case of Listerine mouthwash, produced by Warner-Lambert Company, the company was instructed to run remedial ads saying that Listerine will not help prevent colds or sore throats or lessen their severity. Warner-Lambert appealed the FTC decision through the federal courts and lost in the Supreme Court.

What if the advertising complaint is a local one? As with other forms of complaint, there are some logical steps to follow:

- Complain directly to the manager of the store if the ad in question is a store ad.
- If it is a manufacturer's ad, write a letter to the president of the company. Be sure to give specific details.
- Inform the local or state consumer protection agency, Chamber of Commerce, or Better Business Bureau of your grievance.
- Let the various media that ran the ad know about your annoyance.

CONSUMER PRODUCT INFORMATION

Lack of Information

The current trend in government regulation of trade appears to be to assist consumers in the quest for information. Many "secret" pricing practices and even "secret" formulas are now going public so that consumers can compare and choose on the basis of advance knowledge. The call for product information is coming for nearly every product. Air-conditioner efficiency ratings, appliance energy usage figures, insulation R-values, and EPA auto mileage ratings are but a few examples of information now accessible to consumers. In the areas of eyeglasses, lawyers' services, and drugs, where prices were formerly a mystery to consumers, price schedules are becoming common. This trend is certainly in the best interest of all consumers, for an informed consumer is the best customer.

The Food Label. In 1977 alone, more than sixty bills were introduced in Congress to bring more information to consumers via the food label. The public is demanding such information, especially nutritional labeling. Present regulations require labeling of nutrients only on products that make a nutritional claim or are fortified with nutrients, although many companies are already including a great deal of nutritional labeling voluntarily. Proposed legislation would eventually require:

- open dating of products. This would involve putting latest-sale-date labels on all perishable foods.
- unit pricing. Some states and cities already require unit pricing, but there are many areas of the country where it is not required. Under unit pricing, stores must post a price per standard unit (ounce, pint, etc.) for each product so that consumers can more easily compare prices.

- drained weight. This law would require the label to list the weight of the product without the syrup or other liquid.
- percentage listing of ingredients. While ingredient lists on food items rank ingredients in order of quantity, little is known about the percentage of each item included in the food product.
- storage advice.
- elimination of exemption of many foods from ingredient labeling. The Food and Drug Administration now exempts 284 food products—for example, ice cream and mayonnaise—from ingredient labeling. Proponents of elimination of exemptions say that people who are allergic to certain foods or chemicals (or even salt) cannot tell from the label if the foods contain such substances.

Prescription Drugs.   For years the prescription drug buyer had no choice but to buy the brand-name drug prescribed by his or her doctor at a pharmacy that refused to advertise, post prices, or even quote prices over the telephone. But all that is changing now. Besides a brand or trade name identifying it with a particular company, every drug has a generic or common name, and over thirty states have now passed some form of legislation permitting pharmacists to substitute less expensive generic drugs that are chemically equivalent to expensive brand-name prescription drugs.

Representative William Marovitz, the chief sponsor of the Illinois Generic Drug Bill, contends that "the biggest savings will come in the areas of antibiotics, sedatives, tranquilizers, and antihypertensives. Brand-name drugs are three to five times more expensive than their generic equivalents."[2] According to the Food and Drug Administration, Miltown, a popular tranquilizer, sells for an average of $6.50. One generic version, which is marketed by another large company, costs $3.10. A drug firm that markets only generics sells its version for $1.40.[3]

Funeral Services.   One of the many areas in which the Federal Trade Commission is pushing for more price information is that of funeral services. The FTC would like to see funeral directors make available price lists for their various services. These price lists would break the services

[2]"Generic Drug Law Hailed as Boon to Poor. Foes Doubt It," *Chicago Tribune,* October 2, 1977, p. 4.
[3]"Latest in Health 'Mystery Buy'—Malpractice Repeaters—Generic Drugs," *U.S. News & World Report,* June 26, 1978, p. 61.

down so that consumers could see specifically what they were paying for. The FTC contends that package prices, refusal to advertise prices, and widespread use of embalming services that are not required by law are costing consumers dearly.

False Information

With the advent of information labeling comes the problem of identifying false information. The Federal Trade Commission says that testimony presented at public hearings shows strong evidence of inaccurate care labeling on clothing. After recent hearings, John Gray, the presiding FTC officer, said that 56 percent of those testifying had reported that clothing care instructions were inaccurate, and that 54 percent had indicated that the instructions were overly cautious. Many labels called for dry cleaning when washing was permissible. Some called for no bleaching when bleaching would not have harmed the product. Such misleading information can be expensive for the consumer.

Confusing Information

Another movement by consumers has been directed at forcing business to present information in a simpler form so that it can be more easily understood. In the past contracts have been so complex that many consumers gave up trying—often to their detriment. Only lately have businesses, especially in the consumer credit and insurance fields, attempted to make their literature and contracts more readable. The readability drive involves shortening contracts and policies and changing terms such as "the named insured" and "the company" to "you" and "we." A listing of definitions, boldface headings, and larger type also make the documents easier for laypeople to understand.

A Minnesota law requires that policies be printed in legible type and conform to a readability formula. A more controversial law passed in New York State requires that corporations use "plain English" in all agreements with consumers involving sums of money, goods, or services valued at $50,000 or less. This move by business and government should ensure that the warning "Read All Information Carefully" results in fewer disgruntled consumers.

Too Much Information

How much information should a consumer acquire before buying a product? There are consumers who conduct an exhaustive search in comparison shopping for a can of peas. The best rule of thumb is the "cost versus energy" guideline, where you equate time with money. This means that you set a limit on the amount of time and energy you devote to comparison shopping for a single product. In the case of food shopping, this does not mean that you should ignore the nutritional benefits of some foods over others because evaluating them takes time. A better approach is to learn to pick up the information you need quickly. A glance at the unit price, the nutritional label, and the freshness date of a product may still be efficient, whereas driving from store to store with a handful of cents-off coupons may not be of much value. A busy consumer who is new at grocery shopping might be well advised to make an initial visit to several grocery stores armed with a list of most frequent purchases and personal requirements. On the basis of this visit he or she can then select a store in which to shop regularly.

When you are dealing with mortgage rates on homes, interest on borrowing, large-ticket durable purchases, and insurance, large variations in cost make more extensive investigation practical. However, as the information gathering on these items progresses, you will eventually come to a stage at which the cost of information reaches a point of diminishing return. As you become more adept at information gathering, you will get an inner feeling when you have reached this saturation point.

BUYMANSHIP GUIDELINES

There are three basic ways of finding out about a product. The first is through past experience or judgment. The second is through an independent source of information, such as *Consumer Reports.* The third is through the seller of the product or service. Quite obviously, there are vast differences in the motivation bases of these sources and hence in the types of information you will receive. Consider information from all three sources before you buy.

Warranties and Guarantees

Know the manufacturer's warranties and guarantees before you make a purchase. The Magnuson-Moss Warranty Act requires that warranties be available for inspection before purchase on products that cost more than $15. This allows the comparison shopper to evaluate not only the product or service but also the extent to which the manufacturer or seller stands behind it.

According to the Magnuson-Moss Warranty Act, warranties must be labeled full or limited. A full warranty means that a defective product will be fixed or replaced free; even removal and reinstallment, if necessary, must be performed free of charge. If the defective product cannot be fixed, you have the right to choose between receiving a new one and getting your money back.

A limited warranty means that you share some of the risk. In the case of a limited warranty, there are several things to watch for:

- Does the warranty or guarantee cover the entire product or only certain parts, and is labor included?
- Is there a certain repair service that must repair the product?

Of course, it is also important to note the length of time that the warranty is in effect.

One problem with the warranty law has been that since manufacturers were not required to offer a warranty, many dropped from full to limited or from limited to none at all. This is especially true in the furniture industry.

However, if a product does not include a written warranty, the consumer is still covered by an implied warranty. Sometimes called a *warranty of merchantability,* the implied warranty means that if the article does not perform in a normal way, the customer may return the product to the seller.

In addition to the warranty, another type of protection provided on certain types of merchandise is a service contract. The decision as to whether or not to purchase a service contract can be put in money terms: How large a repair bill can you afford, and how big a risk are you willing to take? Researchers at the Massachusetts Institute of Technology's Center for Policy Alterations found that common first-year service-contract prices ranged from about $21 for refrigerators, ranges, and air conditioners and $26 for washers to $80 to $100 for color TVs.[4] According to the researchers, people tend to buy excessive service contracts on TVs, refrigerators, room air conditioners, washing machines, and cooking ranges.

Even when a service contract is in force, it is only as good as the store that is doing the repairs. If you do decide to purchase a contract, read it carefully before purchase and reevaluate it as the product becomes older.

A good service contract

- guarantees speedy repair service
- allows you to cancel (and to get a refund) or to transfer the contract to another party

[4]"A Skeptical Look at Service Contracts," *Changing Times,* August 1976, pp. 29–30.

- gives more than one free service call where applicable
- covers the whole product and not just some parts
- covers parts and labor (no hidden charges).

Unless the service contract does something a warranty does not, it is best for the customer to wait until after the warranty expires to add the service. Even this should generally be done only if there has been trouble with the product.

Private Labels

Consider buying private-label brands. Private brands can save a great deal of money, especially on the purchase of major appliances, where estimates of private-label volume run as high as 50 percent. Private labels are also a big factor in the food markets, where studies have shown little difference between store-brand and brand-name merchandise as far as drained weight, taste, and texture. A rule of thumb here is that if the private label costs less and the national brand is not noticeably better in quality, then buy the private label at the lower price.

Unfortunately, not all products are sold under private labels, however. Housewares such as coffee makers, can openers, hamburger makers, and personal-care appliances are most often sold only under brand names. And with a few exceptions, private labels in audio/hi-fi equipment have generally been confined to speakers.

Quality

When buying a product, keep in mind its intended purpose. You may be able to use a lower-grade food for cooking, for example. If the item is one you expect to keep for a long time, buy one with low maintenance requirements from a business that will provide good service when and if maintenance is needed. In clothing, washables and permanent press will save time and money.

Sales

First, make sure when buying "sale" goods that the item is genuinely on sale—too often people buy on impulse because a colorful display makes an item appear to be on sale.

Second, buy ahead only if you are quite sure you will use all of the merchandise. A sale is not a bargain if you end up throwing any part of the product away.

Use of buying calendars, which tell when merchandise is normally

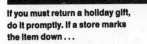

If you must return a holiday gift,
do it promptly. If a store marks
the item down . . .

JANUARY

For Planning, for Good Buys

Storewide postholiday and inventory sales

Bargains: Toys, books, Christmas wrapping and decorations, cosmetics, drugs, furs, diamonds, costume jewelry, shoes, clothing (for men, women, children, infants), blankets, furniture, china, glassware, housewares, floor coverings, rugs, lingerie, luggage, notions, fabrics, stationery, radios, TVs, phonographs, small appliances, freezers, refrigerators, stoves, water heaters, cars, tires, art supplies, bicycles, baby carriages, clothes dryers

Food: Hams, holiday luxury foods, turkeys (if you have freezer room)

Vacations: Europe, Bermuda (early in the month), Caribbean cruises

Chores: Start 1978 income tax file. Make personal calendar and list of year's needs, yearlong gift list

FEBRUARY

Final Winter Clearances

Washington's & Lincoln's birthday sales

Bargains: All the things you may have missed in January (selections not as good). Also sports equipment, bedding, curtains, hosiery, used cars, car seatcovers, storm windows, laundry appliances, air conditioners

Food: Steaks are usually less expensive now than later. Buy and freeze some extras for summer barbecues

Vacations: Europe at off-season prices

Chores: Begin gathering data for income tax returns. Order tulip, hyacinth, narcissus bulbs; for Easter bloom, start them in containers soon (save on high prices of plants and flowers next month—for yourself and for gifts). Prune trees, bushes, grape arbors.

January and February Home Care: Paint interior as needed • Clean and repair summer screens, outdoor furniture, hoses, garden tools

MAY

Putting Winter Away

Mother's Day (14th), Memorial Day (29th) sales

Bargains: Clothes for the whole family, blankets, linens, handbags, tablecloths, towels, housecoats, lingerie, jewelry, children's camp clothing, paint and wallpaper

Food: Cheese, milk, ice cream

Vacations: Between-season prices in Florida, Caribbean, southern Europe (including Greece), North Africa

Chores: Mothproof woolens; store winter items. Get out spring and summer clothes and gear. Make lists of summer things needed (if you didn't buy them at end of last year's end-of-summer sales)

JUNE

Father's Day (18th)

Special sales of dairy products, frozen foods

Bargains: Sportswear, outdoor furniture and playthings (after midmonth), men's wear, floor coverings, furniture and bedding, building materials and lumber, tires, cut roses

Food: Cheese, ice cream, milk, fresh strawberries, asparagus. Best buys of the year in frozen food!

Vacations: Best buys now are Florida, Caribbean, ski resorts, some national parks and Canada. Europe is soaring toward its yearly peak in prices and tourists, though a few parts are still at between-season prices

Chores: Work in flower beds and vegetable gardens; plant late vegetable seeds, second plantings of lettuce, last of flower seeds

May and June Home Care: Clean, repair, paint and store storm windows • Paint exterior as needed (every 4-5 years), but never when temperature is above 90° • Put up screens

FIGURE 5-2. A Buying Calendar. (Reproduced by courtesy of *Consumer Views Newsletter*, published by Citibank.)

███████████

... from the original price, you could have trouble getting a credit or refund for the amount paid

MARCH

An Early Easter (26th)

After-Easter and special-purchase sales

Bargains: Washers, dryers, winter coats for whole family, boys' and girls' shoes, luggage, hosiery, skates, ski equipment. Wait until after Easter to buy spring clothes

Food: Fish, spring greens

Vacations: Europe; some ski resorts start dropping prices

Chores: Finish gathering tax data. Check summer camps, make summer vacation plans. Start indoor seeding and planting of annuals and vegetables; fertilize lawns (right on top of snow if it hasn't melted)

APRIL

The Cruelest Month: Income Taxes

After-Easter sales will continue

Bargains: Children's clothes, lingerie, infants' wear, washers, dryers, kitchen ranges, outdoor paints, garden items

Food: Eggs (early in the month), after-Easter ham sales

Vacations: In Arizona and other parts of the Southwest, Florida and the Caribbean rates start to drop after midmonth; between-season prices in most of Europe

Chores: Store furs, take winter clothes to cleaners. Start outdoor seed planting, set out hardy seedlings, plant gladioli bulbs, pansies, lily of the valley

March and April Home Care: Finish indoor painting and cleaning • Hunt for termites and call exterminator if needed • Inspect and repair roof, chimney, outside walls, drains, gutters, downspouts, driveway, terrace, walks

JULY

Summer Clearances

Watch for after-4th-of-July sales, fur events

Bargains: Summer clothes, sportswear, bathing suits, sporting goods, stereo equipment, home appliances, air conditioners, freezers, outdoor furniture and games, fuel oil, firewood, pressed logs, garden equipment, storm windows

Food: Fresh lima beans, peas, cucumbers, string beans, raspberries, canned fruits and vegetables, frozen foods

Vacations: Best buys are in ski resorts and in Florida, Caribbean, Mexico

Chores: Apply for student loans. Tend garden, harvest vegetables

AUGUST

Final Clearances (Often Half-Price) on Summer Clothes

Car clearances begin

Bargains: '77 cars (earliest shoppers get best selections), white sales, back-to-school sales, furs, coats for the whole family, storewide summer clearances—sporting goods, fans, linens, bathing suits, men's clothing, major appliances, curtains, floor coverings, housewares, paints, housewares, lamps, home furniture

Food: Fresh corn, beets, carrots, summer squash, peaches, spinach, watermelon

Vacations: Highest-cost month to travel; near-at-hand places are better buys, or explore Mexico

Chores: Plan for children's back-to-school needs

July and August Home Care: Clean furnace (annually) • Clean chimneys (every 3 years)

CITIBANK⊕

399 Park Avenue
New York, N.Y.
10022

Member
Federal Deposit
Insurance Corp.

SEPTEMBER

Labor Day Sales (4th)

Farmer's markets offer low harvest prices

Bargains: Home-improvement products, season ticket offers for theater, musical performances, dance, etc. Also, dishwashers, freezers, china, glassware, paints, fabrics, bicycles, cars ('77 models), car batteries, mufflers, snow tires

Food: Fresh tomatoes, squash, cabbage, eggplant, early apples. Buy and freeze turkeys for Thanksgiving, parties, year-end holidays

Vacations: After Labor Day, prices drop in Cape Cod, California, Florida, Canada, Mexico, for Caribbean cruises and are low in ski resorts

Chores: Plan tax-deductible expenditures for year-end, and those more tax-saving to defer to '79. Order bulbs, rosebushes, shrubs

OCTOBER

Columbus Day Sales (9th)

Car sales (last of '77 models)

Bargains: Coats, floor coverings, lamps, electric blankets, silverware, school clothes, school supplies, men's wear, fishing equipment, cars ('77 models)

Food: Apples, grapes, cranberries, cabbages, celery, pumpkins, squash, onions, potatoes. Buy and freeze chickens and turkeys

Vacations: Between-season prices in Europe; off-season prices in Florida, California, Mexico, for Caribbean cruises

Chores: Order holiday gifts from catalogs. Put away summer things. Get winter clothes ready, furs out of storage. Plant rosebushes and shrubs. Refurbish house for winter holidays

September and October Home Care: Batten up for winter • Caulk, weather-strip, insulate, put up storm windows, doors • Check total heating system • Look at, repair roof and flashings • Clean and repair gutters, downspouts, drains • Paint outside (before it's below 40°)

NOVEMBER

Veterans Day on the 11th in All States

Thanksgiving Day (23rd), Election Day, post-Thanksgiving sales

Bargains: Fall clothing, special purchases for holiday gifts, bicycles, car seatcovers, fabrics, quilts, water heaters, wines and liquors

Food: Cranberries, nuts, small onions, winter squash

Vacations: Best buys of year in Europe, especially Spain, Italy, England, Ireland, southern France; also in Caribbean, Mexico and Bermuda

Chores: Plant grass seed (best time for it); fertilize and lime lawns. Plant trees, bulbs, shrubs; mulch roses, winterize vegetable garden and flower beds. Send holiday gifts overseas and across the U.S. early; address greeting cards

DECEMBER

Enjoy!

Post-Christmas clearances: cards, giftwraps, decorations

Bargains: Gift certificates (for better buying values later). If your gift shelf is well stocked with year-long purchases, you can escape the high gift prices usual this month. Same for your pantry—turkeys, luxury foods are at a premium now

Food: Citrus fruits, pomegranates

Vacations: Best prices of the year in Spain, England, Italy, Florida

Chores: Get checks off before Dec. 31 for 1977 income tax deductions. Write thank-you notes. Phone the family at best economy hours. Don't throw all diet to the winds. HAVE HAPPY HOLIDAY

November and December Home Care: Drain and turn off outside faucets (before freezing weather) • Inspect electrical wiring • Repair inside walls, stairs, floors • Paint interior as needed • Finish all cleanup for end-of-year festivities

placed on sale, can help you to take advantage of sales when making major purchases. Figure 5-2 illustrates one such calendar from Citibank's *Consumer Views Newsletter*. The calendar lists not only the bargain buys, but also chores, inexpensive vacations, and foods for certain times of the year. For example, note that bargains in summer clothes are available after July fourth.

The buymanship principles presented here are general guidelines; for more specific hints on purchasing particular items, read articles, books, and other publications on consumer issues and personal finance. If you continually add bits of information to your base of general knowledge by reading such works on a regular basis, it will be easier to make an informed choice when the time is right. One of the unfortunate effects of inflation was the general reduction of spending on periodical literature, for the consumer-aid features found in magazines and newspapers can be very valuable in consumer money management.

QUESTIONS FOR DISCUSSION

1. What does the term "consumerism" mean to you?
2. What advantages do computer checkouts offer?
3. What information is represented by the numbers found on the universal product code designation?
4. How does the IGA grocery store differ from the chain store? From the cooperative?
5. What are the advantages and disadvantages of the factory outlet?
6. What are the advantages and disadvantages of mail-order buying?
7. Do you think sex-related advertising has an effect on consumer purchasing?
8. Do you feel that all advertising should be informational?
9. In a court action on a dishonest advertising charge, what remedies may the FTC request?
10. Do you feel that more information should be disclosed on food labels? What are the advantages and disadvantages of making such information available?
11. Describe the "cost versus energy" concept of shopping.
12. What is one of the negative effects of the Magnuson-Moss Warranty Act?
13. Looking at the buying calendar, determine some basic rules for buying that could aid a consumer who does not have a formal buying calendar.

PERSONAL EXPERIENCE PROJECTS

1. Conduct a survey of consumers to determine the main influence on their buying choices—price, quality, service, advertised specials, brand names, or safety. Determine differences between the attitudes of people who buy on impulse and those of shoppers who plan their purchases.

2. Compare several findings in *Consumer Reports* magazines with the experiences of consumers you know. Evaluate the value of this source of product information.

3. Conduct research in preparation for the purchase of a major item (television, refrigerator, washing machine, stereo, etc.). Use consumer-magazine articles, product information from manufacturers, and discussions with salespeople. Also compare prices and services of various stores that sell the product.

4. Compare prices of various food products at a variety of stores. Determine cost differences among brand names, store brands, and generic brands. Also find examples of open dating and unit pricing information.

5. Discuss with a home economist or nutritionist the comparative nutritional value of meals at home, in restaurants, and in fast-food businesses. Also obtain information on the differences in nutritional value among fresh, frozen, and canned food items.

6. Compare the amount of advertising various food products receive with the nutritional value of the products. Attempt to determine why certain products are advertised more than others.

7. Contact food manufacturers, food chemical manufacturers, the Food and Drug Administration (5600 Fishers Lane, Rockville, MD 20852), and the Center for Science in the Public Interest (1755 S Street, N.W., Washington, DC 20009) regarding the purpose and safety of various food additives.

8. Contact members of local food cooperatives for information on the operation and benefits of their organizations. Evaluate the effectiveness of the food cooperative in saving consumers money. (You can obtain further information on cooperatives from the Cooperative League of the USA, 1828 L Street, N.W., Suite 1100, Washington, DC 20036.)

9. Examine labels of various brands of a food product for ingredients, nutritional information, freshness date, and food additives. Suggest ways consumers can use this information to make the best buying decision. Write the Food and Drug Administration, 5600 Fishers Lane, Rockville, MD 20852, for information on current and proposed labeling requirements.

10. Conduct a survey of consumers to determine the usefulness and influence of advertising. Identify some advertisements that have enticed people to buy something and some advertisements that have helped consumers to make wise choices. Use this information to create guidelines for viewing and evaluating advertising.

11. Contact the Federal Trade Commission, Pennsylvania Avenue at Sixth Street, N.W., Washington, DC 20580, regarding guidelines and rules for advertising verification or substantiation. Write the presidents of several companies requesting substantiation of the claims made in their advertisements. Evaluate the replies to determine whether the information provided is satisfactory or whether the advertisement might be considered misleading.

12. Read articles in *Advertising Age* magazine on government regulation of advertising, new-product development by companies, and new advertising approaches. Prepare a list of suggestions of ways in which this information could be used by consumers to improve their buying choices.

13. Conduct a survey of consumers' habits. Determine preferred fibers, brands, styles, and types of stores where purchases are made.

14. Examine various clothing labels for information on fabric composition, cleaning instructions, and manufacturer's identity. Evaluate the usefulness of these labels and make suggestions for improvement.

15. Contact the Consumer Product Safety Commission, 1111 18th Street, S.W., Washington, DC 20207, for information on the products that most often cause injuries to consumers. Their toll-free number is 800-638-2666. Discuss with consumers the problems they have had with injuries, and determine whether the injuries were product-caused (due to malfunction or unsafe manufacturing) or product-related (due to consumer misuses).

16. Examine guarantees and warranties for a variety of products. Compare the restrictions, length of coverage, and aspects covered by each. Evaluate the benefit of these in relation to the cost of the product and the responsibilities of consumers to get service under the warranty.

17. Interview an appliance store salesperson or manager about the service contracts available on the products the store sells. Determine the cost, benefits, and coverage of several agreements.

6
SHELTER

Rent or buy? The cost of the average home is so high that most newly graduated college students would not even think about buying one. But the American dream still includes home ownership, and in a few years you may be considering such a purchase.

Homeowners are much younger than many people suspect. The U.S. League of Savings Associations studied 8,500 home buyers who took out conventional loans in 1977 and found that, in the first-time buying group, 24 percent were twenty-four years of age or under, and 63 percent were under thirty. The experts were surprised to find that 25 percent of the first-time home buyers were single. The study showed that the statistical average homeowner was thirty-two years of age, married, had 2.7 members in the household, and had an annual income of $22,700.

Home ownership is often regarded as "the best game in town" in terms of investment opportunity. There are, however, several advantages to renting a home rather than buying one. This chapter explores the characteristics, advantages, and disadvantages of various forms of shelter.

RENTING SHELTER

One of the best reasons for renting is to retain the ability to move from place to place with relative ease. Landlords often require a lease, but most leases are not longer than a year in duration, and some landlords do not require a lease at all. This may be a psychological as well as an economic advantage if changes are anticipated in one's job, family, or economic situation. If new job demands call for a move, a renter can relocate in a new geographic area without worrying about property values. If family size increases, it is generally quite simple to move from a one-bedroom to a two-bedroom apartment, or to move from a flat to a townhouse. If belt tightening is necessary, it is equally easy to move to a smaller apartment or to one without frills, such as swimming pools, tennis courts, and athletic fields.

Another major advantage of renting is that the dollar outlay for housing can be estimated accurately. Often heat, garbage disposal, water, and other services are included in the rental, whereas in addition to these monthly costs the owner of a home may be unexpectedly faced with the costs of breakdowns of the furnace, water heater, and other household appliances. And while a new homeowner is tempted or forced to buy hundreds of items to furnish, repair, maintain, or upgrade a home, the apartment dweller can much more easily control and avoid such costs. Even property tax increases have a limited effect on renters. Unless the lease provides otherwise, apartment dwellers continue to pay a fixed amount until their lease expires.

A third advantage is the ease of upkeep of an apartment. Mowing the lawn, painting the house, or washing windows holds little appeal to some young apartment dwellers. These and other tasks take time and money that many feel could be put to better use.

The purpose of this part of the chapter is to provide some guidance for those who decide to rent rather than buy shelter.

Financial Considerations

Most important, you must first determine what you can afford. Consumer economists have long attempted to estimate how much individuals can spend on housing and still have an adequate amount of money for other needs. The traditional guideline is that a family should spend no more than 20 to 25 percent of its income on housing. In reality, however, wide differences in percentages spent for housing are quite common. In a recent year, the U.S. Bureau of Labor found that in the New York–northeastern New Jersey area, the lower-income group (median income $11,000) spent 10 percent of their incomes on housing, while the middle-income (median income $19,000) and upper-income (median income $30,000) groups spent 25 percent. Each individual must consult his or her own budget to arrive at a dollar amount available for housing costs.

Analyzing Tastes

Obviously the second step in renting is to decide what you want. Considerations include the type of community desired, community services and facilities wanted, and transportation requirements. You should also think about the type of building and location you would prefer, as well as the type of people you would like as neighbors. In addition, you need to have an idea of how much and what type of floor space you require. This includes living space, storage space, and recreational space.

The Search

The next step is sometimes a difficult one. In some areas of the country, it is hard to locate *any* affordable apartment in a geographically desirable area. If you decide to use the services of a rental-referral agency, be sure their listings are different from or more exclusive than those you can find in newspapers, by word of mouth, by driving around, or by inquiring of friends and acquaintances. Instead of using a referral service, which generally costs between $20 and $50, you might be better off seeking the assistance of a licensed real estate firm that handles apartment rentals. Realtors generally do not charge a fee for telling you what they have to offer. These firms are listed in the yellow pages under "Apartment rentals."

Before you begin looking at apartments, it is useful to obtain or construct a renter's checklist of what to look for in an apartment. Following are some items you might want to include:

- Is there adequate closet and storage space? Kitchen cabinet space is important.
- Are there enough electrical outlets? Most people need two or three per room.
- Is the security adequate? Deadbolt locks are a must in most buildings.
- Is the refuse disposal frequent and convenient?
- Are laundry facilities available in the building? Check the number and quality of washers and dryers. Studies show that one washer and dryer is needed for every ten apartments.
- Are entrances and exits adequate and accessible?
- Do elevators function properly?
- Check the water pressure and drainage in toilet, shower, and sinks.
- Do the appliances work?
- What type of heating and air conditioning is furnished?

- In cold climates, are there storm windows? This is particularly important if you pay for heat and face the north.
- How sound-resistant are the walls separating you and your neighbor(s)?
- If you drive, what type of and how much parking is provided?

Signing the Lease

Step four is a technical-legal one. Reading the terms of a lease will reduce unpleasant surprises to a minimum. Knowledge of the terms of payment, grace periods, interest provision on security deposits, and the form of payment required is a necessity. The following checklist outlines matters a lease should cover:

- What is the responsibility of the landlord for maintenance? Care of the exterior and public areas is generally assumed by the landlord.
- Who will pay for utilities?
- What is the amount required for a damage deposit? In some states a landlord must pay interest on security deposits.
- What are the rules regarding subletting?
- What is the liability for rent? This is especially important in situations where roommates occupy the premises, for in most cases simply having everyone sign a lease does not protect the last
- person in the apartment if the roommates move out. It would take an individual lease with each of the roommates to legally protect each tenant from having to assume the entire rent if other roommates left before the lease expired.
- What are the arrangements as far as apartment maintenance and as far as the physical conditions of the apartment at moving-in and moving-out time?
- Are there any special restrictions on how the apartment may be used? For example, are pets permitted? Is conducting a business from the apartment permitted?
- When does the landlord have access to the premises?
- Does your lease contain a confession of judgment clause?

The confession of judgment clause has the effect of giving away your day in court. Below is an example of such a clause:

Tenant irrevocably authorizes any attorney of any court of record in any state of the United States from time to time to appear for the tenant . . . in such court, to waive process, service and trial by jury, to confess judgment in favor of owner . . . against tenant, for any rent and interest due hereunder from tenant to owner and to owner's costs and reasonable attorney's fees, to waive and release all errors in such proceedings and all right to appeal, and to consent to an immediate execution upon judgment.

If your lease does have such a clause, you might want to attempt to have it removed.

The lease should say it all. Oral promises to repair or replace certain items are not binding. Even if they were, it would be almost impossible to prove them. In the absence of state or local laws regarding maintenance, the lease may even include more than the above items.

A checklist of existing damage signed by the landlord before you move in is helpful when questions about the security deposit arise at moving-out time—Figure 6-1 provides a sample inventory checklist. Pictures will further reinforce your case.

Laws and ordinances on renting vary considerably from area to area. As a prospective renter it would be wise to learn about your rights and responsibilities before signing a lease. And remember that even a standard-form lease can sometimes be changed to the mutual satisfaction of the prospective tenant and the landlord.

Disputes

Many of the landlord-tenant disputes that fill small claims court calendars could have been avoided through mutual understanding of a carefully negotiated lease, and through the tenants' observance of the normal responsibility to keep the premises sanitary and to obey the rules. If disputes do arise, however, state and local governments, tenants' associations, and small claims courts are all possible sources of assistance.

State and Local Governments. Nearly all states require that rental housing comply with local building codes, safety codes, and the local definition of habitable. City building inspectors enforce these codes. In addition, many state and local laws allow a tenant to make minor repairs and then deduct the cost from the next rent payment. Check your local ordinances by calling your city hall. A number of states also limit the amount that can be taken in a security deposit, and some require the landlord to pay interest on the security deposit for the time it is held.

In most states the attorney general's office will handle complaints that a tenant cannot resolve on the local level. A simple one-page complaint form will generally be supplied to you upon request. In addition, most states have a consumer fraud division located in the state capital, and some states also have regional offices. Your local library and telephone white pages (under state offices) will have more complete information.

This inventory form is for your protection.

You and your landlord should fill it out within three days of your moving in. Then, at least one week before moving out, you should arrange a time to make the final inspection. Both you and your landlord should sign and receive a copy of the form following each inspection.

In completing the form, be *specific* and check carefully. Among the things you should look for are dust, dirt, grease, stains, burns, damages and wear.

Additions to this list may be made as necessary. Attach additional paper if more space is needed, but remember to include a copy for both parties. Cross out items which do not apply.

Apartment Name and Address ....

.... Unit No. ....

	ITEM	QUANTITY (If applicable)	CONDITION ON ARRIVAL	CONDITION UPON DEPARTURE Note deterioration *beyond reasonable use and wear* for which tenant is alleged to be responsible
KITCHEN	Cupboards			
	Floor Covering			
	Walls and Ceiling			
	Counter Surfaces			
	Stove & Oven, Range Hood, (broiler pans, grills, etc.)			
	Refrigerator (ice trays, butter dish, etc.)			
	Sink and Garbage Disposal			
	Tables and Chairs			
	Windows (draperies, screens, etc.)			
	Doors, including hardware			
	Light Fixtures			
LIVING ROOM	Floor Covering			
	Walls and Ceiling			
	Tables and Chairs			
	Sofa			
	Windows (draperies, screens, etc.)			
	Doors, including hardware			
	Light Fixtures			

FIGURE 6-1. Inventory Checklist. (State of California, Department of Consumer Affairs, *Education Update,* Education Series No. 8, Jan./Feb. 1978.)

ITEM	QUANTITY (If applicable)	CONDITION ON ARRIVAL	CONDITION UPON DEPARTURE Note deterioration *beyond reasonable use and wear* for which tenant is alleged to be responsible.
BATHROOM			
Floor Covering			
Walls and Ceiling			
Shower and Tub ((walls, door, tracks)			
Toilet			
Plumbing Fixtures			
Windows (draperies, screens, etc.)			
Doors, including hardware			
Light Fixtures			
BEDROOM			
Floor Covering			
Walls and Ceiling			
Closet, including doors & tracks			
Desk(s) and Chairs			
Dresser(s)			
Bed(s), (frame, mattress - check both sides for stains-pads, bx sprng)			
Windows (draperies, screens, etc.)			
Doors, including hardware			
Light Fixtures			
HALLWAYS OR OTHER AREAS			
Floor Covering			
Walls and Ceiling			
Closets, including doors & tracks			
Light Fixtures			
Air Conditioner(s) Filter			
Heater Filter			
Patio, Deck, Yard (planted areas, ground covering, fencing, etc.)			
Other (please specify)			

Beginning Inventory Date _____ Signature of Tenant _____

Signature of Owner or Agent _____

End of Term Inspection Date _____ Signature of Tenant _____

Signature of Owner or Agent _____

Inventory prepared by University of California, Davis Housing Office

Tenants' Associations.   Renters across the country have found that banding together in tenants' organizations is an effective means of getting their grievances heard by management. And laws in over half the states protect a tenant's right to activism within a tenant's organization.

Small Claims Courts.   Chapter 11 includes a complete discussion of small claims courts, including a table of the maximum amounts for which one can sue in the various states. In most states, an entire small claims action costs well under $30. Many tenants have found this to be a useful, painless, and inexpensive method of recouping losses.

BUYING SHELTER

For more than twenty-five years, homeowners have been a national majority. Two-thirds of American families seem to be convinced that buying a house is a good investment. Even singles, who were a small portion of the housing market years ago, accounted for about 15 percent of all the home sales in a recent year.

There are various options open to the prospective home buyer, such as co-ops, condominiums, or mobile homes. The vast majority, however, prefer the single-family detached dwelling. According to findings of *Professional Builder Magazine*'s 1978 Builder Survey on Housing, 97 percent of the active shoppers in 1978 wanted to buy a single-family detached home.

Why buy at all? Inflation has skyrocketed the prices of homes. Young married women must continue to work longer and longer in order to provide the second income necessary to jump aboard the home-buying bandwagon. A 1978 study by the economists of the U.S. League of Savings Associations indicated that 47 percent of all homes were bought by families with two incomes. Once the husband has become well established in his field and begun to earn a larger salary, the payments become more manageable and the couple can begin to support a family with one income. In many cases, however, the wife continues to work and the husband helps to raise a family.

In addition to the satisfaction people find in owning their own homes, there are three major financial benefits of owning a home.

First, home ownership seems to offer the best chance for an individual to amass capital in any significant amount. The mortgage payment is, in a way, forced savings, for money must be put aside to meet the mortgage payments, and as the mortgage is paid off, the portion of the mortgage payment going for ownership of the home gradually increases. Some people need this type of pressure to build some financial reserve.

Second, there is always the possibility of making a large profit on the eventual sale of the house. Dramatic increases in the values of homes in certain locations have put many homeowners ahead when they sold their homes. Suppose a first-time home buyer had bought an average-priced home in 1965, at a cost of $20,000. If the individual had sold the house in 1977, the profit on the sale would have been enough for a down payment on the average new home, with a price tag of $55,000. On top of it all, the new home would be larger and contain an extra half-bath, air conditioning, and probably a larger garage.

The above is based on average figures for the housing market. However, remember that there is no such thing as *the* housing market. Values vary greatly from area to area—in some areas homes are depreciating. And every prospective home buyer must wonder whether the present trend of appreciation in the value of homes can continue. Opinion seems very mixed, for inflation and land and energy costs cloud the issue considerably.

A third reason for the wide popularity of home buying is that it is indirectly subsidized by the government, for one does not pay income tax on income spent on property taxes and mortgage interest. According to the U.S. Department of the Treasury, in a recent year the federal government lost $10.7 billion in tax from deductions for property taxes and interest on owner-occupied homes.

Financial Considerations

If you do decide that you want to purchase a home, the next question is how much you can afford. Until recent years, the rule of thumb was that your outlay for shelter should not exceed 2½ times your annual income. Today, housing costs have risen so rapidly that alternatives to the "2½ times rule" are being considered. In many cases people have simply committed themselves to paying more and made sacrifices to obtain their goal. In its 1978 study, the U.S. League of Savings Associations found that 38 percent of the buyers—nearly two out of every five—bought houses on which the monthly costs exceeded 25 percent of their family income. Fourteen percent actually incurred monthly costs that exceeded 30 percent of monthly income.

If you have the down payment and can meet the mortgage payments on your dwelling and still have money left over for closing costs and emergencies, there is no problem. In most cases, however, this is not the situation. The real problem comes in deciding just how much a family should "stretch" to buy the dwelling they want.

To get a maximum affordable monthly payment, you might work backwards from after-tax income, subtracting all your normal fixed expenses and good estimates of your normal variable expenses. Remember that housing costs are not restricted to the cost of the mortgage. Property taxes, insurance, heating, electricity, water, telephone, maintenance, and special fees for services such as garbage collection must be considered as well. One rule of thumb to use in computing the monthly cost of maintaining a house is to divide 1 to 2 percent of the purchase price by twelve. By asking homeowners you can get a more accurate estimate of the cost of insurance, heat, electricity, water, and waste pickup. Taxes are a matter of public record. If you find that you have $500 per month available for shelter and you estimate that taxes, utilities, and maintenance on the type of house you want would run $300, you can see that you have approximately $200 for monthly payments.

Now find out from your savings bank, savings and loan association, or credit union how large a mortgage you could obtain with a $200 monthly payment. (See Table 6-1 for monthly payments on representative amounts at various rates.) Then add this amount to whatever sum you can afford as a down payment. The total is the approximate amount you can afford to pay for a home.

TABLE 6-1. Estimating Monthly Mortgage Payments

Mortgage Interest Rate	$30,000	$33,000	$36,000	$39,000	$42,000	$45,000	$48,000	$51,000
9½%	262.11	288.32	314.54	340.75	366.96	393.17	419.38	445.59
9¾%	267.35	294.08	320.81	347.55	374.28	401.02	427.75	454.49
10%	272.62	299.88	327.14	354.40	381.66	408.92	436.18	463.44
10¼%	277.92	305.71	333.50	361.29	389.09	416.88	444.67	472.46
10½%	283.26	311.58	339.91	368.24	396.56	424.89	453.21	481.54
10¾%	288.63	317.50	346.36	375.22	404.08	432.95	461.81	490.67
11%	294.04	323.44	352.85	382.25	411.65	441.06	470.46	499.86
11¼%	299.48	329.42	359.37	389.32	419.27	449.21	479.16	509.11

Figures are for interest and principal for a twenty-five-year term. They do not include annual property taxes and insurance premiums.

Now that you have a better idea of what you can afford, step back and take another look at the rent versus buy decision. The key here is a realistic estimation of costs.

Annual Costs Associated with Owning
Annual mortgage and other loan payments   ————
Property taxes   +————
Maintenance   +————
Homeowner's insurance   +————
Utilities   +————
  Total cost of owning   ————

From the total cost of owning subtract tax savings from ownership. Savings and loans, banks, real estate agents, and the public library will have books that separate monthly payments on mortgages of various sizes, interest rates, and durations into principal and interest. Once you have the annual interest figure, add it to your yearly prop-

$54,000	$57,000	$60,000	$63,000	$65,000	$70,000	$75,000	$80,000
471.80	498.01	524.22	550.43	567.91	611.59	655.28	698.96
481.22	507.95	534.69	561.42	579.24	623.80	668.36	712.91
490.70	517.96	545.23	572.49	590.66	636.10	681.53	726.97
500.25	528.04	555.83	583.63	602.15	648.47	694.79	741.11
509.86	538.19	566.51	594.84	613.72	660.93	708.14	755.35
519.54	548.40	577.26	606.12	625.37	673.47	721.57	769.68
529.27	558.67	588.07	617.48	637.08	686.08	735.09	784.10
539.05	569.00	598.95	628.90	648.86	698.77	748.68	798.60

erty taxes. Then take the percentage of the total that corresponds to your tax bracket.

Mortgage interest		_____
Property taxes	+	_____
Total		_____
Tax bracket	×	_____
Tax savings		_____

Since this result is the approximate amount of money you will save on your income taxes, it can be subtracted from the total cost of owning to give the annual adjusted cost of owning.

Total cost of owning		_____
Tax savings	−	_____
Adjusted cost of owning		_____

Now you are ready to compare your adjusted owning costs to the cost of renting an apartment. Construct a list of expenses in renting:

Annual Costs Associated with Renting	_____
Annual rent	_____
Utilities	_____
Renter's insurance	_____
Total cost of renting	_____

This comparison shows only fixed expenses—hardly the total of all expenses associated with renting or owning. The cost of furnishings and fixtures, for example, should be considered before you make a final decision.

Another consideration is the merit of putting savings into a down payment on a home rather than into some other investment. The interest you could earn by placing the money into passbook savings, for example, should be compared to the amount of appreciation you can logically expect. The value of real estate, under normal economic conditions, usually increases about 5 to 8 percent a year. Too often the eager homeowner neglects to consider the opportunity cost in lost return from an alternative investment.

If the decision you make is to buy, proceed to the next step—analyzing tastes.

Analyzing Tastes

Today's home buyer has many choices in housing. If your goal is to obtain a new single-family or multi-family house, do you want it prebuilt or built to your specifications? Do you want it stick-built or prefab? Both offer a wide variety of styles and floor plans. Most of the same styles and floor plans are available in previously lived in houses, often at a more reasonable cost. If low personal maintenance is your goal, the condominium or cooperative may be more suitable. The costs of these two forms of housing run from economical to luxury class. The mobile home may also be a viable alternative that fits your tastes. The old axiom "houses appreciate and mobile homes depreciate" is not universally true today. In some areas of the country mobile homes can truly be considered an investment.

In discussing needs, it is impossible to generalize about housing styles and tastes. In his book *The Builders*, Martin Mayer cites the following example:

> In the Northeast and especially the Middle West, people like basements under their homes; and these basements, ready to be finished as rumpus rooms, may add five or six hundred square feet of usable floor space to an apparently small home. You might as well build a basement in the Middle West, because the foundation has to be dug beneath the frost line anyway. In Texas and California, almost nobody has a basement: soil and climate conditions are such that basement walls would have to be impervious to water beyond normal capacities to make space usable.[1]

Not all such differences make so much sense, however. Mayer goes on to point out that carports rather than garages are acceptable as far north as Chicago, but in the more mild climate of California the demand is for garages. In the East, formica-surfaced kitchens help to sell a house, but along the Pacific it's ceramic-tile surfaces. In Florida, most single-family detached dwellings are built with lightweight bricks despite the abundance of America's sturdiest lumber, the Southern yellow pine. Building codes, tradition, and union regulations may also indirectly dictate differences in housing tastes and the end product.

Basic wants should be discussed in some detail. The merits of a house in the suburbs, country, or city might be compared at this stage. General taste considerations such as style (ranch, split-level, or two-story) and

[1]Martin Mayer, *The Builders* (New York: W. W. Norton and Company, Inc.), 1978, p. 35.

outside construction (stucco, brick, aluminum siding) are also worth discussing early in the decision-making process. The size of the lot, amount of privacy, and type of neighborhood are important too. The potential buyer should begin reading about the subject and talking with friends who have bought homes. The buyer who is new to the community will face more of a challenge in finding out about the housing market, but it pays to take the time to search for information.

Some ideas of what your house should be will be modified when the search actually takes place. But advance study, discussion, and information gathering will make shopping easier and less time-consuming.

The Search

Many consumers, especially first-time buyers, start their search for that perfect dwelling by driving around in neighborhoods they have selected. They attend open houses and generally ask around about prices, values, and drawbacks. Signs in yards and newspaper ads are common sources of leads.

Eventually, however, most people turn to the services of a realtor. The major reason for using a realtor is their access to the multi-list service. And since the realtor's commission is paid by the seller and not the buyer, the buyer has nothing to lose. You might wish to select a realtor who is a member of the National Association of Realtors (NAR). Membership in the NAR does not guarantee honesty, of course, but the organization does try to ensure that its members adhere to its code of ethics. In addition, relatives and friends who have worked with realtors in the past may provide recommendations.

Several points are useful to keep in mind when using the services of a realtor. First, realtors in a sense work for the seller, since their income is dependent on selling a house. Most realtors work for a 6- to 8- percent commission. Second, the realtor is not a home-inspection expert, a lawyer, or the last word in appraising the quality of town or city services. The realtor can, however, answer questions about taxes, community services, and transportation routes.

Once you have chosen a realtor whom you trust and who is interested in you, be honest with that person. Tell the realtor the amount you wish to spend and what types of needs and wants you have already determined. It is the realtor's job to bring the buyer and seller together in a satisfactory business transaction. Remember that the realtor you select probably hopes to receive your business if you should decide to sell the property.

When you shop for houses, there are things to ignore and others that you should look for. Learn to ignore decorations, mirrors, lighting, blooming flowers, and neatly stacked closets. Remember that the seller has added such little touches here and there in order to make the house more marketable.

Be sure to ask about heating bills, home improvements, taxes, damage, and the seller's reasons for moving. Most people look for homes that they will be able to resell, since the average family moves often. In this connection you must consider location as the most important factor. After location you should consider schools, public facilities, zoning, transportation, and the trend in property values. Zoning refers to regulations governing the type of activity (industrial, residential, or multiple-dwelling) for which a building may be used.

PROSPECTIVE HOME BUYERS

Check heating bills and taxes.
Consider location as the major factor in resale value.
Try out the dwelling's floor plan.
Find out about community facilities.

You should also examine the floor plan of a prospective dwelling. Three distinct zones should be allocated in a dwelling—a work zone, a shared-activity zone, and a private-activity zone. The size of these zones will depend on the individual's entertaining, cooking, and equipment needs, and on tastes in study and sleeping quarters. To determine whether the rooms have been placed in positions that fit your needs, try out travel patterns from one zone to another.

After the general considerations come the specific points to look for in the particular type of dwelling you want.

A New Home. You may decide that you want to be the first one to live in a house. If so, you will not be alone. Over 2 million new homes were built in 1978, just a few more than in 1977 (see Figure 6-2). These homes were built at record costs, partly because the prices of lumber, concrete, insulation, painting, drywall, electrical work, floor covering, excavation, and millwork (called *hard costs*) had risen 36.2 percent since 1975. Not all of the increased cost of the average new house came about as a result of a rise in hard costs, however. The size and cost of the average lot and the size of the average house (1,666 square feet) also increased.

There are many advantages to buying a new house from a builder. In most cases, the builder offers a number of popular styles. Also, new

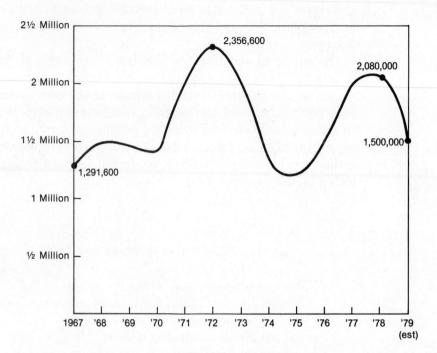

2½ Million
2,356,600
2 Million
2,080,000
1½ Million
1,500,000
1,291,600
1 Million
½ Million

1967 '68 '69 '70 '71 '72 '73 '74 '75 '76 '77 '78 '79 (est)

FIGURE 6-2. New Housing Starts. (U.S. Department of Commerce.)

plumbing, heating system, and appliances are certainly incentives to select such a house—the buyer can anticipate living in the house for a number of years before major repairs become necessary. Many of the new homes are also more energy-efficient, and energy efficiency is now uppermost in the homeowner's mind.

There are drawbacks to buying a new home, however. The overriding drawback of the new house is its cost. Near the end of 1979, the median cost of a new house was $62,900 (compared to $55,900 for a used home) and climbing. And in addition to the building costs, there are other expenses, such as that of landscaping. Many lots are bare of trees, shrubs, and grass—all of which are extremely costly. A second problem is the possibility of shoddy building. Some individuals who buy too hastily later find they have selected a poorly or cheaply constructed house. The Council of Better Business Bureaus reports that complaints against home builders soared by 39 percent in 1977 and 12.6 percent in 1978. Many complaints involve high-volume builders such as Kaufman & Broad, who agreed to an FTC order to make specified repairs on more than 20,000 of their homes. Other home builders large and small violate building codes and even zoning laws.

Following are some of the things to check for in a new house.

LOCATION

Schools	Neighborhood
Churches	Zoning
Work	Tax base
Utilities	Flooding
Traffic volume	

CONSTRUCTION

Asphalt shingles with self-sealing tabs
Insulation
Double-glazed windows
Laminated drywall
100-amp electrical service (220 line for electric stove or dryer)
Neat carpentry
Gutters and downspouts
Proper ventilation
Screens and storm windows
Heating system (with humidifier)
Electrical outlets
Moisture barrier in the basement
Exhaust fans in the bathrooms
Location of registers
Door locks
Lighting (interior and exterior)
Septic system or sewer
Sump pump
Copper pipes
Support beams every ten feet
Type of driveway

INSIDE FEATURES

Quality of appliances
Quality of wall and floor coverings
Hardware on drawers and cupboards

The Custom-Built Home. Many people who can afford to do so choose to have a new house built especially for them. This may merely mean selecting a readymade floor plan, but more often it involves the higher cost of hiring an architect, which requires an investigation of the types and quality of homes previously designed by various architects and a comparison of fees charged. The home buyer also must shop for a lot that complies with zoning needs, has proper drainage and good terrain, and is located conveniently with respect to water, electricity, sewers, and other urban amenities.

Most people who have homes built for them hire a contractor who has a good reputation for building high-quality dwellings at the lowest possible cost. However, some people who want a custom home attempt to save the general contractor's fee of approximately 20 percent by serving in that position themselves. Securing architectural plans, obtaining financing, shopping for materials, supervising work, and dealing with local government officials are duties that come under this job title. If your contractor's duties are over and above the obligations of a time-consuming regular job or if you tend to make mistakes, the savings can easily be erased. But while the risk is high, the savings is worthwhile enough that many undertake the task.

The Prefab Home. The term prefab (prefabrication) conjures up thoughts of a modular dwelling closely resembling a mobile home. Actually, prefabs come in a variety of attractive and even exotic forms. Most prefabs are panelized; this means that the house is assembled in panels containing the inside and outside walls, windows, and even siding. The standard panels are arranged around posts, beams, foundations, and floors. The advantages of the prefab are the shorter amount of time required to erect it (one-third of the time it takes to enclose a stick-built home), the varying floor plans available, and the uniqueness of the designs of many prefab homes in comparison to local builders' plans.

The cost of the prefab may not necessarily be lower than that of other types of homes, for the saving in carpentry labor is usually balanced by the higher cost of shipping the panels. The materials used in building the prefab home are generally high quality. A trap may, however, await the unwary home buyer if a poor local contractor is hired to put a prefab together. Following are some guidelines for the prefab buyer:

- Ask for the names of local customers of the contractor and of the prefab company as references.
- Inspect some of the prefab homes completed by the contractor.
- Check local building codes for requirements that prefabs must meet.
- Study the financial arrangement carefully to be sure that you can meet all the obligations.
- Do not make any changes in plans without a written agreement signed by both parties.

Warranties. A new type of protection available to many buyers of new homes is the Home Owners' Warranty (HOW) initiated by the National Association of Home Builders. It combines a warranty program with an insurance program that guarantees a home, townhouse, or condominium for up to ten years. The coverage costs $2 per $1,000 of the selling price. The HOW requires member-builders to repair major structural defects as well as replace faulty materials during the first year of ownership. During the second year, the warranty covers faulty wiring, piping, and duct work. In subsequent years, the insurance covers major structural flaws. Currently most states have HOW programs. Each of the 124 HOW councils has a list builder-members. If you write to the Home Owners' Warranty Corporation, 15th and M Streets, N.W., Washington, DC 20005, they will send you a directory of the HOW councils.

A Used Home. The new home has the advantage of requiring fewer expenditures for remodeling or repair. But the older home or even slightly used home has advantages as well. A purchase price that is 10 to 15 percent lower is one of the most prominent benefits. Also, the older home may have the advantage of being in an established neighborhood on an already landscaped lot. When you buy a used house, however, you must make a close inspection if you are to avoid or at least minimize the need for costly repairs.

The prospective buyer of a used home should look for the following items:

LOCATION

Schools   Neighborhood
Churches   Zoning
Work   Tax base
Utilities   Flooding
Traffic volume

CONSTRUCTION

Floor plan that suits your activities
Sound driveway
Rust-free downspouts and gutters
Concrete supports from the ground to the house (to keep out termites)
Outside walls free of crumbling
Basement free of dampness
Roof free of missing or poor shingles
Adequate water pressure
Condition of bathroom tiles
Condition of fireplace
Septic tank or sewer

Condition of windows and sashes
Solid beams
Attic ventilation
Adequate insulation (six inches plus vapor barrier in attic floor)
Levelness of the house
Yard condition
100-amp electrical service with 220 line for electric dryer or range
Walls free of cracks
Adequate number of working electrical outlets
Heating system
Adequate water heater
Condition of plumbing
Sump pump

OTHER FEATURES

Quality of appliances
Screens and storm windows
Lighting fixtures
Air conditioner
Water softener
Yard drainage and condition
Healthy trees

In addition, the prospective used-home owner (and even the prospective new-home owner) may want to take advantage of a new service that has sprung up in many parts of the United States. The service is referred to as home inspection. It is used when (1) a potential home buyer is not knowledgeable about how to check for building infirmities; (2) a home seller wants to present a potential buyer with a "clean bill of health" signed by a disinterested party; (3) a homeowner contemplates replacement of a major item—a furnace, for example—and does not trust the judgment of the furnace company alone. Home inspection services are performed by private firms that provide an oral and/or written report. Inspections generally cover central heating, cooling, interior plumbing, electricity, rooms, walls, ceilings, doors, foundation, and basement.

While most home buyers who employ a professional home inspector buy the home regardless of the results of the inspection (92 percent), their usual reaction to learning of flaws is to lower the amount of their offer. In any case, they enjoy peace of mind from knowing approximately how long major systems will last before they will have to be repaired or replaced. Some buyers require a satisfactory inspection report as a condition of the sales contract itself.

In some areas it is possible to purchase a used-home warranty in conjunction with a private or realtor-sponsored inspection. Then if any flaws do appear in the house within a year, the inspection agency pays for repairs. However, homeowner repair and replacement of equipment certified as unsatisfactory may be required in order to maintain coverage under the warranty.

A termite inspection is also a necessity—and sometimes even a law —in certain areas of the country.

A Condominium or Cooperative. The advent of the condominium and the cooperative has extended the possibility of home ownership to apartment dwellers. Many people attempt to identify these forms of ownership with a particular type of building, but building type is not involved.

Condominium ownership implies having full title to living space and joint ownership of certain common grounds—for example, swimming pools and tennis courts—with other owners in the same building complex. By law, the owner's "unit" is a separate parcel of real estate for purposes of purchase and sale, recording of titles, taxation, and financing (a default by one unit owner does not affect other owners in the same condominium). Thus although the condo owner must abide by the association rules, he or she is free to sell when it becomes necessary or desirable to do so.

The condominium concept is relatively new in the United States, having originated in 1961. Some condos are referred to as townhouses and may have a garage, basement, and two other floors. Others may actually be single-family detached dwellings in which the developer keeps control of the surrounding land. In cities, condos are often apartments that have been sold by former landlords to former tenants. Very often this happens because the economic climate and government regulations have made it unprofitable for the landlord to continue renting the property as an apartment building. In other areas, it is speculation that has fueled the condo market. The chance of doubling, tripling, or even quadrupling an initial investment over a two-year period has brought a booming conversion market to the North Shore of Chicago.

The cooperative is a different and more restrictive form of ownership. In a co-op the tenants own a corporation that owns all the property, including dwellings, so each tenant actually has a lease on a dwelling space. Since you do not own your dwelling directly, you must receive permission to sell it to another party.

As co-owner of a condo or co-op you are a partner in a business. You must take responsibility for its success or failure. Co-ownership may mean carefree living with no grass mowing or snow shoveling by the owners. But the owners do have the responsibility to pay to see that these tasks get done. This bill is separate from the mortgage, insurance, and tax payments on the individual units; it covers all managerial, operational, and repair-maintenance costs.

All the owners are part of a homeowners' management association. The association should be controlled by a board of directors elected by the unit owners; it should not be controlled by the developers of the area. In a large condominium complex the board of managers may hire a professional manager. Remember, you will only have a say in how your condominium is run if you actively take part in its management.

Before buying a condominium or co-op be sure to:

1. Read the bylaws carefully. Bylaws should include requirements that all owners be notified in advance of all association meetings and have access to all minutes, that financial books be open to owners and their accountants, and that the proposed budget be available in advance of the budget meeting.
2. Get a full breakdown of the condominium or co-op maintenance budget, and show it to a professional for comparison with other such budgets.
3. If the development is under construction, make sure down payments go into an escrow account and not into construction accounts. You should not have to provide an advance maintenance payment.
4. Ensure that the condominium association maintains a sufficient capital reserve to take care of emergencies (10 to 20 percent of the total assessment should be on reserve).
5. Hire a structural engineer to look over the condominium or co-op.
6. Hire a lawyer to review the contract.
7. Check the building as you would any apartment house. Many of the same rules apply.

The condo or co-op can offer many advantages to the first-time home buyer. Often the savings by the builder in land and materials makes it less costly to purchase. The maintenance offered by the association is also a selling point for people who do not have a desire to become involved with home repair. In resort areas, time-sharing plans make it possible to buy a condo for just a certain week or weeks of any year or years. The varieties are limitless. But construction quality in condos and co-ops varies widely, and the same caution that is used in buying homes is also important in buying a condo or co-op.

A Mobile Home. Mobile homes are particularly popular with young families and retired people. These two groups account for 70 percent of all mobile-home owners. The size of the mobile home has increased dramatically, from the old twelve- to fourteen-foot widths to today's twenty-four- to twenty-eight-foot spans. The cost of the mobile home has risen rapidly as well. Some specialty and deluxe models cost as much as $30,000.

The mobile home does have two major disadvantages. First, it still suffers from some image problems. Second, in most states mobile homes are still considered vehicles rather than houses, although they are not exactly mobile, and thus the financing of a mobile home is often based on the higher interest rates used for automobile loans rather than a simple mortgage computation. In some areas of the country it is difficult to finance a mobile home at all.

On the other hand, the mobile home offers some advantages. The condo owner does not have the right to change the outside surroundings, while the mobile-home owner generally does. Additions, carports, fences, and other amenities can be added to personalize the environment.

The U.S. Department of Housing and Urban Development recently imposed new standards that have strengthened the construction of mobile homes and that require every new mobile home to carry a consumer manual of information similar to an auto owner's manual.

Finally, of course, mobility is the major advantage of the mobile home.

A thorough check of a mobile home should include an examination of the floor, walls, amount of room, insulation, and exterior. Then before you sign the sales contract, shop around for financing. The dealer may not be offering the lowest APR or the best terms on such matters as missed-payment penalties. Also, be sure to have in writing who is to transport the mobile home to your park.

The California Departments of Consumer Affairs, Housing and Community Development, and Motor Vehicles have produced an excellent booklet entitled "Mobile Homes, A Consumer's Guide," which may be obtained by writing to the Department of Consumer Affairs, 1020 N Street, Sacramento, California 95814. The following excerpt is their answer to the question "What should I look for in a mobile home park?"

It is important to find a space *before* you actually buy your mobile home. You can't very well park a ten-ton mobile home on your front porch while you search for a site to set up your new home. You should check the park's:

a. *Location.* What neighborhood is the park in? How far is it to stores, schools, and your job? Check the availability of water, utilities, and mail service.

b. *Condition.* Are the community areas clean and well kept? In case of heavy rain, how is the drainage system? California law requires mobile home parks to meet certain health and safety standards. The park construction, including lighting, drainage, garbage disposal, and grading, is regulated.

c. *Facilities.* Look for extra storage areas and second-car parking if you need it; check the recreational facilities and the laundry area; if you have children or pets, consider their play areas; examine the park's utility system. California law regulates how park management bills you if a "master meter" utility system with sub-metering to each lot provided by the park is used. With this system, the park management must give all tenants their own beginning and ending meter readings and individual bills for the money owed each billing period. The management should post the billing rate where you can easily see it. In some parks, though, the utility company provides individual meters for each tenant and bills you directly.

d. *Rules.* Is special landscaping of your mobile home space required? Does your mobile home have to be of a certain style or have skirting and awnings? What are the hours for using the recreational facilities? Are children, pets, and guests allowed? California law does not allow the mobile home park owner to charge you extra fees for members of your immediate family, for guests who stay less than two weeks in any month, for enforcing the park rules, or for pets unless the park has special facilities for them.

The rules can legally allow the management to rent to adults only, and if you like a particular space, you should find out if the park rules will accept you before you buy your mobile home. However, discrimination on the basis of race, sex, religion, color, nationality, or marital status is not allowed.

If you are considering a park, talk with the park residents. Ask if they are happy with the park, what problems they have, and how the owner and manager are. When you find a space, put a deposit on it, if possible, to hold it for you. But before you sign a lease or rental agreement, read it and the park rules very carefully. The park management must give you a copy of California's mobile home park tenancy laws which you should read and keep for future reference.

The process of buying a home may be a short one or a long one. It is not too unusual for buyers to take a year to decide before buying, particularly if their situation permits a "no hurry" approach to finding the right dwelling. In any case, be sure that you think carefully about what you want before you even go into the market, because in these days of escalating prices of real property you may have to move fast or lose out.

Making an Offer

When you have selected a home, the next step is to make an offer. Many buyers are shocked to find that once they make an offer—whether it is called a purchase agreement, a contract, or a binder—they are bound by it if the seller accepts. Thus the best time to hire a lawyer, if you wish to do so, is before you make an offer and not after you have committed yourself to a legally binding agreement. The practice of hiring a lawyer is especially common among first-time buyers, buyers unfamiliar with an area, or buyers who are buying directly from the owner.

The offer form is usually a standard form purchased at a stationery shop. It will include the purchase price you are offering, method and dates of payment, a legal description of the property, closing date, right to cancel under certain conditions (such as inability to get financing), and a description of personal property to be included in the sale. Make sure when you make an offer on a house that you spell out what items you expect to get with the house. Appliances, carpeting, and other furnishings are often used in the price-bargaining process.

The offer you make is usually accompanied by a "binder" or "earnest money" or "deposit" that shows your good faith in making the offer. You will get back your deposit only if the seller fails to meet the agreed-upon conditions or if you fail to get financing.

The reality of the contract unsettles many first-time buyers. Try to keep a "cool head" in the negotiation process and look at the drawbacks as well as the positive aspects of the dwelling. The amount of your offer should depend somewhat on the market in the area and the circumstances facing the seller.

Raising the Money

Finding financing for the deal is a process that can be done informally at an earlier date so that the transaction can move quickly and smoothly when an offer is made and a favorable appraisal of the property has been obtained.

It pays to shop around for a mortgage, since such a large amount of money is involved. Mortgages are usually available from savings and loan associations, savings banks, commercial banks, and life insurance companies. Recently federal credit unions were given the power to grant mortgages.

Government-Related Loans.　The FHA (Federal Housing Administration) conducts a loan program geared to serving moderate- to low-income households. The FHA does not really lend the money. Instead, it will insure the entire amount of a loan up to $60,000. According to FHA rules, the minimum down payment on a house purchased with such a loan is 3 percent of the first $25,000 of the home's appraised value, plus 5 percent of the remainder. The loans may be written through an FHA savings and loan for up to thirty years.

A second type of government-backed mortgage is the VA (Veterans Administration) mortgage. An estimated 30 million people who have served in the military are eligible. To find out whether you qualify, simply check with the nearest VA office. Terms for such mortgages are even easier than for the FHA mortgages. Since the Veterans Administration guarantees up to $25,000 of a veteran's mortgage, some savings and loans will waive part or all of the down payment. The maximum term of the mortgage is thirty years.

While both of these mortgages sound easy and are certainly cheaper (the 1979 rate of 10 percent does not compare to the 1979 conventional rate of at least 10¾ percent), there are drawbacks. First of all, since financial institutions will refuse to lend the money unless they get the going rate, the seller of the property must make up the difference—and most are reluctant to do so if there is any possibility that a borrower with a conventional mortgage will come along. Each percentage point of difference between the FHA or VA mortgage and the going rate on a conventional mortgage is called a *point*. And each point costs the seller 1 percent of the total mortgage amount. Therefore, a one-point difference on a $50,000 home would cost the seller $500 (.01 × $50,000).

A second drawback of the VA or FHA mortgage is the delay that occurs while the loan is being evaluated in terms of quality standards that have been set by HUD (Department of Housing and Urban Development). The application for an FHA or a VA mortgage is first submitted to an approved lending agency. The agency forwards the application to the FHA or the VA, which then appraises the house to see if the price is equitable and investigates the borrower for credit worthiness. Then the home is inspected to see if it passes HUD standards for wiring, plumbing, etc. All of this requires time—time during which the seller must take the property off the market. Sellers are reluctant to do this, for they must assume the risk that the house and the applicant will not qualify at the agreed-upon price.

Thus it is quite difficult to obtain government-related mortgages in a good real estate market. It is still worth a try, however, as the benefit to the borrower is great—especially if the borrower does not have a large enough down payment for a conventional mortgage.

Some cities and states are now getting into the mortgage business. Over forty cities are already participating in a HUD program called Urban Homesteading, in which abandoned property is turned over to the city by

HUD and sold by lottery for amounts as little as $1. Home repair loans with interest rates as low as 3 percent are then made available to the new owners. The cities are hoping that this will spur revitalization activities.

Conventional Mortgages. The major drawback of the conventional mortgage is that a large down payment is often required. Accumulating a 20-percent down payment, standard in today's market, is almost impossible for many potential homeowners, especially young ones. For some, the answer may be to rent with an option to buy later. Others begin with a less expensive condo or mobile home.

Table 6-2 shows that savings and loans are the primary source of conventional home mortgages. Predictions for the future point to insurance companies, credit unions, pension funds, and commercial banks to begin or step up mortgage activity, especially as the distinctions among financial institutions become more blurred. Until that happens, however, the savings and loans will continue to do the lion's share of the mortgage lending, so you might want to check several savings and loans. In times of tight money it helps to have an account where you apply for your mortgage.

The amount you can borrow on a house will be limited by the value of the house you want to buy. This is not the sale price of the house— it is the value at which the lending institution appraises the house. The loan usually cannot exceed 70 to 80 percent of the house's appraised value. This makes it doubly important that your purchase price be in line with local market conditions.

A conventional mortgage is set up so that interest is paid on the unpaid balance of the mortgage. Since your balance is very high at the beginning, the portion of the payments devoted to interest is much higher than that going into paying for the house itself. For example, on a twenty-five-year $42,000 mortgage at 11 percent, the monthly payment

TABLE 6-2. Sources of Conventional Mortgage Financing

Mortgage bankers	19%
Savings and loans	48
Commercial banks	23
Other sources (such as savings banks)	10

Source: Thomas R. Harter, chief economist for the Mortgage Bankers Association of America, in *Chicago Tribune*, October 22, 1979.

would be $411.65. The interest for the first month would be $385, and the principal would be only $26.65 ($42,000 × .11 ÷ 12 months).

One surprise for many first-time home buyers is the fact that they must pay a service charge, or points. In the case of an FHA or a VA loan, the seller pays them. But in the case of a conventional mortgage, the buyer may pay the financial institution anywhere from 1 to 3 points (1 to 3 percent of the mortgage) in a lump sum at the time of the closing of the sale. Although most of these front-end fees are tax-deductible, they can be a problem for home buyers who have already stretched their finances thin.

One recent innovation that should be of help to first-time home buyers is the GPM (graduated payment method). With the GPM, the buyer makes low monthly payments at first and larger payments later. Table 6-3 illustrates five such plans unveiled by the FHA (similar plans are available for conventional mortgages). The first three plans level off in the sixth year, and the other two level off after the tenth. The annual increases for the first five years are 2.5 percent in Plan 1; 5 percent in Plan 2; 7.5 percent in Plan 3. The annual increases for the first ten years in Plans 4 and 5 are 2 and 3 percent, respectively. Since initial payments under the 7.5 plan (Plan 3) are the lowest, that is the one chosen most by FHA buyers, and it is expected that conventional buyers will do likewise.

The GPM appeals especially to young couples who are thus able to

TABLE 6-3. Graduated Payment Plan Payment Schedule for a $50,000, Thirty-Year Loan at 10 Percent

	Plan 1	Plan 2	Plan 3	Plan 4	Plan 5
year 1	$400.29	$365.30	$333.52	$390.02	$367.29
year 2	410.29	383.56	358.53	397.82	378.31
year 3	420.55	402.74	385.42	405.78	389.66
year 4	431.07	422.88	414.33	413.89	401.35
year 5	441.84	444.02	445.41	422.17	413.39
year 6	452.89	466.22	478.81	430.61	425.79
year 7	452.89	466.22	478.81	439.23	438.56
year 8	452.89	466.22	478.81	448.01	451.72
year 9	452.89	466.22	478.81	456.97	465.27
year 10	452.89	466.22	478.81	466.11	479.23
remaining payments	452.89	466.22	478.81	475.43	493.60

Source: Department of Housing and Urban Development.

afford "as much as $5000 to $8000 more, and buy that house much sooner than they could under a standard fixed mortgage," says James M. Mataya of the United States League of Savings Associations.[2]

As of July 1, 1979, federal savings and loans could offer another type of mortgage called a VIR (variable interest rate) mortgage. Under this plan, the Federal Home Loan Bank Board will determine the cost of funds each January and July. If the cost goes down, the lender must decrease the mortgage rate. If it goes up, so does the mortgage rate. The maximum amount the mortgage rate may be increased is 2.5 percent above the original rate. There is no downward limit. This new type of mortgage may make it easier for people to get loans, since the lender assumes less risk that the rate of return will look smaller in five or ten years.

While the stated rate of interest is currently very high, a borrower's effective rate is actually somewhat lower, because he or she can deduct the mortgage interest from income when itemizing deductions on an income tax return. Table 6-4 shows, for example, that a person who has a taxable income (not the same as gross income) of $17,000 and who borrows at a rate of 11 percent is in effect paying at a rate of 7.92 percent after the tax deduction. For many, this takes some of the sting out of paying high mortgage rates.

Closing the Sale

The formal execution of the contract to buy the home is called the settlement or the closing. At the closing session the buyer has to pay all the fees called for in the contract. Often first-time home buyers neglect to budget for these costs. They are of vital importance, however, as they

TABLE 6-4. Effective Mortgage Interest Rates

Your Taxable Income	Your Tax Bracket	Interest Rate on Mortgage			
		10%	10½%	11%	11½%
$11,000	22%	7.80%	8.19%	8.58%	8.97%
17,000	28	7.20	7.56	7.92	8.28
23,000	32	6.80	7.14	7.48	7.82
29,000	39	6.10	6.41	6.71	7.02
35,000	42	5.80	6.09	6.38	6.67
41,000	48	5.20	5.46	5.72	5.98

[2]"GPM's: The Affordable Mortgage," *Everybody's Money,* Autumn 1979, p. 22.

must all be paid before the new owner can take possession of the house. Possible closing costs to the buyer are listed below.

1. *Contract Sales Price.* This is the price of the home agreed upon in the sales contract between buyer and seller. This price is usually reduced by the amount of earnest money already paid to the seller. The balance is divided between the mortgage from the lender and the buyer's down payment.

2. *Loan Origination Fee.* This compensates the lender for expenses incurred in originating the loan, preparing documents, and doing related work.

3. *Points.* A lump-sum percentage charged by some lenders for making a loan.

4. *Appraisal Fee.* This charge compensates the lender for a property appraisal made by an independent appraiser or by a member of the lender's staff.

5. *Credit Report.* A charge paid to a credit bureau for providing the lender with a report on the status of the buyer's credit.

6. *Adjustments or Pro-Rations.* These amounts represent prorated adjustments of certain costs, such as real estate taxes, utilities, and fuel. Such adjustments are often made in order to charge the seller for the period he or she owned the property (up to settlement) and to charge the buyer for the period after settlement. For example, where settlement occurs October 1, 1979, and the seller has paid the real estate taxes in advance for the entire year, a typical adjustment would be for the buyer to compensate the seller for one-fourth of the real estate taxes for 1979, that is, those for the period from October 1 through December 31.

7. *Prepaid Interest.* This charge covers interest that will accrue from the date of settlement to the beginning of the period covered by your first monthly payment. For example, if your mortgage payment is due on the first of each month, but settlement occurs on April 20, the prepaid interest at settlement will cover the period from April 20 to April 30. Thus your June 1 payment will not have to include an extra amount of interest for the period before May 1.

8. *Prepaid Hazard Insurance Premium.* This is the portion of the premium prepaid by the buyer at settlement for purchase from a private company of insurance against loss due to fire, windstorm, and natural hazards. This coverage may be included in a homeowner's policy that insures against possible additional risks, such as personal liability and theft.

9. *Reserves Deposited with Lender.* These funds are placed by the buyer in an "escrow" or "impound" account maintained by the lender to assure an adequate accumulation of funds to meet charges for real estate taxes and hazard insurance when they become due; and also, if applicable, for mortgage insurance, annual assessments, homeowner's association fees, or flood insurance. If your down payment is high enough, you may not have to place funds in escrow. In that case, you may not want to do so unless the financial institution pays interest on funds in escrow. One advantage of paying insurance premiums yourself is that you have more freedom to change insurers.

10. *Title Insurance.* A one-time premium may be charged at settlement for a policy that protects the lender's interest in the property against land title problems, including those that might not be disclosed by a title search and examination. Whether the buyer or seller pays for this varies with local custom.

    The buyer must request and pay for an additional owner's policy if he or she wants this protection for his or her interest in the property. There are many areas where an owner's policy can be obtained at a modest additional charge if issued simultaneously with a lender's policy. In some areas, the seller pays for the owner's title insurance policy.

11. *Government Transfer Taxes and Charges.* The fees and taxes in this section are generally levied by state and/or local governments when property changes hands or when a mortgage loan is made. Depending on local custom, these charges may be paid by the buyer or seller or split between them.

No two closings are alike, but all involve numerous fees and forms. A number of home buyers choose to have a lawyer at the closing to help with the necessary paperwork, especially if they are unfamiliar with closings.

Moving

Once the papers have been signed, all that remains is the moving chore. The ICC sets interstate moving rates. As a result, different interstate movers are likely to charge about the same amount. The difference lies in the quality of the movers' work, their honesty, and the accuracy of their estimates.

The Interstate Commerce Commission (ICC) releases statistics each year on performance of the nation's largest moving companies. Two sets of statistics are available:

- the number of complaints registered by the ICC from consumers against the large interstate carriers of household goods
- "Performance Reports" on the various moving firms.

You can obtain the reports by writing the Consumer Affairs Offices, Public Information Office, ICC, 12th Street and Constitution Avenue, Washington, DC 20432. Local movers who are not bound by ICC regulations may be considerably cheaper on an in-state move. Once again, however, reputation is important.

HOMEOWNER'S INSURANCE

Types of Policies

Homeowner's policies usually come in three levels of complexity and price. The lowest amount of protection is found in the basic homeowner's policy, which usually protects against eleven perils to property:

- fire and lightning
- wind and hail
- explosion
- riot
- aircraft
- loss (through fire or other perils) of property removed from premises
- vehicles
- smoke
- vandalism
- theft
- breakage of glass

More expensive but covering more perils is the broad form. In addition to the eleven perils named above, it covers:

- rupture of heating systems
- falling objects
- weight of ice or snow
- collapse of buildings
- accidental discharge of water or steam from plumbing

· freezing of plumbing
· heating and air conditioning systems and domestic appliances (includes most electrical shocks)

The most expensive form of homeowner's insurance, called comprehensive, covers all perils except earthquake, landslide, floods of various kinds, sewer back-up, seepage, war, and nuclear radiation.

All three plans cover personal property (contents), usually up to half the value of the policy. If your belongings are damaged, however, you can only collect the current retail cost less a deduction for your usage. For full replacement coverage, you would have to get a replacement value rider. If you have valuable jewelry, furs, or stamp or coin collections, a personal property floater should be purchased to more completely cover these items. In any case, every homeowner or tenant should keep an inventory of valuables and possessions (pictures are even better) in a safe-deposit box in order to be prepared for loss or destruction.

Besides covering property damage, a homeowner's policy also provides liability coverage for those family members living at home. Liability covers lawsuits in which people accuse you, your family, or your pets of causing damage to their property. Liability coverage on various policies ranges from $25,000 up to $1 million.

Medical payments insurance is also a part of homeowner's insurance. To receive payment under liability coverage a victim must show negligence, but to receive payment under medical payment insurance a claimant needs no such proof of liability. Most policies will pay up to $500 per injured person.

For tenants, much of the same coverage is available. Tenants can insure against damage to personal property, theft of personal property, liability, and medical payments. A slightly broader form of insurance protects the condo owner from the extra perils resulting from common ownership of certain areas and grounds.

Replacement Value

Most homeowner policies pay the full amount of a damage claim only when the house (not including the lot) is insured for at least 80 percent of its replacement value. This practice is called *coinsurance*. For example, if you have a house that has a replacement value of $50,000, you must insure it for $40,000 if you want to collect the full amount of a damage claim of $40,000 or less. Replacement value is the actual cost of materials and not the market value. If you wanted to insure for a complete $50,000 loss, you would have to purchase an additional $10,000 worth of insurance.

Suppose your $50,000 home was insured for only $25,000. In the event of a partial loss of $4,000, you would collect:

$$\begin{array}{c} \$50,000 \\ \times \quad .80 \\ \hline \$40,000 \end{array} \qquad \frac{\$25,000}{\$40,000} = \frac{5}{8} \qquad \frac{5}{8} \times \$4,000 = \$2,500$$

In the event of a total loss, you would collect $25,000.

Most people do not deliberately underinsure their property—inflation is the culprit. To protect homeowners against this creep in costs, many insurance companies have introduced an inflation guard program in which the amount of insurance you buy is increased each quarter to match the market value of your home.

Deductibles

One way to decrease the cost of your home insurance is to increase your deductible. The deductible is the portion of each repair bill that you pay out of your pocket before the insurance company assumes the claim. Increasing your deductible from $100 to $250 will save you approximately 10 percent on your premium; an increase to a $500 deductible can reduce the insurance premium by 20 percent.

As in every other aspect of consumer money management, before buying insurance on a home, apartment, condominium, or mobile home, investigate all aspects of the coverage and costs.

QUESTIONS FOR DISCUSSION

1. What case can be made for renting housing rather than purchasing it?
2. What is meant by the statement that "home ownership is subsidized by the government"?
3. Why may a prebuilt (prefab) home cost nearly as much as a stick-built home?
4. How is a home inspection useful for a home buyer? Why is it as important to inspect a new house as it is to inspect an older one?
5. Does the shape or style of the building have anything to do with the definition of a condominium? Explain what a condominium is.
6. How do home mortgages and mobile home loans often differ? Why do you think this is true?

7. What are the advantages of buying a dwelling through a realtor?
8. Why do many home sellers resist a sale to a VA or an FHA buyer?
9. Define "in escrow."
10. A dwelling worth $70,000 is insured for $42,000 by a policy with an 80-percent coinsurance clause. If the owner sustains a $10,000 fire loss, how much will be collected?

PERSONAL EXPERIENCE PROJECTS

1. Visit the sales offices and models of apartments, condominiums, and housing developments. Obtain floor plans and other information needed to compare costs, features, and facilities of various housing alternatives.
2. Interview loan officers at various banks and savings and loan associations to obtain information on their interest rates, credit requirements, and other factors regarding a mortgage.
3. Read articles in *Apartment Life* magazine on leases, security deposits, and other legal aspects of apartment renting. Cite information that would be of assistance to you in avoiding housing problems.
4. Interview a legal aid employee or other legal counselor who deals with landlord-tenant problems. Discuss the aspects of an apartment lease that are designed to protect the rights of the landlord and those designed to protect the tenant.
5. Conduct a survey of apartment dwellers to determine the problems they have had and the reasons they have selected apartment living over other housing alternatives.
6. Conduct a cost comparison of renter's/homeowner's insurance for an apartment or a house. Discuss with various insurance agents the factors that affect the cost of insurance.
7. Survey condominium owners regarding satisfaction with their housing facilities. Discuss costs, benefits, the ownership association, and problems encountered by residents.
8. Interview mobile home salespeople and owners to determine costs, features, safety, and mobility of mobile homes. Ask owners if they are satisfied with their living arrangements.
9. Visit a real estate office to discuss the price range of homes, taxes, and facilities in a certain neighborhood.
10. Compare buying a house and renting an apartment in terms of costs, tax benefits, flexibility, and maintenance.

7

AUTOMOBILE TRANSPORTATION

Why should a whole chapter in this money management book be devoted to automobiles?

The first good reason is the cost of operating a motor vehicle. According to Runzheimer and Company, Inc., of Rochester, Wisconsin, a consulting firm specializing in travel and living costs, a consumer who purchased a new subcompact in 1978 will have spent nearly $10,000 on it by 1982. For consumers who bought a 1978 luxury model, the cost over the four-year period will be more like $17,000. In other words, by the time the consumer trades in the car (based on an average four-year, 56,000-mile ride), the cost will have become double the ticket price of the car. Why that much? The extra money is spent on depreciation, loan-interest charges, insurance premiums, license fees, taxes, gas, oil, maintenance, and tires. Gas prices alone went up 39 percent between August 1978 and August 1979. If the consumer has to pay to park the car or to drive on toll roads, the cost is still greater. Consequently, Americans spend almost 20 percent of what they earn on automobiles.

A second good reason for devoting considerable attention to the automobile is that the automobile has an extremely significant impact on the economy. According to former General Motors Chairman James Roche, 61 percent of all rubber consumed in the United States, 20 percent of all steel, 10 percent of all aluminum, and one-third of all glass

153

is used in the production of the automobile. And in his book *Snap, Crackle and Popular Taste,* Jeffrey Schrank amusingly states that there were so many automobiles in the U.S. in 1977 (1 for every 2.6 humans in the country) that the "entire nation could sit more or less comfortably in the front seat of all the cars."[1] If American taste changed overnight from the automobile to some other mode of travel, the economy would be thrown into turmoil.

The third reason is that a chapter on automobiles can develop some basic principles of buymanship that apply to many durable items. Previous chapters have concentrated more on nondurable items than on durables. The consumer faces a special problem in buying large-ticket durable items: because so much time elapses between purchases, previous knowledge about the product either has been forgotten or is no longer applicable. This is especially true of cost data, but it also applies to new technology. In the case of the automobile, the consumer faces the additional psychological dilemma of cost versus the "you are what you drive" syndrome. Many consumers find it difficult to distinguish between their own dissatisfaction with the performance of the old car and the effect of advertising campaigns cleverly designed by auto companies to create consumer desire for a new, shiny, and more powerful car.

THE COST OF OPERATING AN AUTOMOBILE

Purchase Price

Although the purchase price of an automobile is, as we have said, merely the first of many car expenditures, it is the most visible. While cars have become smaller, the costs of production have kept increasing. Some attribute this to inflation and retooling expenses, while others blame the lack of competition in the auto industry, which makes it possible for manufacturers to automatically raise prices.

To actually analyze the purchase-price component of the annual cost of operating an automobile, the concept of depreciation must be employed. *Depreciation* is the difference between what is paid for the car and what it would be worth if sold or traded. As a rough estimate, Hertz Corporation figures that a car depreciates 2¾ percent per month if kept for two years. It depreciates 2¼ percent per month if kept for three years, and a little less than 2 percent per month if kept for four years. Obviously, the largest depreciation occurs during the first year. For example, a 1977

[1] Jeffrey Schrank, *Snap, Crackle and Popular Taste* (New York: Delacorte Press, 1977).

Chevrolet Malibu four-door sedan equipped with a 305-cubic-inch V-8 engine and average options depreciated $894 the first year, according to the American Automobile Association. For most drivers, depreciation is the single largest cost of operating a car.

Where can a consumer find information about the value of a used car or about how to estimate the cost of depreciation? The National Automobile Dealers Association's *Used Car Guide* and Kelley's *Blue Book Market Report, Red Book Official Used Car Valuations,* and *Black Book Official Used Car Market Guide* are the most common sources of information about used car prices and values. Banks, credit unions, and insurance agencies are sure to have one of these books on hand. But remember that all these publications are merely guides. If a car is in especially good shape or if a consumer finds an eager buyer, the car may bring a higher price.

Insurance

For some, the cost of auto insurance exceeds that of depreciation. A young urban male driver may pay $1,000 per year for automobile insurance even with an accident-free record. Insurance rates in general are high in large urban areas because of the accident rate and the very high cost of automobile parts and repairs, and the cost of insurance is even higher for young drivers because of their particularly bad accident record.

Interest on Loans

In order to cope with higher prices, lenders have increased both the length of automobile loans and the size of monthly payments. According to Runzheimer and Company, Inc.,

> Loans of 36 months or longer accounted for but 4 percent of all outstanding car loans in 1974, compared with 60 percent of all loans now.
> At the same time, the average monthly payment is inching toward the $200 mark, and is expected to be there by 1981. . . . That figure is double the average monthly payment of 1969.[2]

The longer the auto loan is, of course, the higher the dollar cost. Thus most financial advisors encourage repayment over as short a time as possible, and a down payment of at least 25 percent.

In order to evaluate and compare loan costs, it is best to construct

[2]*Rockford* (Illinois) *Registar Star,* September 10, 1979.

a chart. You will need to tell prospective lenders the exact cost (including options and taxes) of the car less the down payment and the trade-in, which will yield the amount to be financed. They will also need to know how long a loan you require. They will then be able to tell you the amount of the monthly payment, the exact number of payments, the APR (annual percentage rate), and the total dollar value of the loan, along with any other conditions of the loan. Be sure the rate is expressed in APR and not in "so much per $100." Also determine whether there will be an additional charge for credit life insurance; it is probably not wise for young consumers to buy credit life insurance. (For a more detailed discussion of automobile financing, see Chapter 4, page pp. 76–77.)

Gas and Oil

The cost of gas and oil is a variable expense that can be controlled to some extent. With gas shortages forcing prices well above the $1 per gallon rate, control of gas usage has become particularly critical. The cost per mile for AAA's average-sized car was 3.89¢ in 1978, down from 4.11¢ from 1977. In 1979, the cost per mile jumped dramatically, however.

To compute gasoline costs per year, first estimate the number of miles driven per year. Then divide this figure by the estimated average number of miles per gallon delivered by the car to be purchased. (This will be easier with the new EPA figures, which will only give a single average miles-per-gallon number rather than the old city and open-road numbers.) Multiply this result by the current price in your area for the type of gasoline needed. Many of the new cars do not run well on regular-octane unleaded gasoline and need a higher-octane unleaded gasoline—be sure you investigate before buying. This figure will obviously be a rough estimate, for the Environmental Protection Agency sticker figures depend heavily on the way a car is driven and current gasoline prices cannot be relied upon.

Vehicle weight and engine size are the most important items affecting overall fuel consumption. Generally, a car that weighs half as much as another car will consume half as much gasoline. Because they add to the weight of a car, options also cause it to require more fuel. It is possible to improve a car's mileage per gallon by:

· accelerating slowly
· avoiding unnecessary braking
· driving at moderate speeds
· driving at steady speeds
· avoiding excessive idling.

Maintenance, Repairs, Tires, and Parts

Maintenance, repairs, tires, and parts represent another relatively large cost per mile to the car owner. The AAA estimated the cost of these items to be 1.76¢ per mile on the average 1978 car.

During periods of inflation, car owners often skimp on or neglect regular auto maintenance, but this is a decision that can have costly long-range repercussions. The purchase of tires is a decision that requires particularly careful study. The Department of Transportation will soon announce a set of tire standards for consumer comparison. These standards will be based on tread wear, traction, and temperature resistance. The choice of the right tire—bias-ply, belted-bias-ply, or radial—depends on the miles driven per year and even the type of driving.

Other Expenses

Other fixed expenses include annual registration costs, storage fees, and parking fees.

It is easy to see that there is much more to auto ownership than the initial cost of the car. The rest of this chapter will discuss the purchase of new and used cars, auto repair, the future of the automobile, and auto insurance.

BUYING A NEW CAR

How Much Can You Afford?

Car buying, like most other projects, can be carried out in steps. A logical first step is to determine what you can afford by taking a realistic look at your finances. Unrealistic proposed cutbacks in your spending will make you very unhappy when the "new car smell" wears off. It is even a good idea to tentatively arrange financing as soon as you determine how much you can afford so that you do not spend more than you originally planned.

What Is Available?

Automobiles are categorized by size. Subcompacts are the smallest, with compacts, intermediates, and full or standard sizes rounding out the choices. Of course, every size has its luxury or specialty lines as well.

Deciding which one is best for your special needs usually requires some homework. Among the most popular sources of auto research are the *Consumer Reports* April car-buying issue and yearly buying guide. The *Consumer Reports* car-buying issue takes some of the mystery out of price options and, more importantly, gives the results of test-driving. Other periodicals also give price information and auto road-test results. Edmund's *New Car Prices* or *Foreign Car Prices, Car and Driver, Motor Trend, Road Test,* and *Car/Puter's Auto Facts—New Car Prices* are among those which provide such information. All are available on newsstands, and back issues of most are available in libraries.

Another more informal source of information is the dealer's lot. If you want privacy, take a look on evenings or weekends. This phase of comparison shopping will familiarize you with option costs, styles, and even colors.

Such reading and informal shopping will assist you in narrowing your choice within your price range. Remember that many cars share parts, such as chassis, motor, and ornamentation. Within a price range and type of car, it pays to keep your options open. For example, Chrysler Aspen and Volare are as much alike as are some combinations of General Motors and Ford cars.

In making a selection it is necessary to think beyond the ballyhoo of media advertising, which provides little help in disclosing real differences in automobiles. It is also necessary to think beyond the purchase price to the costs of insurance, gas and oil, and maintenance.

The number of years you plan to own the car may affect your selection. An end-of-the-year model tends to be a good buy for the purchaser who plans to keep it for at least five years. On the other hand, a consumer who trades often will lose valuable first year's depreciation at trade-in time, so the end-of-the-year model may not always be a bargain.

This is also the time to compare warranties. American Motors, Ford, and General Motors all greatly expanded, extended, and simplified their warranties in 1978. The Ford warranty is 113 words, down from over 1,000. The General Motors warranty is a combination of words and pictures that describes what is, and what is not, covered in the firm's limited warranty. These warranties should be required reading for all car buyers.

Many auto firms are also offering service contracts on new and used cars. In the case of a new car, a service contract acts to extend the warranty. One company will give twelve months' extra coverage on the motor and transmission for about $75. The same rule applies to the extended contract—read and investigate *before* you sign.

The best way to summarize the second step is *do not hurry,* for you will have to live with the car for some time.

What Do You Want?

The third step begins the action phase. First check with friends and the Better Business Bureau to find out which dealers provide the best service. This is a plus factor while the warranty is in effect. Then visit these dealers and test-drive the cars you are interested in buying. Be sure to drive the car with the engine size you plan to buy. If you test-drive an eight-cylinder car, only to change to a six-cylinder car when placing the order, you may be in for a sad awakening on delivery day, for the six-cylinder is a far different car.

Options, too, should be carefully considered. If a consumer drives a car many years, he or she may want air conditioning, power brakes, power steering, and automatic transmission in any but the smallest car. For those who trade in frequently, it does not pay to overload a car with too many options.

Negotiate

Finally you are ready to find the best price. You have done your research, asked your friends about local service, and even checked with the Better Business Bureau regarding the reputation of various dealers. *Consumer Reports, Car/Puter,* or maybe your credit union or auto insurer has given you a good idea of the dealer cost of the car and its options.

To obtain the best possible deal, time your purchase carefully. August and September are the best months to buy end-of-the-model-year cars, unless they all contain too many options. Mid-winter is the best time to buy a new car because sales are slow. The last few days of a month are better than the beginning of the month because sales managers and salespersons are trying hard to meet their quotas.

Some buying services advertise that they will take the work out of buying a car by doing it for you for $125 over the dealer cost. But James Mateja, an auto editor for the *Chicago Tribune,* tested the claims of several of these buying services and found that it pays to shop the dealerships as well. Most of the buying services could only match the best deals that the dealers themselves offered.[3]

Generally, you are doing well if you get 8 to 10 percent off the sticker price on a subcompact, 12 percent on an intermediate, and 14 percent on a full-sized model. Be sure to stick to the options you have decided you

[3]*Chicago Tribune,* May 14, 1978, p. 39.

want and the price you can afford to pay. Remember that taxes must be added to the cost.

If you have a car to trade in, be sure you have found its estimated value in one of the books previously mentioned. If possible, keep the used car out of the discussion until you have agreed on the new-car price. Otherwise at least ask the dealer to separate the trade-in and new-car prices. That way the dealer's trade-in figure will not impress you because you know the value of the components.

Many consumers sell their used cars themselves for a higher price than they would have been allowed in a trade-in. Remember, however, that in that case you are assuming the responsibility for expending time and effort that would normally be spent by the auto dealer—you have to decide whether it is worthwhile.

You have to watch out for tricks used by some dealers to clinch the deal.

Bushing or Bumping. The seller and buyer agree on a price, and then the dealer pushes it up later. This trick is called bushing or bumping. The price is usually raised under the pretense that the manager "blew his top" when he saw the deal and needs more money to break even. Sometimes the bad news comes when the deal is being made and sometimes when the car arrives after a six- to eight-week wait.

Low Balling. Low balling involves quoting an especially low price on a new car and then backing out when the comparison shopper comes back to buy the car.

High Balling. High balling is a bait-and-switch scheme in which the buyer is quoted an unusually high value on the trade-in. The dealer usually will not put this trade-in price in writing. Then when the actual deal is made or the new car arrives, the trade-in price is lowered. Most contracts include the right of the dealer to adjust the price of the trade-in if the customer has switched options after the deal has been made. A high-ball schemer may accuse the buyer of doing this and deduct money from the trade-in without a good reason for doing so.

Add-on Charges. Add-on charges are hidden charges that arise after the deal has been made. They may include additional fees for dealer preparation (over and above the prep charges included in the manufacturer's price) or for preparing your trade-in for resale. These are only a pretense for the dealer to obtain more money.

Avoid these last-minute pitfalls by having the dealer or an authorized representative sign the contract after you have read it. If there are any "ifs or ands" to the deal, be sure they are written into the agreement.

BUYING AND SELLING A USED CAR

A how-to guide to used cars must include both the buying and the selling side, for a growing number of consumers are coming to believe that they can get more for their car by selling it outright than by trading it in. The market seems to be in their favor: three to four times as many used cars as new models were sold in 1978.

Selling

What should be done to a used car to enhance its real value? Generally, the best investment is to take the time to clean the car thoroughly inside and out, polish it, and touch up minor scratches. The car should be made ready for a good and thorough test-drive by the prospective owner. This includes checking fluids and air pressure and replacing burned-out bulbs or defective windshield wipers. It is probably not profitable to repaint or make major repairs at this late date.

When you find a buyer who wants an option on the car, insist on a 5- to 10-percent binder to hold the car. Otherwise you may be discouraging other potential buyers for no reason. When a buyer does make the purchase, the final price should be paid with cash, a bank check, or a certified check.

When you receive the money, you should provide the buyer with a written bill of sale. No particular form is required, but the document should list the seller's name, the serial number of the car, and the price. Keep a duplicate copy for your own records. It is also a wise idea to write "as is" on the bill of sale. If you have made no false promises, this may help to relieve you of responsibility if the car breaks down after it is out of your possession. In most states, a signed certificate of title must also be provided to transfer ownership.

Remove the license plates and vehicle stickers before turning over the car. The plates often may be transferred to your next car. The vehicle stickers could get you into trouble if the new owner gets a parking ticket and the officer writes down the vehicle sticker numbers.

Buying

According to *Motor Trend* magazine, 40 to 70 percent of used cars sold are now traded between private parties. This seems to make private purchase the most desirable source of used cars. However, this is not always so! Table 7-1 compares the advantages and disadvantages of the various sources of used cars.

Warranties are a problem in nearly all categories. Many dealers offer

TABLE 7-1. Sources of Used Cars

	Advantages	Disadvantages
New-car dealer	more late-model cars better maintenance (especially among suburban dealers) by the original owners extensive service departments better finance terms	higher prices most warranties are 50/50
Independent used-car dealer	may be willing to accept trade	older models (may be cast off from new-car dealers)
Private sellers	possibly lower prices knowledge of car and owner (if buying from a friend)	few warranties no financing shopping is time-consuming more paperwork
Major lease/rental lot (corporately owned—not franchised)	lower prices better warranties possibly better maintenance	limited selection (usually standard models) no credit extended

50/50 warranties. This means that you and the dealer split the cost on all repairs.

Eddie is a typical victim of a 50/50 warranty. He bought a used car. On the second day he owned it, the car burned six quarts of oil. He took it back. The garage put in a new gasket. The next day it burned even more oil, so he took it back again. This time a different mechanic told him that the problem, among other things, was a main seal. The mechanic gave him two quarts of oil and told him to call the manager, Ralph. When Eddie called Ralph, he was told the whole job would cost in excess of $500. Later that day the brakes failed. Luckily for Eddie, he was covered by a warranty. The only trouble was that the warranty was one of the 50/50 types where the customer pays half and the garage pays half. Now all the garage needs to do is inflate its half by 100 percent and Eddie pays 100 percent. Too bad, Eddie!

So if there is a choice between a full short warranty and a long 50/50 warranty, the full warranty is usually the better bargain.

Some used-car and new-car dealers are offering extended service warranties on used cars. The private seller rarely provides any warranty at all, except in some states, where the seller may offer (and the buyer should demand) a warranty that the car will pass state safety and emissions inspection.

The FTC has formulated new rules that, if enacted, would make used-car buying less of a mystery. All used-car dealers would be required to disclose in window-sticker form (Figure 7-1) whether sixty different automobile functions were "OK" or "NOT OK." The dealers would then have to give an estimate of how much it would cost to fix all of the functions marked "NOT OK." The FTC rules would also require the dealers to disclose the car's prior use.

How old a car should one buy? The most reasonable balance between the newest used car and the lowest operating cost seems to be when the car is three to four years old. At this stage, car costs are reduced by the greatest amount of prior depreciation.

How many miles can a car have on it and still be a good buy? According to *Motor Trend* magazine, "20,000 miles or less, you expect relatively little wear; more than 50,000, and you can be sure it's had one or two brake jobs, 2–3 sets of tires and that little things (and maybe some big ones) are beginning to go wrong."[4]

Can the odometer reading be trusted? This question is still open to debate. It is unlawful for any person to disconnect, reset, or alter the odometer of any motor vehicle with the intent to change the recorded mileage. Federal law subjects offenders who sell over a certain number of cars a year to fines of up to $50,000 or one year in jail or both. However, sellers are still sometimes tempted to try it. Fortunately, there are other ways for a potential buyer to estimate the age of a car. The easiest way is to simply multiply an average of 10,000 to 15,000 miles by the age of the car. For example, a six-year-old car × 10,000 miles per year = 60,000 miles. Wear on the arm rests, pedals, seat cushions, and ignition lock is also an indicator of high mileage. Finally, the service stickers, when they are available, are helpful in checking mileage.

Mileage, however, is not always an indication that the car is in poor shape. Much depends on the previous owner. It is not uncommon for a car to go 100,000 miles without a major engine repair. A better guide is your personal inspection of paint, uneven tire wear, body rust and damage, oil leakage, steering wheel "play," brakes, and drivability. If the car passes your inspection, take it to your mechanic for a thorough check-up. If the

[4]J. Joseph, "Used Car Buyers Guide," *Motor Trend*, June 1977, p. 95.

Here's Who Pays if Something Doesn't Work

When You Buy

Items Marked "OK"

If anything we've marked "OK" is not OK, state law says we have to fix it or give you back some money. And, if the problem's bad enough, you can make us take the car back. **This is true whether you buy with a warranty or "as is".** You get a reasonable time after you buy to make sure that items marked "OK" are really OK. Tell us as soon as you know that something's not OK.

Items Marked "Not OK"

You pay all the costs to fix things marked "not OK".

OK	NOT OK		OK	NOT OK	
☐	☐	Frame & Body	☐	☐	Brake System
☐	☐	Engine	☐	☐	Steering System
☐	☐	Transmission & Drive Shaft	☐	☐	Suspension System
☐	☐	Differential	☐	☐	Tires
☐	☐	Cooling System	☐	☐	Wheels
☐	☐	Electrical System	☐	☐	Exhaust System
☐	☐	Fuel System	**NO**	**YES**	
☐	☐	Accessories	☐	☐	Flooded or Wrecked (once an insurance "total loss")

What's wrong with things marked "not OK" and how much repairs should cost: _____
_____
_____
_____

(Look at the back of this form for the details of our inspection.)

After You Buy

☐ **No Warranty ("As Is")** This means you will pay all costs to fix things that break after you buy. And you will also pay all costs to fix things marked "not OK" above. But we have to pay to fix things marked "OK" if you find the problem in a reasonable time after you buy.

A seller's spoken promises may be no good when you buy "as is". Ask us to put all promises in writing. You can make a seller keep written promises even when you buy "as is".

You lose your implied warranties when you buy "as is".

About Implied Warranties

State law gives you an "implied warranty" that your vehicle will be good enough for ordinary use. And, if you tell us to pick out a vehicle for some special use, you get another implied warranty that your vehicle will meet those special needs.

☐ **Full/Limited Warranty** on: _____
_____

for_____. We will pay_____of the cost to repair these items if they break down during the warranty period.

Ask us for a copy of the warranty. **This warranty adds to our responsibilities for items marked "OK".**

A seller's spoken promises may be no good. Ask us to put all promises in writing.

Implied warranties may give you more rights than this warranty.

☐ **A Service Contract** is available from _____
for $_____ extra. Ask us for a copy.

Past Use(s)

☐ Private Owner	☐ Daily/Weekly Rental	☐ Taxi
☐ Private Lessee	☐ Driver Education	☐ Unknown
☐ Commercial Owner	☐ Dealer Demonstrator	☐ Other: _____
☐ Commercial Lessee	☐ Police	_____

Mileage

☐ **Right** The mileage on the odometer is correct.

☐ **Wrong** The mileage on the odometer is not correct. The true mileage was _____ miles when we bought this vehicle.

☐ **Unknown** We don't know the true mileage for this vehicle.

Dealer: _____

NAME   ADDRESS   SEE FOR COMPLAINTS

Vehicle: _____

MAKE   MODEL   MODEL YEAR   VEHICLE ID NUMBER

The information on this form is part of any contract to buy this vehicle.

FIGURE 7-1. Used-Car Disclosure Form. (Federal Trade Commission.)

seller refuses to submit the car to this type of inspection, forget it and leave.

PROSPECTIVE USED-CAR BUYERS

Check for uneven tire wear.
Inspect the body for rust.
Look for oil leakage.
Test the steering and brakes.
Know the car's *Blue Book* value.

How much should you pay for a used car? The used car manuals listed earlier in the chapter are all good indicators of price, especially when they are combined with your own bargaining skills.

Which models have particularly good past histories? The *Consumer Reports* April buying issue and annual buying guide record the repair experiences of readers. The May 1978 issue of *Motor Trend* magazine presents a selection of their top forty used cars. There are, however, many exceptions to any list of best cars. Each car will have to be considered on its own merit.

Financing a used car may be a bit more costly than financing a new one. Lenders are often reluctant to risk making a long-term loan on a heavily depreciated car. Resist any pressure to finance through the used-car salesperson until you have compared rates. The used-car salesperson's "easy credit" usually costs more than a third-party loan. Even better than that is to pay cash.

AUTO REPAIRS

Joan Claybrook, head of the National Highway Traffic Safety Administration, estimates that 40¢ of every dollar spent on auto repairs ($20 billion or $150 per car) is wasted on unneeded parts, incompetent repairs, over-frequent preventive maintenance, wasted fuel, and vehicle design defects. Outright fraud is estimated to account for 10 percent of the money spent on unnecessary work—this amount is $2 billion a year.

Michael Pertschuk, Chairman of the Federal Trade Commission, says that one out of four new-car owners is unhappy, compared with less than one out of twelve owners of other warrantied products. He testified at the 1978 Senate Commerce Committee hearings that inspections of

5,000 cars at a Department of Transportation diagnostic center revealed that 24 percent of all repairs were unnecessary. This amounted to a waste of 33¢ of every dollar spent on auto repair.

The ball-joint trick is one of the most common. The customer brings the car in for routine work or a front-end alignment. When the customer returns to claim the car, the garage employees shake their heads and move toward the owner's car, which is still on the rack. They explain with great concern that the front ball joints are worn and need replacing. To prove their fear, they wiggle the front wheels back and forth to demonstrate the "play" in the wheels. To further convince the customer of the seriousness of the problem, they explain that the wheels will soon fall off or collapse. Luckily for the customer, however, they have a special on ball joints that day.

It is true that ball joints sometimes need replacing, but very often the problem is merely that the "play" in the wheels is normal and not a sign of damage.

The Insurance Institute for Highway Safety also lays part of the blame for auto-repair problems on the manufacturers. They say that the manufacturers are still making bumpers that allow cars to sustain hundreds of dollars of damage in accidents at low speed, when they have the technology to reduce the damage to zero. Table 7-2 shows the cost of repairing cars driven into a concrete barrier at various speeds by Insurance Institute testers.

Selecting a Repair Service

Keeping a car in good repair is a challenge, and the key is to establish a good relationship with a repair service. Being able to discuss repair problems and to feel confident that one's car is in good order provides a consumer with peace of mind, as well as better gas mileage, fewer repair costs, and more time between costly car purchases. In selecting auto repair services, the consumer has many choices.

Dealer Service. The car dealer's mechanics are usually the ones most familiar with the type of car the dealer sells, and while the warranty is in force the dealer's lot may be the only place the owner can have repair work done on a new car. Cost of dealer repairs is generally high, however, because of overhead and equipment. And the dealer repair shops are also most likely to replace rather than repair auto parts. Always get a receipt for all warranty-item repairs at a new-car dealership even if they are free. This will protect you in case the problem recurs when the warranty is no longer in effect.

Independent Garages. The driver can usually get more individual attention at an independent garage. The independent garage owner is more likely to spend some time with the car owner, personally discussing and diagnosing problems. In addition, the independent garage owner is often more flexible with time schedules and less dependent on the manufacturers' rigid standards and very high prices.

Specialty Shops. When the car owner is sure that a specific repair is needed—for example, brakes relined—a specialty shop may be the best choice. This form of repair establishment may be cheaper and quicker, and it will have the parts needed. However, if the car owner is not sure of the specific repair problem, there is considerable risk that he or she will get the specialty anyway, even if it is not needed.

Mass Merchandisers. Taking advantage of advertised specials at auto centers located in large shopping centers can save car owners money. In addition, these establishments offer convenient working hours. Drawbacks to this kind of service, however, are that the owner may not really need the advertised special, and that the repairs will be made by mechanics who are less than expert.

Service Stations. Many consumers have work done at a neighborhood service station because it is convenient. Most experts agree that the service station is the best place for routine maintenance. Consumers are cautioned against getting major repairs done there, however, especially when gas is being pumped by the same individual who is repairing the car.

Most auto repair experts agree on several rules in looking at an auto repair shop:

- Is the equipment used up-to-date? This equipment may range from engine-performance and tune-up testers to diagnostic computers and chassis dynamometers. Check whether up-to-date repair manuals are being used in the shop.
- Look for a clean, well-organized shop and, at the same time, a busy one.
- Check the shop's reputation with a variety of sources, such as the AAA or friends. You might find out where fleet owners, such as city fire and police departments, have their service work done. Good auto repair reputations spread rapidly, so you will begin to hear the same names mentioned again and again. A good shop will have a reputation for fair dealings (including guarantees on their work), thorough diagnosis, and accurate estimates (provided for

TABLE 7-2. 1978-Model Low-Speed Crash Test Results

Model	5 mph Front into Angle Barrier	5 mph Rear into Pole	10 mph Front into Angle Barrier
Intermediate:			
Chevrolet Impala	$319	$200	$849
Chrysler Cordoba	273	138	875
Ford LTD II	273	151	820
Averages:	288	163	848
Compact:			
AMC Concord	372	248	914
Buick Skylark	237	201	735
Chevrolet Chevelle	226	173	937
Chevrolet Monte Carlo	238	107	1,068
Ford Fairmont	282	278	858
Plymouth Volaré	200	203	789
Volvo 244DL	171	13	1,306
Averages:	247	175	944
Subcompact:			
Chevrolet Chevette	206	121	586
Chevrolet Monza	122	229	741
Datsun B210	421	329	940
Ford Fiesta	146	126	677
Ford Pinto	290	195	639
Honda Accord	206	231	735
Plymouth Horizon	110	90	532
Toyota Celica	186	206	620
Toyota Corolla	384	258	861
VW Dasher	15	406	921
VW Rabbit	231	111	1,152
Averages:	211	209	764
Overall Averages	$234	$191	$836

10 mph Front into Rear			Total Damage All Tests
Front Damage	Rear Damage	Damage to Both	
$199	$160	$359	$1,727
300	369	669	1,955
316	195	511	1,755
272	241	513	1,812
62	136	198	1,732
185	258	443	1,616
90	143	233	1,569
39	105	144	1,557
304	248	552	1,970
130	131	261	1,453
49	4	53	1,543
123	146	269	1,634
7	181	188	1,101
155	212	367	1,459
73	84	157	1,847
9	165	174	1,123
230	210	440	1,564
20	60	80	1,252
66	17	83	815
28	137	165	1,177
140	188	328	1,831
6	88	94	1,436
14	151	165	1,659
68	136	204	1,389
$115	$154	$270	$1,531

Note: Each damage appraisal was prepared by three members of an independent damage appraisal service using a labor rate of $11 per hour.
Source: Insurance Institute for Highway Safety, March 23, 1978.

owner authorization before any repairs are undertaken).

Find out whether or not a shop's mechanics are certified. To cope with the fact that for every trained practicing mechanic there are two without training or skill, the National Automobile Dealers Association has established a program of certification through its National Institute for Automotive Service Excellence. Since 1972, more than 102,000 mechanics have been certified. The Institute offers certification in eight areas: engine repair, automatic transmission, manual transmission and rear axle, front end, brakes, electrical systems, heating and air conditioning, and engine tune-up. The insignia is worn as a shoulder patch by the mechanic and is posted in certificate form in the garage (see Figure 7-2). Since experience seems to be a very important factor in passing the exam, the preparation stresses apprenticeship.

It is generally advisable to use a certified mechanic if you can find one. Remember, however, that one certified mechanic in a shop does not mean that all of the employees are certified.

The Institute publishes a booklet about certification of mechanics, available for a small fee from the National Institute for Automotive Service Excellence, 1825 K Street, N.W., Washington, DC 20006.

Know how the shop computes labor charges. Labor charges are generally arrived at in one of two ways. In the *clock-hour method,* the cost is calculated by multiplying the garage's charge per hour by the number of hours worked. The *flat-rate method* involves the use of a flat-rate manual, which shows the estimated amount of time it will take to perform the work. The number of hours is then

FIGURE 7-2. NIASE Insignia

multiplied by the hourly rate to determine the cost of labor. For example, the flat-rate manual may say that it should take 4.00 hours to replace a retainer and seal in an intermediate Buick with a manual three-speed transmission. The 4.00 figure is multiplied by the hourly rate, which may be $15 per hour, to arrive at a labor cost of $60.

The flat-rate method has the advantage that the charge is set even if the job takes longer. It also prevents a garage from dishonestly charging for time wasted. The flat rate also encourages many repair shops to speed up the work, for if they can do two four-hour jobs during a four-hour period, they can increase their profit.

Protecting Your Interest

Many of the problems in auto repair result from the failure of the auto owner to take an active interest in the operation of the car.

Some of the strange things that happen to a car during a trip could be avoided through even the most minimal owner attention. If you get out of the car for gas refills, you can ensure that fan belts and tires are not slashed, alternator wires pulled, and gas caps stolen, and that oil is not "poured" from an empty can. Vigilance is the best protection.

With only a little more effort, you can add considerably to your knowledge. A brief reading of your auto manual will tell you much about the types of routine maintenance a car requires. This information is particularly helpful in preventing overmaintenance. And numerous courses are available to provide owners with basic knowledge of what is going on under the hood. Many women have recently become very interested in repairing cars.

A growing number of informed owners are doing their own routine maintenance work. Much of this work is done at home, but recent estimates indicate that at least a hundred "rent-a-bay" garages have sprung up. These professional surroundings may even include an in-house mechanic to provide advice if needed.

A little bit of knowledge should not be relied upon too heavily, however—many owners make the mistake of prescribing what work should be done rather than merely helping to identify the source of the problem. Some shops will then simply do what the customer asks, whether the car needs it or not.

Filing Complaints

If, in spite of your best efforts, you run into problems with auto repairs, how can you register a complaint?

The first place to go with a complaint is the shop or dealer. Beyond this point, much will depend on your locality; consumer agencies, Better Business Bureaus, small claims courts, and attorney general's offices are all good sources of aid for consumers. (See Chapter 11 on Pursuing Consumer Complaints.)

Another relatively new form of assistance for the new-car buyer is AUTOCAP. Some 2,000 dealers across the country support the Automotive Consumer Action Panels. An unhappy car buyer simply looks up AUTOCAP in a local phone directory and reports the problems to a representative. AUTOCAP relays the complaint to the accused party, whether it be a dealer or a factory. The dealer or factory then has ten days to reply to the complaint. If the two parties cannot settle the issue, the case comes before a panel of three dealers and three consumer representatives. AUTOCAPS have a good track record thus far. Though they exist now in only eighteen states, they are expected to spread soon to the rest of the fifty states.

The federal government has a consumer hotline that provides information and advice to unhappy used-car buyers. The hotline is manned by a team of operators representing the National Highway Safety Traffic Administration. The hotline number is 800-424-9393, and a call to that exchange will get a used-car buyer information on manufacturer recalls or suspected defects.

AUTO OF THE FUTURE

Will the automobile cease to exist in the near future? It would be very difficult for most people to suddenly abandon their cars, even if gasoline prices continue to escalate. Over a long time span, though, it is possible that more people will live closer to where they work, ride the bus, or, in the case of two-car families, abandon one of the family cars. As auto populations shrink, fewer dollars will be collected in gas taxes and thus fewer dollars will be available for road repairs. The pothole will be a common sight and obstacle.

The average car will probably be smaller and lighter, as federal law requires that by 1985 auto makers produce cars that use less gas (an average of 27.5 miles per gallon). Bubble plastic has already been used to lighten some new cars. According to Minnesota Mining and Manufacturing, the company that developed bubble plastic, a car averaging 20 miles per gallon consumes about 5,000 gallons of gasoline in its 100,000-mile lifetime. If 400 pounds of weight were trimmed, the same car would require 700 fewer gallons of gasoline.

The government is also experimenting with the electric car. Developers hope to come up with an electric car that has a 75-mile range without recharging; recharges within six hours; has a top speed of 50 miles per hour; accelerates to 30 miles an hour in ten seconds; and has appropriate safety equipment, heater, and defroster. Such a low-pollution, energy-saving vehicle may be one answer to our transportation problems.

AUTOMOBILE INSURANCE

Auto insurance is becoming a very controversial issue. In a series written for *Motor Trend* magazine in 1977–78, Jack Scagnetti found the following points of contention:

- Estimates indicate that as many as 25 percent of the registered automobiles in California and as many as 40 percent of those in New Jersey are being driven with no liability insurance.
- The average driver sees little or no resemblance between his or her insurance company's annual report to the shareholders and the amount he or she pays for insurance.
- General Insurance Company of Florida claims that 70 percent of bodily injury claims in Miami are fraudulent. This is why the unmarried male Miami driver under twenty-five has to pay over $1,300 annually for minimum insurance coverage required by the state.
- It is not unusual for insurance companies to refuse to renew a policy because of a single nonaccident traffic ticket.
- There is a widely held opinion that most state insurance regulations have been drafted by the insurance companies themselves, or at least that they have had great influence in the writing.[5]

It is against this backdrop that the average driver must try to get a policy that suits his or her needs from a company that will charge a fair premium and will pay if an accident should occur. The shopper must choose among the more than 900 companies operating in some or all of the states in the United States, all offering many sorts of policies.

Types of Agents

Contacts between companies and consumers are made through agents of various types.

An *insurance broker* negotiates insurance contracts on behalf of

[5]Jack Scagnetti, "Auto Insurance—Friend, Foe, or Fraud," *Motor Trend,* December 1977.

the people he or she insures. The broker then sells these contracts to insurance companies that agree to accept the terms the broker has negotiated. The broker is not tied to any particular company and is paid on a commission basis. The public is generally not familiar with this form of insurance selling because it is used by large business firms and large organizations that carry heavy insurance protection which is very costly.

Consumers are much more familiar with the *independent agent* (also informally called a broker), who represents more than one insurance company. The independent agent has a separate contract to sell for each insurer; this guarantees that the agent is not dominated by one company. The independent agent system is considered advantageous to the consumer because the choice of company, service, and price can be tailored to individual customers. One disadvantage for the unwary customer is that commissions vary from insurerer to insurer and the size of the commission may influence the agent's choice of policy.

The third type of sales system is that of the *exclusive agent,* also called a captive agent or direct writer. This form of agent represents only one company and may or may not act as an employee of the firm. Contractual agreements vary with the insurer and the exclusive agent. Many direct writers work exclusively through the mail or over the phone —it is still possible to offer many services in this manner.

Types of Insurance

Auto insurance may be purchased as a total package or broken down into desired components.

The base of an auto policy is *liability coverage.* Every state has some form of financial responsibility law. In most states it takes the form of requiring liability coverage. The minimum liability coverage required varies from state to state. The minimum liability coverage sold, however, is usually $10,000 for one person for injuries and $20,000 for all persons injured in an accident. The third part of liability coverage involves property damage to the other driver's car by the driver at fault. Minimum coverage for this risk is usually $5,000 (10/20/5).

Sometimes liability coverage combines the three-part maximum into a single limit. If you were to purchase a $100,000-limit liability, it would cover any or all bodily injury and property damage you caused up to $100,000.

The basic liability coverage is the most expensive. Additional amounts may be added for a relatively small fee. With today's high damage settlements, 10/20 ($10,000 for one person and $20,000 for all injured) may not go very far. In liability coverage the old adage applies: "You need not be a millionaire to be sued like one." Whatever policy you choose, it is important that the coverage you buy be in force even when you are driving other people's cars or other people are driving yours with your permission.

While liability coverage pays for other people's personal injury and property damage, it does not pay for the insured. Medical payment insurance must be purchased in states with no-fault laws and is optional in others. *Medical payment insurance* covers the insured and members of the immediate family and guests of the insured who occupy the car. Medical payment insurance pays even if the insured is riding in someone else's car or is injured as a pedestrian.

Collision and comprehensive coverage are required by most lending agencies until a car is paid for. *Collision* pays for damage to the insured's car when the injured hits another vehicle or any other object, even if the accident is the insured's fault. The car is insured for its cash value (cost of car minus depreciation). *Comprehensive* pays for damage that results from fire, wind, theft, vandalism, collision with animals, explosions, floods, and lightning. Comprehensive coverage also includes glass breakage, which is not covered by collision.

Both collision and comprehensive premiums are based on the present value of the car. When a car becomes older, it may no longer pay to carry collision and comprehensive coverage. Collision and often comprehensive are sold in deductibles ranging from $50 to $500. The higher the deductible, the greater the saving on premiums. Even if the insured should sustain a loss, part of the deductible may be an income tax deduction as a casualty loss.

It is important to include *uninsured motorist coverage* in case the insured or his or her immediate family is struck by an uninsured hit-and-run driver while driving or walking. The only problem with uninsured motorist insurance is its limitations. In most states it only applies to bodily injury. And it is most often limited to the state minimum liability coverage, regardless of how much you choose to carry personally for liability insurance. The hit-and-run driver must be the one to blame for an accident in order for you to collect under uninsured motorist coverage. Your property damage in a hit-and-run accident is already covered by your collision insurance, but only after you pay the deductible. You can also collect on your medical payment insurance, but it is written only in very small amounts.

Other coverages that are available include wage loss (in no-fault states), road service, and accidental death and dismemberment.

Insurance Rates

Insurance rates are based on the following driver characteristics and environmental factors:

Principal Place of Garaging. Each locality has its own set of rates. Where population is dense and the risk of theft is high, insurance rates are very high. Some insurance companies have been accused of "red lining" certain areas—either not offering insurance there or strictly limiting the amount they will underwrite.

Use of the Car. The company will want to know whether the car is driven for business or only for pleasure. If you regularly drive more than ten miles to work, you will pay a higher premium.

Type of Car Driven. "Muscle cars" and expensive sports cars are charged higher rates, especially for collision and comprehensive coverage.

Age, Sex, and Marital Status of Drivers. The under-twenty-five driver is said to cause 36 percent of all accidents. This is a greater percentage than the proportion of drivers in that age group, so this group is charged a particularly high rate. Single drivers are charged more than married drivers. Drivers in certain occupations are sometimes charged high-risk rates unless they have good safety records. Because males have more accidents than females, they pay more for insurance. (This may be due to the larger number of miles they drive.)

Driving Record. The driving records of the members of the family who drive the car may affect the insurance rate. The number of claims made by the insured as well as the amount of each claim may also affect the premium cost.

Comparison Shopping

Is it possible to learn more about the strengths of various insurers? A limited amount of helpful information does exist. A good start is to ask around. Good news travels. If consumers find a company to be fair and reasonable in claim dealings, they are eager to spread the news. It would be difficult, however, to get a recommendation on anything other than price from individuals who have never filed a claim for settlement.

A series on auto insurance in the June and July 1977 issues of *Consumer Reports* contains a great deal of information on readers' opinions of service provided by specific companies. Another source of information on auto insurance is the *Best Ratings* found in most public libraries. The A. M. Best Company rates insurers mainly on their financial stability. Since all their ratings sound favorable, a rating of less than excellent is a warning signal about the company's financial stability.

It is advantageous to compare prices of auto insurance coverage.

RATING INFORMATION

Name_____

Number and Street_____

City, State, and Zip_____

	Age	Sex	Marital status	% Use of car	Accidents or moving violations in past 3 years
Principle operator					
Other driver(s)					

	Make	Model	Year	Miles driven to and from work in a week	Approximate annual mileage
Auto 1					
Auto 2					

COVERAGE

Annual premiums

	Company A	Company B	Company C
Basic Coverage			
Liability_____per person			
_____per accident			
Bodily injury_____per accident			
Property damage_____per accident			
Uninsured Motorist			
Liability_____per person			
_____per accident			
Bodily injury_____per accident			
Collision			
_____deductible			
_____per accident			
Comprehensive			
_____deductible			
_____per accident			
Medical payments			
_____per person			
Other Coverages			
_____			
Total Annual Premium			
REPUTATION			

FIGURE 7-3. Automobile Insurance Cost Worksheet

Different companies have different discounts available to consumers, as well as variations in how certain occupations and territories are rated, so prices can be significantly different. Remember, however, that price is second in importance after claims payment record.

Figure 7-3 is a worksheet that may be used to compare insurance rates. The top portion is for filling in the rating information agents will need to have. The lower portion is for filling in the various rates agents will quote. Some space has been provided at the bottom for personal findings regarding company reputation, claims settlement record, or financial stability.

The Future of the Insurance Industry

No-Fault. Professor Jeffrey O'Connell of the University of Illinois and Professor Robert Keeton of Harvard University introduced the idea of no-fault insurance more than a decade ago. The concept is simple—it is very much like that of fire insurance, where if your house burns, the company pays for it. It makes no difference how careless you were or whether someone else started the fire. Under no-fault auto insurance your insurance company reimburses you and the other driver's company takes care of reimbursing its claimant.

Under the traditional common law system, a driver files a claim against the other driver, alleging fault or contributory fault. The victim may sue for "out-of-pocket losses" and may place a value on pain and suffering. Under no-fault, the insured driver is reimbursed monthly for out-of-pocket costs, such as loss of income, medical bills, and household assistance. No payments are ever made for pain and suffering. Thus under no-fault, premium dollars traditionally used for attorneys' fees and pain-and-suffering claims go to claimants to compensate for real economic losses. The U.S. Department of Transportation has found that under the old system, the larger the economic loss to a driver, the smaller is the percentage paid to the driver. Lawyers' contingent fees alone take one-third or more of the settlement in such cases.

Many states have now passed some form of no-fault insurance. However, only the state of Michigan has an almost pure no-fault law that covers unlimited medical expenses and a maximum of over $46,000 for wage loss and eliminates fault claims unless a victim suffers death, serious disfigurement, or serious impairment of body function. Recently, the Department of Transportation issued a statement saying simply that no-fault insurance works.

Why hasn't no-fault been adopted in all states and even on the federal level? No-fault insurance bills have been proposed on the federal level many times since 1970. Each time they have been sidetracked. Trial lawyers have been particularly successful lobbyists. They are fighting a pocketbook issue, and at the same time objecting philosophically to paying damages to every involved party whether guilty or innocent. The National Association of Independent Insurers opposes no-fault on the basis of higher costs. The American Mutual Insurance Alliance is opposed to imposing the same law on all states; the alliance supports the McCarran-Ferguson Act of 1945, which allows the states rather than the federal government to regulate the business of insurance. However, an insurance industry group called the All-Industry Research Advisory Committee noted in a recent study that 81 percent of accident victims in no-fault states collected their money within three months and 90 percent within six months. In non-no-fault states, the three-month collection rate was 46 percent and the six-month rate was 62 percent. For this reason, much of the insurance industry supports federal no-fault legislation.

The Merit System.   Another issue affecting the insurance industry is that of rate equity. Critics of the present rate-setting system see it as discriminatory. Irate center-city dwellers, whose rates are the highest, want to ban insurers from rating by location. Proponents of the merit system are trying to shift the system from one dependent on group behavior to one that depends on the individual's driving record.

Opponents of the merit system say that such a system is unworkable because the time and the expense required to set individual rates would affect the drivers' premiums. Opponents feel that the fact that sixteen-to twenty-four-year-olds cause a disproportionate number of losses and that city drivers file more claims than suburban drivers justifies the present system.

Rate Control.   A final issue that may never be resolved in full is the rising cost of auto insurance claims. The rise in the cost of repair parts and medical fees, the increase in the number of accidents due to unsafe equipment and poor roads—all have contributed to rising premiums. Political battles will continue over requiring air bags and other safety equipment, placing lids on medical costs, and policing car-crash part costs.

The driver has done his or her share in contributing to high insurance rates. Drinking and drugs are factors in at least half of the 50,000 fatalities caused annually by the automobile. And the consumer does not seem to take a great deal of interest in safety equipment. It is estimated that only 25 percent of all automobile occupants wear seat belts. Even the 55-mile-per-hour speed limit brought on by the energy crisis, which studies show is favored by a majority of motorists, is widely disobeyed. Insurance rate reduction will require the strong cooperation of many segments of the economy—business, government, and the consumer. The stakes are very high in terms of economic loss and, more seriously, the loss of more and more lives every year.

QUESTIONS FOR DISCUSSION

1. What are the "after costs" of owning an automobile? How can these costs be reduced?
2. What is meant by the statement that cars often share the same parts? Cite as many examples as you can of cases where this has happened.
3. When are new-model cars often cheaper to buy?
4. Outline a strategy for buying a new car with no trade-in.
5. How would the strategy in question 4 change if you had a trade-in?
6. What are the advantages and disadvantages of purchasing a used car from a private seller?
7. What are some things to look for when selecting a source of auto repair?
8. How can the certification program by the National Institute for Automotive Service Excellence help to upgrade the quality of auto repairs?
9. Compare the flat-rate and the clock-rate methods of computing repair costs. What are the advantages and disadvantages of each?
10. What kinds of major accidents could easily cost up to the value of your property damage liability coverage?
11. Why would an insurance company red-line a given geographical area? What could be done to share the risk?
12. What are the advantages and disadvantages of no-fault auto insurance?
13. Do you think that rate equity based on an individual's driving record is a feasible method of determining auto insurance premiums?

PERSONAL EXPERIENCE PROJECTS

1. Obtain an estimate of automobile operating costs from consumers, automobile rental companies, and the U.S. Department of Transportation, Office of Consumer Affairs, Washington, DC 20590. These should include money spent on gas and oil, depreciation, insurance, maintenance and repairs, tolls, parking fees, and tires.
2. Conduct a survey of consumer preferences for certain automobile makes, models, and options. Determine reasons for preferences and what causes changes in these preferences.
3. Obtain costs for automobile insurance for you or a member of your family from a couple of different insurance agents. Determine whether the differences in cost are justified by differences in service. (For information on automobile insurance company service, read

"Managing Your Auto Insurance, Part 2: Which Companies Give the Best Service?" *Consumer Reports,* July 1977, p. 375.)

4. Conduct a survey of various sources of used cars—dealers, private parties, auto rental companies. Compare the quality of the vehicles, the prices, and guarantees or services provided.

5. Compare the restrictions and costs of financing an automobile purchase through a consumer finance company, a bank, a credit union, and a car dealer. (For additional information on auto financing, read "How to Save on a Car Loan," *Consumer Reports,* April 1978, p. 201.)

6. Conduct a survey of gas station prices. Be sure to note differences in octane levels, self-service versus full-service stations, and local taxes.

7. Compare repair costs for several routine operations at a new-car dealer, a service station, and an automobile repair shop. Analyze these costs based on discussion with consumers of their satisfaction with the service received.

8. Interview salespeople and mechanics who are employed by retail tire stores to obtain information regarding the uses and durability of the tires they sell. Compare the prices of various tires at tire stores, department stores, and discount stores.

9. In the annual auto issue (April), the buying-guide issue (December), or any other issue of *Consumer Reports,* read articles comparing various models of new cars. Determine whether consistency exists between the test results of Consumers Union and the "frequency-of-repair" records as reported by *Consumer Reports* readers.

10. Compare the costs of various options (air conditioning, stereo tape player, etc.) when factory installed and when installed by a dealer, service station, or department store auto center.

11. Compare prices of the purchase and installation of a battery, muffler, and shock absorbers at a car dealer, service station, specialty shop, and department store.

12. Obtain information about no-fault automobile insurance by reading "Managing Your Auto Insurance, Part 3: Insurance Crisis: Causes and Cures," *Consumer Reports,* August 1977, p. 484.

13. Contact the Federal Highway Safety Administration, Department of Transportation, Washington, DC 20590, and the Center for Auto Safety, 1346 Connecticut Avenue, N.W., Washington, DC 20036, for information on current and proposed automobile safety features and laws. Interview various consumers and auto dealers regarding the costs and benefits of various auto safety features.

8

FRAUDS
AND
SWINDLES

The consumer must be constantly on guard in order to survive in the present economic world. The unwary buyer is fair game for all sorts of fraudulent or deceptive marketplace "pitches." While the outright defrauders are estimated to comprise somewhere in the neighborhood of 5 percent of all business people, deceptive practices are engaged in by a much larger number.

There is a rip-off for every individual, regardless of type, age, economic bracket, or taste. There are "get-rich-quick schemes" for the greedy, "charity rackets" for the needy, and "fad diets" for the meaty. The auto owner is fair game, but then so is the homeowner, retiree, single person, and even the businessman.

Some schemes deal in pressure—"Buy now or forever lose the chance"; while others soothe the victim with "It's only a standard form —just sign here." Many come-ons lure the consumer through flattery— "You have been specially selected"; others appeal to the pennywise shopper—"Yours absolutely free" or "You can save up to . . ." Still others begin with salespersons coming to the door and saying, "We are taking a survey . . ."

CON GAMES

The oldest form of fraud is the "con" game. While the types of con games have not changed much over the years, the use of these "bunko schemes" is actually on the increase. There are always new twists to the old favorites.

The Pigeon-Drop Game

An older person is approached by a younger, well-dressed person of the same sex who claims to have just found an envelope or package containing a very large sum of money. A third person comes along and offers to ask an attorney about keeping and sharing it. The others agree to the "good deal." The third person departs, soon to return with the advice from the attorney that each should put up $1,000 to show good faith. The older person is persuaded to go to the bank, withdraw the money, and give it to the other two. The two go off, ostensibly to the attorney, never to return again.

The Talented Children Game

Mothers are persuaded to enter their children in a "talent contest" by paying a $200 filming fee. After the mothers pay, they never see their money or the film.

Franchise Game

Successful or potential business people are sold distributorships on payment of a large deposit. They never see their money or the products to be distributed.

Resumé-Writing Game

Young and desperate job seekers are defrauded of several hundred dollars as a charge for writing up "sure fire" resumés. The money disappears, but the job does not materialize.

"Two Fives for a Ten" Game

The accommodating sucker helps out a stranger and winds up with a $1 bill in return for his two $5 bills, for the bill the faker hands the stranger has corners from four different $10 bills pasted onto a $1 bill.

DOOR-TO-DOOR SALES

According to *Money* magazine, 2 million bell ringers did $6 million worth of business in 1976, up 9 percent from 1975.[1] While the door-to-door sellers may offer good buys in reading material, pots and pans, cosmetics, home products, vacuum cleaners, or clothing, don't take it for granted. Some need careful watching.

A door-to-door salesman smooth-talked me into buying $402 worth of cookware. I decided a couple of days later that I didn't want it. I called the salesman and left a message that I wanted to cancel the order. He called me back and said I couldn't have a refund on my deposit [this is not legal], but I could purchase some other goods for the amount of my deposit. I didn't really want anything, but I settled on some steak knives to end the hassle. I've never used them or unpacked them.

In October we signed up our kid to have pictures and a videotape shot once a year for five years by Blank Models Service. The salesman claimed that she would become a child model in no time flat, so we paid the $125 fee. We waited for the modeling offers to come in. Well, last October we tried to call Blank Models about our second set of pictures and learned that their phone is disconnected.

I am twenty-one years old and work as a secretary. Two months ago a salesman came to my apartment to deliver my free cookbook. He ended up staying around for four hours trying to sell me a double cemetery lot. I finally bought one just to get rid of him.

Direct at-home sales offer many advantages to the consumer. Shopping is convenient and comfortable, and the whole family can see and try out the product before buying. Their biggest disadvantage, however, is that they upset rational financial planning. People with low sales resistance often buy items that they have no need for and will never use. Another disadvantage is the higher cost of home shopping. Most marketing people say that door-to-door selling is an expensive channel of distribution. And because of the higher prices, salespeople are often forced to be devious in what they say and do in order to sell.

Fortunately, a new FTC regulation has made it easier for consumers to back out of hastily contracted arrangements. This regulation gives you a cooling-off period of three business days in which to change your mind

[1]David Chagall, "How Door-to-Door Sellers Ring Your Chimes," *Money,* July 1977, p. 65.

about any purchase costing $25 or more that is made in your home or anywhere else except the seller's place of business. The only exceptions are insurance transactions, real-estate transactions, and transactions where the buyer has previously visited the seller's place of business. While it is a bad idea to sign before you compare, this is a way out of a poor bargain struck under heavy pressure. The consumer in the cookware example cited earlier would have been covered under the cooling-off-period regulation. If she had only known the law or read the contract (in which, under the law, this cooling-off-period provision is supposed to be conspicuously displayed), she would have known she was entitled to a refund of her deposit.

PRIZE CONTESTS

All consumers should know that no enterprise can stay in business very long if it gives away merchandise. Ironically, many consumers seem to forget that basic fact when they receive a card telling them that they have won second prize in a contest. This prize entitles them to purchase a $209 sewing machine for $59. Later they find out that the machine is worth only $59.

Frequently merchants advertise some type of contest with three or four substantial prizes. Along with these prizes there are, as additional prizes, thousands of credit checks. However, the prices of the merchandise you can purchase with these credit checks may have been inflated for the contest. And the "prize" may be only the prelude to the purchase of many hundreds of dollars' worth of additional merchandise in the years that follow—a free camera may necessitate long-term developing costs, or a low-cost photo enlargement package may include inflated mailing costs (in fine print, of course).

Even a free vacation may turn out to be a "high pressure" weekend with a land development company. In some cases a registration fee is required to get the three days and four nights in an unknown hotel or motel. Sometimes transportation is not provided—or only one way is provided if you do not agree to buy the land.

MAIL FRAUDS

Mail frauds come in an almost unlimited number of forms. They range from the old scheme of chain letters to the newer version of free cosmetic samples. In one way or another, however, they appeal to the individual's dream of easy money. As long as the consumer continues to be greedy, fraud and deception will continue.

Pyramid Schemes

Many easy-money mail traps are really versions of the pyramid scheme. A pyramid scheme is one in which each participant recruits a number of other participants, who in turn recruit further participants, and so on, so that the organizational structure grows in the shape of a pyramid. The first few in a pyramid scheme benefit; but as more and more people try to sell the same product, distributorship, or secret formula, the sales force soon overpowers the market.

Some magazines advertise any number of such plans. The reader is encouraged to send $1 or more to show good faith or to purchase outright a secret formula for success or a booklet that will describe how to obtain easy money. Often the initial payment will simply buy the advice to take out an ad. The seller will then ask for yet another payment for a book or formula. Eventually the buyer will be allowed to sell the book or formula to other suckers using the same pitch.

The chain letter is another example of a pyramid scheme. The person who starts the scheme may place his or her name at the top of the list, followed by a series of dummy names at addresses accessible to the originator. The originator will collect the benefits before interest in the chain drops, leaving later participants high and dry. Chain letters are mathematically unsound, and the majority of the participants lose money. The U.S. Postal Service has declared that many chain-letter schemes involving cash or bonds are lotteries and are, therefore, illegal.

Unclaimed Bank Accounts

Another form of fraud that appeals to the "easy money" syndrome is the unclaimed-bank-account scheme. One company in New York mailed a large mass of letters to people with the same surname to suggest that they were heirs to an unspecified amount of unclaimed money. The pitch begins with a rather personalized letter telling the people that "research into state records has revealed that an unspecified amount of money . . . has recently been turned over to a state agency." Also included with the cover letter is a Finders Fee Agreement, which includes a schedule of the way the inheritance will be split if, in fact, it does belong to the receiver. The organization will charge 15 percent of the first $10,000 recovered and so on up to 5 percent of any sum over $50,000. The fee schedule suggests large amounts when, in fact, the amounts may be very small. Before any further "research" can be done, however, a research fee must be mailed to the company. The research fee usually ranges from $15 to $35.

Another firm in California sends a legal-looking form that suggests that one of your relatives may have died and that you could have a claim on the money. Actually records such as these are all available from government agencies free of charge to the general public, and your chances of finding a long-lost relative are almost nil.

Who's Who in . . .

Another set of mail schemes involve vanity rather than greed. Fly-by-night "who's who" books imitate the legitimate prestigious *Who's Who* publications. The fraudulent outfits tell everyone whose name is included on a mailing list that he or she has been nominated for inclusion in such a book. The privilege of being included in the book, however, includes the obligation to buy one.

Genealogy

Another version of the human vanity scheme is the genealogy racket, which plays on the now-popular family pastime of tracing roots. Genealogies readymade for a surname are available for purchase at a price of $30 or more.

Work at Home

Mail schemes often appeal to the unemployed, the elderly, or housewives who want to make extra money at home.

Come-ons such as "I made $15,000 in one day at home with the flu" may be used to entice persons to pay for the right (?) to sell a whole variety of cheap items on a commission basis. The ads grossly overstate what can actually be sold.

Addressing envelopes seems to be an easy way to make money at home. It sounds ideal to be able to sit at home and be paid for addressing each envelope. The mistake made by most people is to assume that they will be paid on a piecework basis. Close reading reveals that the addressor is actually only paid a commission on the sale of the product or service advertised on the postcard or in the envelope addressed. A lot of work and expense may yield nothing, as many of the plans provide for the individual to pay the postage on the mailing, as well as to address the envelopes.

Another form of the address-envelopes-at-home scheme requires you to send money in order to have your name included in a directory of people who will address envelopes for money.

There are many other mail frauds. They include high-cost debt consolidation schemes, fraudulent vacations, deceptive land sales, and loan-shark schemes. It is best to forget a promotion pitch that makes getting rich or being happy sound too easy and then asks for money to accomplish your dream.

ELECTRONIC SALES SOLICITATION

The electronic sales pitch is the newest form of selling. It is not necessarily fraudulent, but it is surely regarded by many as a nuisance. An automatic dialer is used to call residents of an area in a telephone number sequence. Even unlisted phone numbers are called when the machine dials in this manner.

Estimates on the number of calls made daily have run from 7 million to 27 million. The return on such calls is good, according to Murray Roman, Chairman of Campaign Communications in New York. "Telephone sales do 2½ to 5 times what mail does," he said. "So the temptation is there to switch from mass mailings to phones."[2] Many businesses and organizations (including Wards Motor Club and various churches) are using the process.

The devices start playing the recorded message when the person called agrees to listen, and they start recording when the person talks. The equipment can sense when a person isn't responding after a question is asked. Then the recorded message will say something like, "Please speak up" or "I can't hear you." "This almost always brings a response," says Jack Heinz of Dycon International Inc., a Dallas equipment maker.[3]

Many people are less than enthusiastic about the phoning devices. The Federal Communications Commission has received thousands of complaints about them. Proposed legislation would limit this type of sales technique to only those persons who do *not* instruct the phone company to omit their names from such phone lists. Automatic dialing has already caused some serious problems for people who needed to use the phone while a recorded message was being played, for you cannot break the connection by hanging up. Such "junk phone calls" are more difficult to disregard than junk mail, which can be dropped into the wastebasket.

[2]Ron Aaron Eisenberg and Michele Oriven, "Hello, 'Junk Mail' Calling," *Milwaukee Journal*, Sunday, July 31, 1977, p. 1.
[3]Stan Crock, "If the Phone Rings and It's Zsa Zsa, Don't Be Surprised," *Wall Street Journal*, Wednesday, August 15, 1979, p. 21.

RETAIL DECEPTION THROUGH ADVERTISING

Retailers are frequently guilty of using deceptive advertising to lure consumers into their stores.

Out-of-Stock Specials

One way this is done is through the advertised special. A store advertises a sale item in the newspaper, but when the customer goes to the store to purchase the item, it isn't available or it is priced higher than in the advertisement. Is this simply a chance error or a "run" on the bargain product, or is it company policy?

In some cases the out-of-stock specials result in an FTC complaint. In 1976, after an FTC complaint alleged that Pay Less Drug Stores Northwest failed to have advertised items in stock, Pay Less was required to have all items available for sale at the advertised price. Recently, the FTC found 13 percent of A&P's advertised items were unavailable or overpriced. A&P was ordered to have the items in stock or to notify customers and to offer a rain check.

The rain check itself may be used to get a customer back into the store. A better solution to the out-of-stock problem is the substitution of another item. If out-of-stock items are not a rarity in your favorite store, you should report this to the FTC or state consumer agencies. While government agencies may not act on one complaint, if many persons call attention to a particular practice the agencies will attempt to correct the trend.

Bait-and-Switch

Bait-and-switch is an old-time sales technique that hooks a customer with an advertisement (the bait) and then lets the customer in on some high-pressure selling of a more expensive item (the switch). Bait-and-switch is universally condemned as a deceptive sales practice and violates federal, state, and local laws. It is quite common, however, in spite of its illegality. An ad may promise three rooms of furniture or carpet for a ridiculously low price, or meat at well below the current market rate. The consumer who answers such an ad can expect to be switched to another product for "a few dollars more" (usually hundreds or thousands). And most of the time the payment schedule calls for time payments at a very high interest rate.

Major department stores as well as small businesses have been caught in the bait-and-switch game. In 1976, Sears, Roebuck & Company was prohibited from allowing salespersons to downgrade advertised items or make misleading comparisons between sale and non-sale items.

Bait-and-switch takes many forms:

· Refusal to show the advertised item.
· Disparagement of the product—"Especially for one of your taste."
· Refusal by the business to take orders on the advertised item.
· Failure by the business to submit the order after writing it up for the customer.
· Displaying, demonstrating, or delivering defective, unusable, or unsuitable sale merchandise.
· Switching or modifying an order after accepting a deposit.
· Failing to deliver within the promised delivery time in order to encourage you to change your order.
· Penalizing a salesperson who sells the advertised item instead of switching the customer to a higher-priced item.

One other variation of bait-and-switch is the referral scheme. A product such as a swimming pool may be advertised at a ridiculously low price. When the consumer goes to the store to investigate, he or she is offered a rebate on a more expensive pool in return for the names of friends who might also buy a pool. In some cases, the shopper is offered a discount under the pretense that the pool will be used as a display for other potential buyers. The bait is the low-priced pool; the switch is brought about through the discount or rebate (often not paid) on a more expensive model. The final price is usually no different or even higher than that of any other pool of similar type in that area.

The best way to avoid being taken in by a bait-and-switch scheme is to refuse to cooperate when you recognize one. If you find that the merchandise is sold out, inferior, or appears to be used or damaged, don't let the salesperson show you anything else. Go elsewhere. If consumers would begin doing this in large numbers, bait-and-switch would disappear.

HEALTH AND BEAUTY AIDS

Most Americans strive to look young, beautiful, and healthy. At first glance we seem to have a lot of aids available to help us. For the overweight, there are machines and devices that purport to allow you to reduce without expending physical effort. For one worried about deficiencies in the food we eat, there are hundreds of vitamin supplements from which to select. And for those who are concerned about physical appearance, there are thousands of health and beauty aids, hair restorers, and breast developers.

But medical experts agree that the best cure for obesity is to get up from the table—fad diets can be dangerous, and there is nothing that one can rub on, bathe in, or heat up that can have any influence on permanently reducing obesity. As for vitamin supplements, the Food and Drug Administration says that the food most of us eat contains adequate amounts of required daily vitamins. And the AMA states that there is no mechanical device or system of exercise that can increase the size of the female breast, nor is there anything you can rub on your head that will restore hair.

Another aspect of health fraud concerns real or imagined physical impairments. Consumers pay for eyeglasses they do not need, hearing aids that promise much more than can be delivered, and operations that are unnecessary. The Public Interest Research Group in a recent report estimated that there are 3.2 million unnecessary operations performed each year. In November of 1977 the federal government said it would begin paying for second medical opinions for Medicare patients before surgery was performed. This was done in reaction to a 1975 study in twenty-six states which showed that "the rate of operations on Medicaid patients for a 12-month period was more than double that for the general population: 18,716 compared to 7,940 per 100,000 persons."[4]

CHARITABLE SOLICITATIONS

Money magazine recently told of a golf pro from California who received nine pounds of solicitations in junk mail during a recent ten-month period. Among the "prizes" were 140 requests from 86 organizations, 17 sets of greeting cards, 8 combs, 3 key chains, 2 ball-point pens, 1 plastic napkin holder, and numerous decorative stamps and gummed address labels. Why? He had given $1,000 to 40 of them and was therefore added to lists in geometric progression.

How can one tell if a charity serves it purported purpose? Charities have two major categories of expenses: those of fund-raising and those of operating the actual program. In some cases, the fund-raising stage takes almost all of the funds; for example, telethons can eat up 40 to 50 percent of the income (although the Muscular Dystrophy Association has reduced

[4]Arthur E. Rowse, ed., *HELP: The Useful Almanac, 1977–78* (Washington, D.C.: Consumer News Inc., 1978), p. 225.

its fund-raising expenses to 20 percent).[5] The purchase of mailing lists and the actual cost of mailing letters or trinkets is also a major expense for many charities—especially the smaller ones. On the other hand, the expense of operating the program may be particularly high for charities in which direct contact is made between the donor and the intended recipient.

At least half of the income taken in by a charity should go toward the intended goal. A figure of less than 25 percent for total expenses identifies a particularly well-run charity. The best way to find out about a charity's budget is to ask the organization for a copy of its year-end financial statement (Form 990) filed with the IRS.

Although tax-exempt status is not necessarily an indicator of a well-run charity, you might check the tax-exempt status of the charity in the Internal Revenue Service list of such organizations in your public library, or call your local IRS office for a copy of the list.

Following are some other possible means of evaluating charities:

· Check with the National Council of Better Business Bureaus, 1150 7th Street, N.W., Washington, DC 20036.
· Check with the National Information Bureau, 319 Park Avenue S., New York, NY 10016. It is a private organization that reviews the operation and practices of charitable organizations.
· Do not give to a door-to-door campaigner for an organization whose name you do not recognize.
· Do not contribute to organizations that offer unsolicited gifts or sell merchandise unless you have determined that they are legitimate charities or social service groups. (Be aware that gifts from charities or other organizations may be kept by the consumer without obligation to subscribe.)
· Do not contribute to an appeal made by a person wearing a uniform, because it is a violation of the law for a police or fire officer to solicit in uniform.
· Be suspicious of mail solicitations that have first-class postage (first-class costs are prohibitively high), a return envelope with prepaid postage (especially first-class), a slick-paper magazine or publication, glossy photographs, computer-generated individual address labels, or handwritten letters. These collection methods are all extremely costly, so it pays to check the fund-raising costs of organizations that use them.

[5]Christine Miles, "Is Charity Obsolete?" *Forbes,* February 5, 1979, p. 51.

Some charities and 70 percent of direct-mail organizations belong to the Direct Mail Marketing Association, so you can reduce the number of solicitations you receive by contacting them. To be removed from the lists of their members, write to the organization at 6 East 43rd Street, New York, NY 10017.

Mail fraud is the province of the U.S. Postal Service, so if you find any deceptive practices in the mailings of charities, complaints may be made to the local postmaster.

WHITE-COLLAR CRIME

The consumer pays heavily for what is now called white-collar crime. The late Phillip Hart of Michigan once estimated that white-collar crime costs Americans $200 billion annually. The U.S. Chamber of Commerce feels that this practice costs a somewhat lower but still startling sum of $40 billion. Even if these estimates are high, the amount spent by Americans as a result of such crimes is shocking.

The term white-collar crime refers to the phenomenon of upper-world law breaking. Examples of white-collar crime include:

- bribery of public and private officials in domestic and international business dealings
- income-tax cheating
- violation of antitrust laws
- shoddy production of automobiles and heavy equipment
- illegal campaign contributions by corporations
- deceptive business practices and conspiracies that result in court-ordered sanctions and cease-and-desist orders from administrative agencies
- excessive charges by professionals engaged in legal- or health-care practices
- embezzlement of public or private funds
- arson for profit
- insurance fraud
- payroll padding
- violation of safety rules and regulations
- kickbacks—public or private
- gifts to public or private officials to influence their decisions
- robbery and embezzlement through illegal use of computers (using computers for personal projects, creating accounts or dummy payroll names to collect money)

- sabotage of computers and other equipment (damage to the computer or excising of records by irate employees)
- illegal passing along of excessive income taxes or utility charges to consumers.

Who is the white-collar criminal? According to W. Steve Albrecht, an expert on employee crime, the average white-collar criminal is just that —pretty average:

> He's older than the typical property offender. He's more likely to be married; less likely to be divorced; less likely to have used drugs or alcohol; more likely to be an active church member; weighs more than average; has more children; has a more stable family life; scores higher on psychological tests of self-esteem, self-sufficiency, achievement; has higher self-control, and is more kind and empathetic.
>
> In fact, the typical offender of the white-collar type turns out to be someone just like the normal citizen who's placed in a situation where he has a great opportunity to steal and is under high situational pressure.[6]

FRAUDS BY CONSUMERS

Businesspeople are not the only ones who perpetrate frauds—frauds are also enacted against business by consumers. Insurance rates are higher today because some policyholders fake injuries, cooperate with towing services to inflate actual costs, and attempt to include old dents as part of collision claims. Prices in retail stores are estimated to be considerably higher than necessary as a result of shoplifting and employee theft. Phoney complaints have caused merchants to adopt strict return policies. Some people are prone, for example, to buy clothes, wear them to parties or weddings, and then return them as unacceptable after the event. Others switch tags in the stores, or write bad checks. The list goes on and on.

While the consumer has the right to safe products, information, redress, and selection, the consumer also has the responsibility to act as an honest individual. The old maxims "Do unto others as you would have them do unto you" and "Honesty is the best policy" are still applicable today.

---

[6]"Surprising Profile of the White-Collar Crook," *U.S. News & World Report,* July 23, 1979, p. 61.

QUESTIONS FOR DISCUSSION

1. What is the difference between fraud and deception?
2. How is an unlisted phone number inadequate defense against an electronic sales pitch?
3. In what circumstances is the cooling-off period not in effect?
4. Describe a pyramid sales scheme. How is a chain letter actually a pyramid scheme?
5. What is meant by a vanity scheme? What are some examples of this form of fraud?
6. How is a referral scheme related to bait-and-switch?
7. What constitutes an efficient charity?
8. Define white-collar crime. Can you think of ways white-collar crime takes place in ordinary situations on a daily basis?

PERSONAL EXPERIENCE PROJECTS

1. Contact the Federal Trade Commission, Bureau of Consumer Protection, Pennsylvania Ave. at Sixth Street, N.W., Washington, DC 20580, to obtain information on common frauds and deceptive sales practices.
2. Watch for "too-good-to-be-true" advertisements for furniture, carpeting, appliances, and automobiles in local newspapers. Contact the businesses to see whether the specials are actually available and to determine whether there are hidden costs for "extras."
3. Contact your local telephone company to obtain information regarding the use of electronic sales solicitation machines by businesses. Find out whether consumers can request to not receive calls from these taped-message machines.
4. Obtain examples of sales-promotion contests and puzzles from newspapers and magazines. Attempt to determine whether there are benefits for consumers or whether the promotions are designed only to increase business for the company.
5. Contact the Consumer Advocate, U.S. Postal Service, Washington, DC 20460, for information on common mail-order frauds and how to avoid them. Find advertisements that may constitute fraudulent use of the postal service.
6. Find examples of deceptive advertisements aimed at young consumers in comic books and teen magazines. Write up guidelines to help young consumers and parents to avoid being deceived by these schemes.
7. Note examples of low-priced specials in local advertisements. At-

tempt to determine if these "loss leaders" are legitimate bargains or gimmicks to attract consumers to the store.

8. Find examples of earn-money-at-home advertisements in various magazines. With the benefit of opinions and experiences of other consumers, analyze the value of the offers.

9. Interview local store managers regarding the various costs of shoplifting. Discuss merchandise losses, security systems, and changes in store operating procedures.

9
INSURANCE

What is insurance? Insurance is protection against financial loss. Buyers of insurance agree to pay a certain amount for a guarantee that they or their survivors will be compensated for specific losses. The contract is the policy in which the buyer of the insurance (the insured) and the insurance organization (the insurer) agree that for a certain payment (the premium) certain benefits will be paid for certain losses.

Insurance companies base premium rates on loss experiences of large groups. To establish a life insurance premium for a twenty-one-year-old, for example, an insurance company might look at a table such as Table 9-1, the National Association of Insurance Commissioners' 1958 Standard Ordinary Mortality Table, which shows that the death rate at age twenty-one is 54.15 per 1,000.

If individuals purchased all the insurance available for every possible risk, they would be insurance poor. The key to allocating insurance dollars is to protect yourself from the most significant financial losses first. Some individuals do just the opposite—they routinely purchase service contracts (a form of insurance) on every appliance they buy, but have inadequate life or health insurance. Actually, many risks can be adequately covered through the keeping of an emergency fund. Other disasters, however,

203

TABLE 9-1. Commissioners' 1958 Standard
Ordinary Mortality Table

AGE	Number Living	Deaths	Expectation of Life	AGE	Number Living	Deaths	Expectation of Life
0	10,000,000	70,800	68.30	50	8,762,306	72,902	23.63
1	9,929,200	17,475	67.78	51	8,689,404	79,160	22.82
2	9,911,725	15,066	66.90	52	8,610,244	85,758	22.03
3	9,896,659	14,449	66.00	53	8,524,486	92,832	21.25
4	9,882,210	13,835	65.10	54	8,431,654	100,337	20.47
5	9,868,375	13,322	64.19	55	8,331,317	108,307	19.71
6	9,855,053	12,812	63.27	56	8,223,010	116,849	18.97
7	9,842,241	12,401	62.35	57	8,106,161	125,970	18.23
8	9,829,840	12,091	61.43	58	7,980,191	135,663	17.51
9	9,817,749	11,879	60.51	59	7,844,528	145,830	16.81
10	9,805,870	11,865	59.58	60	7,698,698	156,592	16.12
11	9,794,005	12,047	58.65	61	7,542,106	167,736	15.44
12	9,781,958	12,325	57.72	62	7,374,370	179,271	14.78
13	9,769,633	12,896	56.80	63	7,195,099	191,174	14.14
14	9,756,737	13,562	55.87	64	7,003,925	203,394	13.51
15	9,743,175	14,225	54.95	65	6,800,531	215,917	12.90
16	9,728,950	14,983	54.03	66	6,584,614	228,749	12.31
17	9,713,967	15,737	53.11	67	6,355,865	241,777	11.73
18	9,698,230	16,390	52.19	68	6,114,088	254,835	11.17
19	9,681,840	16,846	51.28	69	5,859,253	267,241	10.64
20	9,664,994	17,300	50.37	70	5,592,012	278,426	10.12
21	9,647,694	17,655	49.46	71	5,313,586	287,731	9.63
22	9,630,039	17,912	48.55	72	5,025,855	294,766	9.15
23	9,612,127	18,167	47.64	73	4,731,089	299,289	8.69
24	9,593,960	18,324	46.73	74	4,431,800	301,894	8.24
25	9,575,636	18,481	45.82	75	4,129,906	303,011	7.81
26	9,557,155	18,732	44.90	76	3,826,895	303,014	7.39
27	9,538,423	18,981	43.99	77	3,523,881	301,997	6.98
28	9,519,442	19,324	43.08	78	3,221,884	299,829	6.59
29	9,500,118	19,760	42.16	79	2,922,055	295,683	6.21
30	9,480,358	20,193	41.25	80	2,626,372	288,848	5.85
31	9,460,165	20,718	40.34	81	2,337,524	278,983	5.51
32	9,439,447	21,239	39.43	82	2,058,541	265,902	5.19
33	9,418,208	21,850	38.51	83	1,792,639	249,858	4.89
34	9,396,358	22,551	37.60	84	1,542,781	231,433	4.60
35	9,373,807	23,528	36.69	85	1,311,348	211,311	4.32
36	9,350,279	24,685	35.78	86	1,100,037	190,108	4.06
37	9,325,594	26,112	34.88	87	909,929	168,455	3.80
38	9,299,482	27,991	33.97	88	741,474	146,997	3.55
39	9,271,491	30,132	33.07	89	594,477	126,303	3.31
40	9,241,359	32,622	32.18	90	468,174	106,809	3.06
41	9,208,737	35,362	31.29	91	361,365	88,813	2.82
42	9,173,375	38,253	30.41	92	272,552	72,480	2.58
43	9,135,122	41,382	29.54	93	200,072	57,881	2.33
44	9,093,740	44,741	28.67	94	142,191	45,026	2.07
45	9,048,999	48,412	27.81	95	97,165	34,128	1.80
46	9,000,587	52,473	26.95	96	63,037	25,250	1.51
47	8,948,114	56,910	26.11	97	37,787	18,456	1.18
48	8,891,204	61,794	25.27	98	19,331	12,916	.83
49	8,829,410	67,104	24.45	99	6,415	6,415	.50

would be far more than the individual or survivors could face alone. The death of a family's sole supporter, the cost of serious disease or injury, the loss of a home through a fire, or an adverse judgment in a personal liability suit would be ruinous to most of us. This is where insurance is very important.

Since health and income losses are among the most significant an individual faces, and since agents are better at selling insurance than consumers are at shopping for it, this chapter will be devoted to life insurance, health insurance, and Social Security.

LIFE INSURANCE

An estimated nine out of ten families and seven out of ten individuals in the United States carry some form of life insurance.

A major purpose of life insurance is to provide for the care and support of the surviving dependents of the insured. The more dependents a person has, the greater is his or her need for adequate provisions in case of death. The family will have to pay funeral expenses and the cost of settling the estate, as well as various short-term debts. Most important, the family will need income in order to carry on in the manner to which it was accustomed. Settling an estate may take a considerable amount of time and effort, but insurance benefits are available almost immediately upon filing the necessary proof-of-death papers. This is why insurance benefits are often referred to as *instant estate*. Readily available funds are a small but welcome relief to a grief-stricken family.

Another popular purpose of certain types of life insurance is to provide benefits to the insured while he or she is still alive. A portion of the premiums of some policies may be used as borrowings, as collateral for loans, or as a supplement to retirement income.

Types of Policies

There are a number of different types of life insurance policies, each with an even larger assortment of options available. This makes the choice of the right policy a difficult decision for the average consumer. Following are the most common types of insurance policies and options.

Term Insurance. Assume that a consumer buys an automobile theft insurance policy and pays a $100 premium for it. If the car is stolen during the insurance period and is not recovered, the insured will collect for the loss according to the provisions of the policy. Whether or not the car is stolen during the year, the policy ends on the expiration date. The $100 was an insurance expense for protection against theft. This is an example of pure term insurance—protection against loss.

Similarly, term life insurance is protection against death only for the period of time (term) specified in the policy. The term may be one, five, ten, or fifteen years, but when that period expires, the policy has no value.

The premium, which depends on the age of the insured, remains the same (level) for the entire term. Level premiums are computed by averaging the chance of death each year over the entire period. If risks were not averaged, the premiums would have to increase as the risk increased.

It is also possible to obtain *decreasing term* coverage. In the early years of raising a family, the insured may want a large amount of insurance. To anticipate the decrease in family responsibilities after ten or fifteen years, the insured takes out coverage that will provide smaller benefits after a certain period of time. This type of decreasing term coverage is sometimes called family income insurance. Credit life insurance, which is written through lenders on the lives of borrowers and installment buyers, is another form of decreasing term insurance. Mortgage insurance is a type of credit life insurance in which the benefits decrease gradually with the declining balance on the home mortgage.

Another variation of term insurance is *group insurance* written in a blanket master policy to an employer or an organized group for all its members, without medical examination. The rates are usually very low. Remember, though, that the average age of the group is considered when the group premium is computed. So if the premiums are then divided equally among the group members, young employees are subsidizing employees nearing retirement, whose actual risk of premature death is much higher.

Straight Life Insurance. As protection against death, term life insurance is adequate. The straight life—also known as ordinary life or whole life—policy, however, provides not only protection against the financial hardship caused by death, but also a sort of a savings account. Part of the higher premium paid for this type of insurance goes toward the cash value of the policy, also called cash surrender value or loan value.

The straight life policy protects the insured from the day the policy is issued until the insured reaches age one hundred. At that age, the policyholder receives the full face value of the policy—the amount that would have been paid if the insured had died.

The face amount of a policy does not change for the entire policy contract period, nor does the premium. However, the cash value, which determines the amount the insured may borrow on the policy, is constantly increasing. Upon the death of the insured, the beneficiary or beneficiaries named by the insured in the policy receive as death benefits the full (face) amount of the policy, less any borrowings.

If a policyholder stops making premium payments, he or she is entitled to the living benefits of the policy—the cash value that has accumulated up to that point.

Figure 9-1 shows that the cost to the insurance company of a death claim is much greater in the earlier years of the policy. As cash value increases over the years, the portion the company has to contribute in case of death becomes considerably less. If the insured lives to age one hundred, the full amount of the policy is paid in cash that has accumulated from the savings portions of the premiums, which have been earning compound interest over the years.

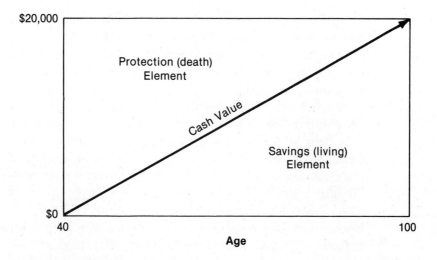

FIGURE 9-1. Protection and Savings Components of a $20,000 Whole Life Policy

Many life insurance policies pay an annual dividend to the insured. It is not the same kind of dividend a stockholder receives from a corporation—it is really a benefit or refund to the policyholder. The dividend may reduce the cost of the premium, be received in the form of cash, remain with the company to earn interest, or be used to buy paid-up additions to the policy. Insurance policies that pay dividends are called *participating policies.* Policies that do not pay dividends are called *nonparticipating policies.* Although nonparticipating policies have lower premiums, participating policies are actually more profitable if the profit and savings history of the company is good.

Only stock companies write nonparticipating policies, but both mutual and stock companies write participating policies. The policy premiums charged by a mutual insurer may be slightly higher than those charged by a stock insurance company, but in a mutual company the excess charge is returned to the policyholders at the end of the year in the form of dividends.

Limited-Payment Life Insurance.   A policy that is closely related to the straight life policy is a limited-payment policy. It is similar to the straight life policy in that the policy runs to age one hundred and the face amount remains level for the entire contract period. It differs from straight life in that the policy is paid up after a limited number of years, such as thirty, twenty, fifteen, ten, or even one, or at a specified age, such as sixty, sixty-five, or seventy. However, the cash value at that point does *not* equal the face amount of the policy. After the premium payments stop, cash value continues to increase as earned interest increases. Cash value and face value are equal only if the insured lives to age one hundred.

Although the premiums are level for the specified premium period, they are larger than the premiums for a straight life policy, and, correspondingly, the cash value grows more rapidly during the period that premiums are paid. This means that the insurer's out-of-pocket risk is less, because the face value is largely supported by premium dollars.

Because of the high cash value, limited-payment life coverage is usually more expensive than straight life insurance. Every dollar spent on life insurance will buy more straight life insurance than limited-payment life insurance.

Endowment Life Insurance.   Some people who have difficulty forcing themselves to save prefer an endowment policy. In this type of life insurance, the cash value on the termination date equals the face amount of the policy.

The endowment policy always has a level amount of coverage and level premiums for the total period of the policy, but at the end of the contract, when the policyholder collects the living benefits, the insurance protection is terminated.

The advantage of endowment life insurance is a rapid increase in cash value. The serious disadvantages are the very high premium payments and the fact that life insurance protection ends.

One of the variations available in endowment policies is a *retirement income* policy, also called an income endowment or retirement endowment policy. This policy provides for the payment of premiums to terminate on a certain date and provides a guaranteed specified monthly income from a predetermined age to death.

The premiums, though high, are level for the total number of premium payments specified in the policy. The date when the insured will start to receive a specific amount of income is also specified.

Combination Policies.   In addition to the four major kinds of life insurance coverage described above, there are many other types of life insurance called combination policies because they are variations and combinations of the basic types.

Variable Life Insurance.   Inflation has resulted in the creation of a new type of life insurance linked with the investment market. It is called variable life insurance. A variable life policy offers a death benefit that fluctuates with the rise and fall of the value of portions of the premiums invested in the stock market. If the stock market is up at the death of the insured, the beneficiaries receive a larger settlement than the face amount of the policy. This element of possibility makes the variable policy more expensive. If the stock market is down at the death of the insured, the beneficiaries receive a smaller settlement, but not less than the face amount of the policy.

Adjustable Life Insurance.   Recently, some insurance companies have begun to market an adjustable life insurance policy. This policy is a combination of straight life insurance and term insurance. The policyholder selects the premium he or she can afford and the face value of coverage needed at various stages of life. The company then writes a combination of term and whole life that will meet these requirements. The main feature of the coverage is that it may be varied (with some limitations, depending on the company) on any given monthly premium date. This flexibility costs more, however, because the amount of coverage desired may not conform to normal policy specifications ($10,000, $20,-000, etc.).

Industrial Insurance.   In many poor urban areas and in some less affluent suburbs, insurance agents used to sell small policies with a face amount of less than $500 or $1,000. The agents collected the small weekly premiums of 10¢, 25¢, 50¢, or $1.00 at the home of the insured. This type of policy was popularly called burial or funeral insurance because it was purchased to pay funeral expenses. Medical examinations were not usually required. The high cost of writing these policies and paying the agents' commissions, plus widespread public criticism, has caused most insurance companies to abandon industrial insurance.

Sources of Insurance

Savings Banks.   Life insurance policies are sold in person or by mail without any commission by savings banks in Connecticut, Massachusetts, and New York. They are available only to residents and to persons employed in the state at the time the policy is purchased. The amount that can be bought is limited by the laws of each state. Savings Bank Life Insurance (SBLI) is not rated in the recognized insurance business reporting publication called *Best's Life Insurance Reports,* but many consumer groups feel that SBLI policyholders are well protected at low cost.

Professional and Business Groups.   Many professional groups and business organizations provide retirement plans and individual life insurance policies to members and spouses. The Teachers Insurance and Annuity Association (TIAA) is only one example of an organization that provides its members with retirement plans and insurance protection at relatively low cost.

Veterans Administration. Since World War I, men and women in service and veterans have been able to buy National Service Life Insurance (NSLI) from the government at very low cost.

State Organizations. The Wisconsin State Life Fund is an example of a state-operated insurance organization. It offers a limited maximum amount ($10,000) of individual straight life insurance to Wisconsin residents.

Fraternal Benefit Societies. Some fraternal and religious benefit societies, such as the Knights of Columbus and the Lutheran Brotherhood, offer life insurance coverage to their members.

Policy Provisions

Designating a Beneficiary. The beneficiary is the person or persons who have been designated by the insured to receive benefits upon the death of the policyholder. The designation of a beneficiary in a policy is a much simpler and less formal matter than in a will. It is, however, no less important that it be done carefully, after thorough consideration. Fortunately, in most cases the designation of beneficiary can be changed by the insured as often as desired—unless a policyholder chooses to designate a beneficiary irrevocably (this means that the beneficiary cannot be changed nor can certain ownership rights be used without the approval of the original designee). It is usually unwise for a policyholder to designate a beneficiary irrevocably, for an irrevocable designee really becomes a part owner of the policy, and this can be bad business in cases of family disputes.

Settlement Options. Upon the death of the insured, the beneficiary may receive the funds in a lump sum or through any of several other options. Unless the insured has made specific arrangements, the choice of options is usually left to the beneficiary. In times of high inflation it is probably better to take the money in a lump sum and invest it somewhere where you will receive higher returns than the insurance company offers (often 2 to 3 percent).

The interest or deposit option provides for the beneficiary to leave the funds with the insurance company. Interest is paid at regular intervals to the beneficiary. The beneficiary may arrange to have limited or unlimited privileges to withdraw funds or to switch to another option.

In the fixed-amount or installment-amount option, the funds are left with the insurance company, and periodic payments are made of both principal and interest as long as the funds last. Withdrawal arrangements may be limited or unlimited, or the option may be changed on a limited or unlimited basis.

In the fixed-period or installment-time option, the funds are left with the company, and periodic payments of principal and interest are made to the beneficiary for a specific period of time.

The selection of an option depends largely upon the management capabilities of the beneficiary, on the return on the proceeds of a policy, and on the alternatives available with other investments. The lump-sum option is the most widely used option. Choosing an option is particularly important and difficult during periods of inflation.

Grace Period. Almost all life insurance policies provide a grace period. This means that the insured is given thirty days after the premium due date to pay the premium, and the policy remains in force during this grace period. In case of death during the grace period, the amount of the unpaid premium is deducted from the face value of the policy. The insured may borrow from the cash value of the policy to pay premiums.

Incontestability. Almost all life insurance policies provide that the insurance company cannot question or contest the policy on any grounds or refuse to pay the policy after it has been in effect for two years. This is very strong protection for the insured.

Suicide. Almost all life insurance policies provide that if a suicide occurs within two years of the date of issue, the company need only return the premiums paid by the deceased.

Double Indemnity. Some insurance companies offer double indemnity coverage. If the insured dies in an accident, such as a car, train, bus, or plane crash, the beneficiary will receive twice the face amount of the policy. Since most persons die from medical causes rather than accidental causes, it is not a good idea to rely very heavily on this option. In assessing the extent of insurance coverage, this option should never be counted as part of a person's overall life insurance.

Policy Loans. Almost all insurance policies except term policies provide that the policyholder may borrow up to the cash value of the policy without discontinuing the coverage. The rate of interest on such loans ranges from 5 to 8 percent. When interest rates on alternative forms of investments such as treasury instruments are high, borrowing by policyholders increases. This practice appeals especially to high-income individuals, who can invest the borrowed money at a higher rate and at the same time deduct the interest on the policy loan from personal income for tax purposes. The danger, of course, is that any borrowing reduces the proceeds to the beneficiary if the insured should die before the money is repaid.

Renewability. Some term insurance policies have a renewability clause. It states that the policy will be valid for another period equal to the term of the original policy without the need for the insured to take a physical examination.

Convertibility. Most term insurance policies contain a convertibility clause. It specifies conditions under which a term policy may be converted to another type of insurance without a physical examination.

Waiver of Premium. Many policies give the insured the option of waiving premium payments in case of total and permanent disability. There is an extra charge for this option.

Choosing the Best Policy

Selecting the best life insurance program requires a multifaceted look at needs, types of policies, insurance companies, and agents. Unfortunately, most life insurance is sold rather than bought. Too often individuals are swayed by a persuasive salesperson's "buy now" arguments. It is true that premiums are lower when a person is younger, but they should be, because the insured will be paying longer. Also, while the chances of obtaining insurance do diminish slightly as age increases, industry estimates show that over 90 percent of applicants are accepted at normal rates. Thus insurance need not be bought in a hurry.

Term versus Permanent Insurance. The real reason for buying life insurance is need—for family protection in case of death and in some cases for a form of savings for old age. So the type of coverage one buys should depend on an individual's personal needs.

PROSPECTIVE LIFE-INSURANCE BUYERS

Decide which type of policy fits your needs.
Estimate family expenses to come up with a face value.
Compare prices.
Examine all policy provisions.

While insurance companies and agents are concentrating on permanent (whole life, limited-payment, endowment) policies, consumers are demanding more time coverage. In 1976, term insurance accounted for 48 percent of the total face value of life insurance policies, versus 40 percent in 1966. Three reasons account for this trend.

The biggest reason is that inflation has dampened the enthusiasm for the more expensive whole life policies, whose returns are 4 to 5 percent at best. As people become more concerned about the time value of money, they are giving more consideration to the lower-cost death protection offered by term insurance.

A second reason why term sales are growing is that the agent's commission on permanent insurance takes an amount equal to one year's premium. The agent usually receives about 55 percent of this during the first year and the remainder spread over a seven- to nine-year period. This commission or front-end load makes permanent life insurance a reasonable buy only if the policy is held at least ten years, and preferably fifteen to twenty years.

Third, the portion of a whole life premium that the insurance company keeps in a savings account will yield more interest if invested in a savings bank or some other form of investment, such as stocks or bonds.

In a comparison between straight life and term insurance it is often pointed out that older people will pay extremely high term premiums while the level straight life premium will remain the same. While this is true, the comparison is often exaggerated by running the term coverage up to age seventy, a time when a policyholder is likely to have, at most, one dependent.

How Much? There is no ready formula for determining how much insurance an individual should carry. Many families have too little life insurance. They are dazzled with the large-sounding face values and do not have any conception of just how long the money will last in an inflated economy.

To determine your insurance needs, first add the following estimated expenses:

1. Funeral expenses.
2. Cost of administering the estate.
3. Estate-tax expenses (based on current federal and state inheritance taxes).
4. Unpaid debts or financial obligations (frequently called "accounts notes payable") likely to be outstanding, such as automobile loans, personal loans, mortgage or installment loans.

5. Cost of college education for the family members who may wish such an education.
6. Family living expenses for one year. Many factors enter into this determination, but the present standard of living can be of some assistance. Studies have shown that many families can limit their spending to 60 or 75 percent of their former annual expenditures. Single spouses or dependents can probably turn down to an even lower percentage of income.

Now estimate income that is likely to be available from various resources to meet the estimated annual expenses. Common sources of income are the following:

1. Social Security, disability, child care, or pension payments (to be discussed later in the chapter).
2. Pension-plan payments.
3. Profit- or income-sharing plan payments.
4. Income from interest and dividends.
5. All family assets including property.
6. Income of the surviving spouse.
7. Cash on hand to meet short-term out-of-pocket expenses.

The total estimated income minus the total estimated expenses provides a fairly reliable indication of the amount of insurance a prudent person who is anxious to provide for surviving dependents may wish to carry. There is a delicate balance between alleviating potential financial loss through insurance and needlessly draining assets through the acquisition of too much insurance.

Cost Comparison. When your needs assessment has been made, the next step is a comparison of costs.

Comparing the cost of term policies is relatively easy, because you need only find the pure death protection that, dollar for dollar, is the best buy.

A cost comparison of permanent policies is a more difficult proposition. Simple comparison of the premiums will not reveal the ultimate benefits of various permanent insurance policies. And FTC studies have shown wide disparities in value among both nonparticipating and participating policies, so comparison is important.

The bottom-line return on a permanent policy is the amount collected versus the amount paid, so cost comparisons must include three factors:

1. Premiums.
2. Dividends (if the policy is participating).
3. Cash values (obviously, the greater it is and the sooner it is available, the better).

These three somewhat isolated factors must be combined in order to compare company products.

Under the *net cost method,* the cost of premiums is totaled, and from this sum the dividends and guaranteed cash value are subtracted. The net cost method may show that the cost of a policy in premiums is less than the amount realized at maturity. However, this method has been largely discredited by consumers and insurance experts. The problems with this method are that dividends may be overestimated (they are not guaranteed), and, more importantly, the opportunity cost of using the premium money for an alternative investment is not considered.

The *interest-adjusted method,* therefore, computes the return to a policyholder by subtracting from the premiums the dividends, the cash value, and the amount that an alternative form of investment would earn. This method still has one flaw that the net cost method has—namely, the insured must rely on projected dividends rather than real payouts.

But although it has its drawbacks, the interest-adjusted method of comparison does give an indication of value. The most common reliable method, it has been used in the compilation of indexes that give cost per $1,000 of coverage. The lower the number, the better the dollar buy. Indexes such as *Best's Flitcraft Compend* or the *Interest-Adjusted Index* published by the National Underwriter Company are available at many insurance agencies and libraries. New York State's Insurance Department also publishes a guide. Called *Consumers' Shopping Guide for Life Insurance,* the New York booklet compares the interest-adjusted method to other cost methods. It is available upon request from the Publications Unit, New York State Insurance Department, Agency Building, 1 Empire State Plaza, Albany, NY 12223.

Another measure that is gaining credibility is called the *average cost method.* This method uses the interest-adjusted cost, but is averaged over a hypothetical group of policyholders with various lapse and mortality rates. A study conducted by the Life Insurance Marketing and Research Association and the American Council of Life Insurance, based on interviews with consumers who had purchased or planned to purchase whole life insurance, showed that the average cost method was preferred (see Table 9-2).

The Final Selection.   The final step in purchasing a whole life policy is to settle on policy provisions. Since you will be relying on your agent for

TABLE 9-2. Reactions to the Cost Comparison Methods

	Would find method helpful*	Most preferred method
1. Out-of-pocket cost method (comparison of premiums)	17%	10%
2. Traditional net cost method	16	9
3. Interest-adjusted cost method	32	24
4. Average cost method	39	30
None of these	9	9
Don't know	16	18
		100%

*Multiple responses.
Source: "Cost Comparisons: Fact, Fiction and Future," *Best's Review*, June 1978, p. 70.

guidance in this final decision-making process, be sure to select one who is experienced, knowledgeable, and professional. Look for an agent who has business degrees, a CLU (Chartered Life Underwriter) designation, patience, and the ability to give thoughtful answers to questions. On the preliminary visit, you should be doing the interviewing. When the right agent has been selected, formal planning can get underway.

Buying life insurance is not easy, but simply being sold some or hiding your head in the sand is not the answer to rounding out this important part of your financial plan.

Periodic Policy Review

A complete and thorough review of life insurance needs should be carried out every two years. Such a review is necessary to take care of circumstances that were not in existence when the policy went into effect.

The most common policy alteration is a change in beneficiary. Failure to remove the names of beneficiaries who have died or have been declared mentally incompetent may cause costly and violent disagreement over who is to receive what.

Another change that may be advantageous is to discontinue an existing policy and buy a new one to replace it. Because inflation has brought significant cost changes in life insurance, many older policies are no longer competitive with new policies. Nonparticipating policies have suffered most from inflation, since they do not pay dividends; thus they may be prime candidates for replacement.

There are many disadvantages, however, to giving up an existing policy:

· The policyholder is again paying the purchase costs involved in acquiring a new policy.
· The incontestability period of two years starts again.
· The suicide-clause period of two years begins again.

Thus a policy should not be replaced unless the insured feels that it is a most advantageous change in the total life insurance program. It should not be replaced as the result of high-pressure salesmanship by an insurance agent. If a replacement is made, the new policy should be in effect *before* the old policy is canceled.

Policy Storage and Security

Many policyholders keep their policies in a safe-deposit box at a bank. This seems like a good security measure, but actually it often causes problems when the insured dies, for the box may not be accessible to the family of the deceased until a state official has inventoried its contents. Also, when policies are kept in a safe-deposit box the insured tends not to review them often enough.

Actually security of the policies is not a vital matter, because copies can be obtained from the insurance companies. Thus it is better to keep insurance policies at home in a desk drawer, a file cabinet, or a small home safe. A list of the insurance companies and the policy numbers should then be placed in a safe-deposit box as a precautionary measure.

HEALTH INSURANCE

Health insurance in its various forms provides protection against sickness, accidents, and disabilities of all types.

Types of Insurance

For most young people, disability and medical coverage are crucial. A long period of high bills and no means of support can destroy an individual's financial health, even far into the future. In the twenty-to-thirty age group, health or disability losses are three and a half times more likely to occur than death.

Basic Coverage.   Health insurance should be purchased in three levels for complete protection. The first of these levels, basic coverage, has three parts.

Medical Expense Insurance.   The cost of medical care rose very rapidly after World War II, and has continued to zoom upwards ever since then. Many individuals have decided to carry medical expense insurance to protect themselves against the high cost of regular medical care.

Medical expense insurance covers nonsurgical physician care in the hospital and generally at home and in the doctor's office. It also may include the various medical tests and laboratory costs related to these medical visits up to a stated amount. Medical expense insurance, in most cases, is one of the less important phases of health insurance, because the average individual can usually afford the cost of regular medical attention.

Hospital Expense Insurance.   Undoubtedly the most popular form of voluntary social insurance at present is hospital expense coverage, commonly referred to as hospitalization. This insurance covers a hospital room, board, operating facilities, laboratory services, medicine, and other related medical treatment services.

The insured is usually allowed up to a certain amount of money for a maximum number of days ranging from 21 to 365 or more. Since hospital costs have skyrocketed in recent years ($65.6 billion in 1978 compared to $3.7 billion in 1950), the cost of hospital expense insurance has increased accordingly.

Although many large commercial insurance companies offer it in their total health insurance program, the best known name in hospital insurance is Blue Cross.

Surgical Expense Insurance.   Closely related to hospital expenses is the fee charged by an individual surgeon or the surgical team now used for most major surgery. The cost of surgical care has increased tremendously as a direct result of the astronomical rise in the cost of malpractice insurance. Every surgical insurance policy has a list of the various surgical operations covered and the maximum benefits allowed for each.

What Blue Cross has done in the hospital expense insurance field, Blue Shield has pioneered in the areas of surgical expense and other doctors' services. Blue Cross and Blue Shield plans are not considered to be insurance in the strict sense. Rather, they are actually prepaid nonprofit agreements between groups of hospitals and/or physicians and groups of individuals who desire their services. Blue Cross and Blue Shield are merely the intermediaries.

Commercial insurance companies also carry surgical expense policies, as well as package deals providing basic coverage—medical expense, hospital expense, and surgical expense.

Major Medical Expense Insurance. Basic coverage has certain limits. What happens in case of an illness that runs into several thousands of dollars? For this, major medical insurance is needed. Major medical is the second level of a sound health insurance program. Major medical allows for more hospital days and related expenses than basic coverage supplies. It also covers more out-of-hospital expenses, such as intensive care by medical specialists in almost all fields (basic coverage pays for specialists for a limited number of selected ailments). Most major medical policies even cover serious mental problems.

Major medical insurance usually has very high maximum limits. Some policies go as high as $100,000 coverage.

Major medical insurance generally has a deductible. This is the amount ranging from $100 to $1,000 that the insured must pay before the insurance coverage begins. The cost above the deductible is generally then shared by the insured and the insurer. This sharing is called *coinsurance.* The deductible and sharing provisions serve to keep down excessive demands for service.

Typical major medical coverage would probably include a $100 deductible to be paid by the insured. On the next $2,000, the company would pay 80 percent and the insured 20 percent. On medical expenses that exceeded the $2,000 level, the individual would be insured 100 percent up to the upper limit of the major medical policy.

Most major medical coverage is group insurance.

A policy that combines the basic hospitalization, surgical expense, and medical expense coverage with major medical insurance is called *comprehensive coverage.* Comprehensive policies are usually group policies offered by employers or schools, and often such institutions pay a large share of the cost.

Catastrophic Expense Insurance. The third and most extensive level of coverage in a complete program begins where major medical leaves off. Catastrophic medical expense insurance covers diseases that run into many tens and even hundreds of thousands of dollars. These very serious ailments include kidney diseases, heart problems requiring open-heart surgery, and cancer. Catastrophic insurance provides a lifetime maximum of from $50,000 to $500,000 for a single accident or illness. Maximum coverage comes with a high deductible.

Other Forms of Health-Related Insurance. Following are the three most common types of health-related insurance.

Disability Income Insurance. Insurance to protect against the loss of income from disability due to work-related injuries and illnesses was one of the earliest forms of social insurance in the United States. Workers' compensation, which started in the early 1900s, has now spread into all fifty states. The employer is responsible for this insurance, which replaces wages lost because of any work-related sickness or disability. Disability protection and benefits also became an integral phase of the Federal Social Security program, which will be described later in this chapter.

Because of the large number of workers' compensation and other group disability plans financed through private business and industry, as well as through government programs, only a relatively small number of consumers carry their own disability insurance. However, many employees make the mistake of thinking they are covered for income loss due to non-work-related accident or illness when actually they are not.

The cost of disability insurance is relatively low. It is based on the time the insured is willing to wait after sickness or accident before collecting. A thirty-day waiting period costs more than a sixty-day waiting period. The income protection usually covers up to 50 percent of income lost. The important clause to watch is the definition of disability. In some policies, if a person can do even little tasks he or she is not considered disabled. Other weak policies will say that a person who is fit to do work in a field other than his or her regular occupation is not disabled.

Dental Insurance. During the past twenty years prepaid dental insurance has become very popular. It is usually provided on a group basis, although individual policies are available. The major group insurers are Blue Cross, Blue Shield, dental organizations, local dental groups, and commercial insurance companies.

The typical dental plan carries a fixed deductible and a predetermined maximum in each category of service. The plan covers diagnostic services such as examinations, consultations, and x-rays. It also covers preventive procedures, oral surgery, restorative treatment, endodontics, periodontics, and prosthodontics.

Dental insurance is now often included in comprehensive medical coverage plans.

Dreaded Diseases or Disablement Insurance. The low premiums on insurance against dreaded diseases or disablement should tell you that companies rarely have to pay for losses under this type of insurance. Rather than insure yourself against a narrow range of risks, it is better to purchase a good health insurance policy that will automatically cover these diseases or disablements.

With the extraordinarily high cost of hospital, medical, and surgical care in this inflationary period, it is almost compulsory for every person, regardless of age or health, to be covered by some form of health insurance. Most large companies are providing group health insurance as a phase of employee benefits. Any person not covered in a group plan should enroll in either a health maintenance organization (see next section) or at least a Blue Cross/Blue Shield type of organization. You cannot afford to take the risk of being solely responsible for large hospital, medical, surgical, or even dental bills. Fortunately, college students up to the age of twenty-three are usually included in their parents' Blue Cross/Blue Shield plans.

If you are covered by group health insurance offered through your employer, the group coverage is terminated if you leave your job. Many private insurance companies will sell "bridge coverage" until you begin your next job. It is best to arrange for such coverage, for the risks of being without health insurance for even a short period of time are high.

The Future of Medicine

The constantly spiraling cost of health care has become a national nightmare: the increasing cost of health care services is a large factor in the current high cost of living.

National spending on health care, which was $3.8 billion in 1940, $12 billion in 1950, and $69 billion in 1970, is expected to be $229 billion in 1980. Government spending alone zoomed to $64 billion in 1978, and this amount is constantly increasing. About 10¢ of every federal dollar is now going for health care (see Figure 9-2). A large part of this money provides Medicare for the elderly and Medicaid for the poor.

The health industry is the third largest industry in the United States after food and construction. Health costs now account for about 10 percent of the total national production of goods and services—double the percentage of twenty years ago.

This rise is largely a result of the tremendous increase in hospital costs—from $40 a day in 1965 to about $200 a day in 1978. Doctors' fees have also been increasing at a higher rate than the prices of other services, partially because of the high cost of malpractice insurance.

There is little doubt that the United States offers the best medical attention in the world. However, 24 million Americans do not have access to it because they do not have health insurance of any kind and cannot

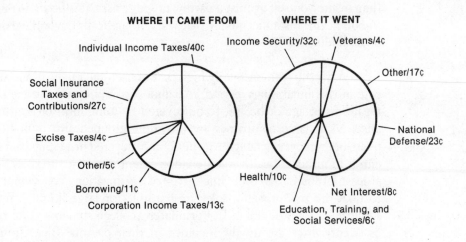

FIGURE 9-2. The 1978 Budget Dollar. (Internal Revenue Service.)

afford to pay the costs themselves. According to the National Center for Health Statistics, approximately another 20 million have what the Center considers inadequate coverage. A less expensive way to provide health care must be found.

National Health Care. One possibility is national health insurance, which is currently the subject of heated controversy. The principal opponents are the suppliers of health services, who are very concerned about their professional right to operate their businesses at whatever compensatory levels they can command.

Informed consumers should investigate national health care and make their views known to their representatives in the legislature.

HMOs. As another alternative to traditional health insurance, the Department of Health, Education and Welfare supports the establishment of Health Maintenance Organizations (HMOs). Passed in 1973, a federal law called the HMO Act requires that an employer of more than twenty-five employees offer HMO membership as an alternative to health insurance if there is such an organization nearby. The law mandates that dental care and diagnostic mental health services for children be provided at these centers.

HEW's goal is to keep more people out of hospitals, for hospital charges account for 80 percent of the nation's health care costs. HMOs are composed of groups of physicians who cooperate to provide complete office and hospital care for a fixed monthly fee. Many tests are given in the physicians' offices rather than in hospitals. The HMO group doctors have little incentive to hospitalize patients unnecessarily, because their monthly fee is fixed. The stress is on preventive medicine and early treatment of illness.

Membership has been on the increase, but HMOs have a long way to go. Only 6.3 percent of the nation's population is currently enrolled in such plans. The government predicts that the problem of finding a family doctor and the frustration of being referred from one specialist to another will bring in many patients and that the high cost of malpractice insurance and the problems of administering private practices will lure staff members.

SOCIAL SECURITY

During the depression there was a great deal of controversy over the extent to which the injured, sick, and elderly should be protected. After a vigorous campaign by the Roosevelt administration and a vicious political struggle, in 1935 Congress passed the Social Security Act, which provided retirement benefits for elderly workers.

In 1939, the law was revised to pay certain dependents upon the death of a worker in industry or commerce. The Act was changed again in the 1950s to extend coverage to most self-employed persons, most state and local employees, household and farm employees, members of the Armed Forces, and the clergy. Today, almost all jobs are covered under Social Security.

In 1954, workers were awarded protection against loss of earnings due to total disability. In 1965, Social Security was again amended to include Medicare coverage, which provides hospital and medical insurance to people sixty-five and over. Medicare was extended in 1973 to people under sixty-five who have been entitled to disability payments for two or more consecutive years, or people with severe kidney disease who need dialysis or kidney transplants.

Inflation results in automatic increases in Social Security benefits, since regulations provide that an increase of 3 percent or more in the CPI results in an equal increase in benefits.

Social Security benefits are paid to the following dependents of a retired or disabled person:

1. unmarried children under eighteen (or twenty-two if full-time students)
2. unmarried children eighteen or over who were severely disabled before twenty-two and who continue to be disabled
3. wife or dependent husband sixty-two or over

4. spouse under sixty-two caring for worker's child under eighteen (or disabled) who is receiving benefits based on the retired or disabled worker's earnings.

Benefits are paid to the following survivors of a deceased worker:

1. unmarried children under eighteen (or twenty-two if full-time students)
2. unmarried children eighteen or over who were severely disabled before twenty-two and who continue to be disabled
3. widow or dependent widower sixty or over
4. widow, widowed father, or surviving divorced mother if caring for worker's child under eighteen (or disabled) who is receiving benefits based on the deceased worker's earnings
5. widow or dependent widower fifty or over who becomes disabled not later than seven years after worker's death or within seven years after checks for care of worker's children have stopped
6. dependent parents sixty-two or over
7. under certain conditions, a divorced spouse.

The Social Security Act covers many programs of social insurance, unemployment insurance, public assistance, and health and welfare services. Only the old-age insurance, survivors' insurance, and disability insurance are administered by the federal government.

The provisions for becoming fully insured under the Social Security Act vary according to age group. In any case, any individual who has worked and paid Social Security for at least one and a half years (six quarters) within the three years immediately before retirement or death is insured.

There are regional and local Social Security Administration offices throughout the United States. They are well staffed to provide information and advice on all phases of Social Security, and they will answer questions in person, on the telephone, or by mail.

Table 9-3 shows that individuals rely heavily on Social Security for retirement income. In view of this fact, the future of Social Security is an important issue. Late in 1977 Congress passed a law increasing the maximum withholding for Social Security to $3,046 in 1987, up from $1,071 in 1978. This increase will only finance those individuals who will be receiving Social Security benefits in 1987. The real crunch will be felt in about 2010, when there will be more people collecting than paying in. Yet employers are already finding it difficult to pay the higher cost of the employer's share of Social Security. Social Security reform is thus becoming a major topic of concern in the U.S. Congress.

TABLE 9-3. Income Sources of Those Sixty-five and Over (approximate percentage receiving income from each source)

	Families headed by individual 65 or older	Single individuals 65 or older
Wage or salary	42%	13%
Property or personal assets	63	52
Social Security or railroad retirement	91	89
Supplemental security income	7	13
Veteran's benefits, unemployment, or workman's compensation	12	7
Retirement pensions	35	22

Source: U.S. Bureau of Census.

QUESTIONS FOR DISCUSSION

1. How is the amount of the premium charged to a life insurance policyholder determined?
2. How does an insurer arrive at a level premium for a life insurance policy?
3. Credit life insurance is actually a form of what type of term insurance?
4. What is the difference between a nonparticipating policy and a participating policy? Does a participating policy guarantee a higher return to the policyholder?
5. How does the concept of variable life insurance attempt to deal with inflation? Why is the concept not widely accepted?
6. What is the major advantage of the loan value of a whole life insurance policy to the policyholder? How may the loan value be used? What is the major disadvantage?
7. What are the main advantages of group insurance?
8. When would an individual be most likely to select a term life insurance policy over a whole life policy?

9. Why must a whole life policy be kept in force for a period of at least ten years in order to be a good investment?
10. Describe the interest-adjusted method of comparing whole life insurance policies.
11. What is the purpose of major medical insurance?
12. Why is the federal government advocating the spread of HMOs?
13. Why is the financial stability of the Social Security system being questioned?

PERSONAL EXPERIENCE PROJECTS

1. Conduct a survey of consumers' life insurance plans. Ask about the company, type of policy, amount of coverage, special features or benefits, and satisfaction with agent and company service.
2. Compare the cost of obtaining various types of life insurance from several insurance agents. Attempt to determine reasons for differences in the costs.
3. Contact your state department of insurance to obtain information on common complaints of consumers. Also inquire as to the function of this state office and request information on the insurance laws in your state.
4. After talking to a number of consumers, compare group health insurance to individual health insurance. Determine differences in costs, restrictions, deductibles, coverage, and satisfaction with service.
5. Collect advertisements and other information on mail-order health insurance. Compare the costs of these policies with those of local agents.
6. Contact a health maintenance organization in your area. Obtain information on costs, benefits, organizational structure, and services provided. Attempt to evaluate the effectiveness of this form of prepaid medical service. (For background information, read "HMOs: Are They the Answer to Your Medical Needs?" *Consumer Reports*, October 1974, p. 756.)
7. Write to your Congressional representatives regarding their position on national health insurance. Obtain information on proposed plans, costs, benefits, and restrictions on coverage.
8. Obtain information from the Social Security Administration, 6401 Security Boulevard, Baltimore, MD 21235, on the costs, benefits, and restrictions of this government insurance program. Obtain opinions on the advantages and disadvantages of Social Security from consumers of various ages.

10
INVESTING IN SECURITIES

Rapidly changing economic conditions have driven many people to consider forms of investments other than the traditional savings accounts, time certificates, savings bonds, and life insurance. The 5¼- or 5½-percent passbook rate looks meager (especially after taxes) against a 10-percent inflation rate. Savers become anxious when they see the dollar eroding each year—they realize that the large sum they had planned to have at retirement may well provide a pretty dim existence by the time they reach age sixty-five. And to the dismay of those who had considered life insurance cash values to be their "ace in the hole" toward a pleasant retirement, in 1979 the FTC issued a report saying that the average return on a whole life insurance policy was actually 1.6 percent—a very weak return.

Investors have even lost faith in the stock market—7 million people fled from the market from 1970 to 1979, leaving mainly older people. According to *Business Week,*

> Younger investors, in particular, are avoiding stocks. Between 1970 and 1975, the number of investors declined in every age group but one: individuals 65 and older. While the number of investors under 65 dropped by about 25 percent, the number of investors over 65 jumped by more than 30 percent. Only the elderly who have not understood the changes in the

nation's financial markets, or who are unable to adjust to them, are sticking with stocks.[1]

The feeling toward common stock is well founded. According to a study by Salomon of Salomon Brothers,

> Since 1968 stocks have appreciated by a disappointing compounded annual rate of 3.1 percent, while the consumer price index has surged by 6.5 percent. By contrast, gold grew by an incredible 19.4 percent, diamonds by 11.8 percent, and single family housing by 9.6 percent.[2]

What are Americans doing with their money to fight inflationary erosion? Fortunately, there are other possible investments—new forms of mutual funds; profitable common stocks within a dreary market; high-yield, good-quality bonds; and even some types of hobby collection-investments have been healthy sources of profit. Finally, the family home has enjoyed a high return on investments.

All of this does not mean that you should avoid savings accounts, savings certificates, treasury instruments. Saving is putting money aside at low risk. The return may be low, but the money will be there when you need it. Investments introduce the promise of a higher return, but they also involve an element of risk. Everyone should save. Unfortunately, by the time funds are set aside for emergencies and the bills are paid, many people have little left over for investing. However, most people are at least indirect investors. Pension funds are invested by employers for employees in an attempt to keep the value of retirement income in line with the economy. And for those who do not have retirement plans, some alternatives are discussed at the end of this chapter.

WHO SHOULD INVEST IN SECURITIES?

Financial securities are neither as liquid nor as safe as savings accounts. Most of them cannot be converted to cash quickly in an emergency without some loss of the original principal or capital invested, and even the best of them may go down in value as well as up. There is, therefore, a much greater element of risk involved in investing money in stocks, bonds, or real estate rather than in savings accounts.

Any consumer who has a limited amount of unspent income to

[1]"The Death of Equities," *Business Week,* August 13, 1979, pp. 55–56.
[2]*Ibid.,* p. 56.

invest should not consider high-risk investing unless he or she has all of the following:

1. *Job Security.* Nobody can ever guarantee unconditionally that he or she will not unexpectedly become unemployed or go out of business for one reason or another. Economic conditions may worsen; businesses may cut payrolls; serious illness may strike. However, a person should have a relatively safe and secure regular income; otherwise that consumer should not even begin to think seriously about investing.

2. *Money Needed for Regular Living Expenses.* The stock market should not even be considered if living expenses are a problem. The consumer must first be certain that all living expenses can be paid comfortably, and if a small amount remains unspent, it should go into a savings account and not into investments.

3. *Adequate Insurance.* The consumer must have the right kind of life insurance for the special need of his or her family: health insurance, including major medical benefits for the whole family; disability income protection; a homeowner's policy covering all possible catastrophies; and car insurance with adequate liability limits.

4. *Cash on Hand for Emergencies.* The consumer should have enough cash in savings accounts to meet any emergencies that might arise, both short-term and longer-term.

5. *The Temperament to Take Risks.* Some consumers do not have the emotional balance to face a high possibility of loss. Such people may become distressed at the slightest price dip in the stock market, or excessively elated when stock prices show increases several days in a row. Such an emotional type will not last long amongst the ups and downs of the stock market.

6. *Time and Patience to Study the Market.* An investment should be the result of considerable study and investigation. Too often the new investor buys or sells solely on the basis of tips, rumors, or hunches. Such decisions are liable to be disastrous.

WHY INVEST IN SECURITIES?

It would be unwise to rule out stocks as a possible investment. Both large and small investors have had success with this investment medium. The only real danger is in saying that *all* stocks are a good hedge against expected or unexpected inflation. The right stock may go up under even the most adverse economic conditions, and the wrong stock may decrease in value under the best of economic conditions.

Over the years, the prices of many common stocks have moved upward. This trend reflects, in part, the continuing growth of American business. There are good economic reasons for believing that this trend will probably prevail, in spite of creeping or galloping inflation or recession.

First, the "real" gross national product, after allowing for inflation, has been increasing for many years at a rate of about 3 percent a year. High-quality stocks are bound to benefit from this increase in gross national product.

Second, consumer prices have been going up since the depression years of the early 1930s, and this inflationary trend will probably continue for some time. Of course, all stocks will not necessarily benefit from a rise in consumer prices. However, many stocks have been moving up in value and have also been paying larger dividends. When either situation occurs to any stock, it is helping its owners to reduce the decrease in purchasing power caused by previous inflation.

Third, pension funds, educational institutions, unions, insurance companies, mutual funds, and foreign investors are still making large security purchases. This constant demand for high-quality securities provides a solid base of support for a continuous upward trend in the price of stocks and bonds.

Fourth, many new investment packages being developed and promoted jointly by investment institutions, insurance companies, banks, and mutual funds (such as tax-deferred annuities) are likely to increase the total amount of investment money on the market.

There are three major objectives to be considered when investing in securities.

1. *Safety of Principal.* Some consumers "play the market" as they would play at the casinos in Las Vegas. Most consumers, however, cannot afford to take excessive risks. The "best bet" is to invest in stocks or bonds with almost as high a degree of safety as most savings institutions provide.
2. *Liberal Dividend Income.* Some prospective securities investors seek an average return on their investment that is at least comparable to the yield on regular or time-certificate deposits in savings institutions. This goal is not in conflict with the safety-of-principal objective. There are many stocks and bonds that offer a high degree of safety *and* a fairly good dividend yield. For example, in recent years most of the public utility stocks and bonds have met both of these objectives.
3. *Growth of Capital.* Ideally, the prudent consumer seeks not

only safety of principal and dividends, but also an increase in the value of the original investment. Fortunately, there are many stocks that combine all of these goals.

Careful investigation and planning are required for all of these objectives to become realities.

COMMON AND PREFERRED STOCK

The stocks and bonds of the 1¾ million corporations in the United States are the major financial securities available to the general public.

A corporation is a legal entity (artificial person) chartered either by the federal government or, in most cases, by a state government. From its very origin the corporation is financed by the sale of shares of stock to stockholders. The stockholders are the owners. The extent of each one's ownership is determined by the number of shares owned. A certificate is issued to each stockholder for the number of shares owned.

Shares that entitle their holders to normal rights in the corporation are called *common stock.* Shares that entitle one to special rights or benefits not given to common stockholders are called *preferred stock.*

The most important of these rights relates to the receipt of dividends. If there are profits from operations, the Board of Directors may decide to declare a dividend. When preferred stock is issued, the amount of dividend, when and if declared, is usually specified in the name—for example, AT&T $4.00 preferred. On the other hand, dividends on common stock depend entirely on the decision of the Board of Directors from quarter to quarter. No dividend can be paid on common stock until the preferred stock dividend has been paid, and preferred stockholders cannot be paid dividends until bond interest has been paid. If the earnings are inadequate, the dividends on all stock may be passed or omitted. Dividends are usually cash dividends, but at times, when a corporation wants to hold on to cash but issue more shares, it will declare a stock dividend.

A second difference between common and preferred stock is in voting rights. As owners of the corporation, the common stock shareholders elect the Board of Directors and vote on certain basic policy matters. The Board of Directors then selects the officers who operate the corporation. Preferred stockholders do not usually have voting rights.

The third major difference involves liquidation priorities. If a company becomes bankrupt or liquidates the business, the common stockholders are the last to share in any of the assets available. The creditors and bondholders are first, and the preferred stockholders are next.

Common Stocks

Characteristics of Common Stocks. Some corporations have more than one kind of common stock. One class of stock may have voting rights that a second class does not enjoy. In past years this distinction was more common than in recent issues.

Another distinction that is becoming extinct is that of par-value and no-par-value stock. At one time, most common shares had a $100 nominal par value. Theoretically, all stockholders were to pay $100 for each share. But since prospective stockholders refused to pay more for a share than they thought it was worth, par value became meaningless. Almost all shares issued now are no-par-value shares. They are sold and bought at whatever price the stock brokers agree on in a particular situation. For corporate tax purposes only, some corporations put a nominal value of $5 or $10 on a new share issued. This nominal value has no relationship to the market value at which it will be sold.

Much more important than par value is the *earning per share* (EPS). How much does the corporation earn on each outstanding share of stock? The prospective investor is very much interested in this figure, for it provides some indication of the potential income that can be expected from the stock. By dividing the EPS into the price per share, the buyer can then determine the stock's *price/earning multiple* or ratio (P/E ratio). Assume that the market price of a stock is $20 and the earnings are $2. The price divided by the earnings gives a price/earnings multiple of 10 ($20 \div 2 = 10$). Whether 10 is a good multiple depends on the stock market averages at the time. It also depends on what the average P/E ratio is in that particular industry under prevailing economic conditions. P/E ratios are generally higher for growth stocks than for income stocks. However, an especially high P/E ratio is usually a warning that a stock is overpriced.

A second factor in determining the attractiveness of a stock is the dividend yield. Assume that the corporation whose stock sells for $20 a share has been paying a yearly dividend of $1 a share. The $1 is divided by the $20 market price to determine the yield on the investment ($1 \div $20 = 5 percent). Since the yields on savings accounts range from 5 to 8 percent, this stock provides a reasonable return on the investment when dividends alone are considered.

The investor must always keep in mind, however, that the dividends used to compute the dividend yield and the earnings used to compute price earnings are last year's figures. There is no guarantee that the same amounts will be earned in the future.

One other factor to consider when looking at a stock is its book value. Net worth is the difference between a corporation's assets (property owned) and its liabilities (debts). The *book value* per share is found by dividing the net worth by the number of shares outstanding. For example, say the net worth of a corporation is $300,000 and there are 10,000 shares outstanding. Dividing $300,000 by 10,000 gives a book value of $30 a share. Book value often bears very little relationship to the market price of a common stock, but some prospective buyers are interested in it as an indication of the capital behind a share of stock. For example, if a stock has a book value of $30 but is selling at $20, it has a good possibility of increasing in price because of the value behind each share. But if the same stock is selling at $40, it must have other attractive features that have pushed the price up.

Common Stock Aftermarket. Once a common share is sold initially, it becomes a part of the aftermarket. The share is registered by the corporation to its original owner, and when it is traded to someone else the subsequent owner's name and address are recorded by the issuing corporation. Most daily newspapers follow the progress of the majority of stocks, especially those traded on a regional or national stock exchange. Figure 10-1 shows the format of a newspaper report on the trading progress of common stocks A and B.

The figure shows that during the past year the selling price of stock A reached a high of $22 and a low of $17. While stock A pays an annual dividend of $1, stock B pays no dividend. Because stock B has a P/E ratio of 20, we know that its company made a profit last year but decided to retain it, possibly for expansion, rather than pay it out to the shareholders. Owners of stock A have invested $10 for every $1 in earnings, while stockholders of B have invested $20 for every $1 of earnings. The sales column indicates that 50,000 shares of A and 210,000 shares of B were traded during the day. Both common stocks fluctuated in price during the day, but only A closed at a different price than it had the day before (change). The price/earnings ratio and dividend yield were computed on the closing price for the day.

Securities that are not listed on any stock exchange are sold by dealers operating business firms devoted to buying stocks from companies and selling them to investors. This is called the *over-the-counter (OTC)*

Yearly High	Low	Stock	Dividend	Yield	PE	Sales 100s	High	Low	Close	Change
22	17	A	1.00	5	10	500	20	19½	20	– ½
16	12	B		20	20	2100	15	13½	14	...

FIGURE 10-1. Common Stock

Stock	Dividend	Sales 100s	Bid	Asked	Bid Change
OTC CO.	.10	60	6	6½	+ ¼

FIGURE 10-2. Over-the-Counter Stock

market. The prices asked by the sellers of OTC stocks are fed into the central computer of the National Association of Securities Dealers Automated Quotation System (NASDAQ). The resulting report is illustrated in Figure 10-2. While most over-the-counter stocks are reported only in the region in which the corporation is located, the more widely held stocks are reported nationally.

The name of the firm, the annual dividend, and sales figures are listed in much the same manner as for an exchange stock. The bid and asked prices are much more approximate, however, because of the diversity of trading outlets. It is much more difficult to keep a record of the last transaction of the day for an OTC stock than for a share of stock traded on the floor of a single exchange. According to Marshall Blume, one of the nation's leading experts on the securities market, many small investors prefer trading OTC: "Individuals tend to own different stocks. They invest heavily in over-the-counter issues, whereas the institutions prefer the companies listed on the New York Stock exchange."[3]

Preferred Stocks

There are two classes of preferred stock, first and second. Holders of the first preferred stock are entitled to receive dividends before they are paid to any other stockholders. Holders of second preferred stock receive dividends only after the first preferred dividend has been paid. Either first or second preferred stock may fall into one or more of the following categories:

Cumulative Preferred Stock. Assume that a corporation cannot pay dividends to the preferred stockholders for several years, and then the earnings become adequate to pay some dividends. The company must pay the cumulative preferred stockholders all the unpaid dividends in full before other preferred and common stockholders receive their dividends.

[3]Interview with Marshall E. Blume. "Safe Strategies for Small Investors," *Changing Times,* November 1978, p. 35.

Participating Preferred Stock.   Assume that earnings are large enough to leave a surplus after all preferred and common dividends have been paid. The participating preferred stockholders share with the common stockholders in the distribution of the surplus dividend income.

Cumulative Participating Preferred Stock.   Cumulative participating preferred stock combines the special advantages of cumulative preferred stock and those of participating preferred stock and therefore sells at a higher price.

Callable Preferred Stock.   The corporation retains the right to buy back all outstanding callable preferred stock, usually at a premium above the original price at which it was issued. It may do so either because it wishes to bring out a new issue of preferred stock at a lower dividend rate, or because it wishes to sell bonds with a lower interest rate.

Convertible Preferred Stock.   Convertible preferred stock can be converted to common stock by the stockholder at a stated ratio. If the ratio is 1.1, for example, one share of Company A preferred stock may be changed into 1.1 shares of Company A common stock. Thus, 100 shares of preferred $4.00 stock may be converted into 110 shares of Company A common stock. If the common has been paying regular dividends of $4.50 a share, versus $4.00 for the preferred stock, conversion will increase the annual yield from $400 to $495. Sometimes the common may even be selling at a higher price than the preferred—this may also be a factor in the decision to convert preferred to common stock.

Preferred stock prices are quoted in the same manner as their common counterparts. Figure 10-3 indicates that the A Corporation has sold both common and preferred stock. The preferred issue is designated by a pf next to the name of the stock.

Choosing Stocks

What are the rules for picking the stocks that will be winners? If anyone knew for sure, he or she would be rich. Those who sell formulas for riches

Yearly High	Low	Stock	Dividend	Yield	PE	Sales 100s	High	Low	Close	Change
22	17	A	1.00	5	10	500	20	19½	20	– ½
50	40	A pf	5.00	10	. . .	10	51	48½	50	. . .

FIGURE 10-3. Preferred Stock

usually make their money on the books people buy from them. These are some general rules worth noting, however:

1. Choose stocks of companies in industries that are or will be sound and essential.

2. Diversify—don't put all of your money into the shares of one company. For example, if you have all your money in a utility and a nuclear accident shuts it down, you will be in trouble. On a $10,000 investment, you should have stock in at least five different companies.

3. Look at *blue-chip stocks*—stocks that provide, in addition to the promise of market-value growth, a dividend that is as high as the return on a savings account. Such stocks are generally issued by recognized leaders in important industries.

4. Look at stocks whose earnings per share have been increasing each year; this is a clear indicator of demand for the product or service. Some companies with increasing earnings will plow the money back into the company rather than pay dividends. The stocks of such firms are called *growth stocks.*

5. Buy at the end of a long decline in market prices and the start of a steady gain. It is hard to second-guess when the market has reached its bottom level, so it is best to wait for a sign of recovery.

Of course, a person who invests in stock will anxiously await the results. Be patient, but don't keep the stock too long if it is losing dramatically. Good luck!

BONDS

Characteristics of Bonds

A bond is a promissory note given to a lender as evidence of a loan by a borrowing corporation (or government body). The bond may be payable in five, ten, twenty, fifty, or more years. The long-term maturity date does not worry the bondholder, however, because the bond can be sold through a stock brokerage firm at any time.

Since a bond is a debt of the corporation and not a share in the ownership of the company, a bondholder's income is limited to the stated interest rate. Interest is generally paid at this fixed rate twice a year. The rate of interest depends on the interest rates being paid for this type of bond at time of issue. This interest rate stays the same until the bond matures and is redeemed by the corporation.

The element of risk in investing in a good bond is much smaller than in investing in the common stock of even a good corporation, for interest must be paid to the bondholder before any of the shareholders receive any dividends. In case the business fails to pay the interest on bonds or becomes bankrupt, the bondholders must be paid before any of the stockholders receive anything.

In a period of prosperity or inflation, bond prices and interest rates on stocks and savings accounts go up. In a recession, depression, or deflationary period, good bonds go up because the bondholder continues to receive the stated rate of interest while dividends, prices, and interest rates on stocks and savings accounts go down.

Income from dividends and interest is taxable as unearned income on federal and state income taxes, while some federal, state, and municipal bonds are tax-exempt. This saving in taxes makes bonds an attractive investment for consumers in the higher tax brackets.

The quality of individual bonds is rated by several financial service organizations. Among the best known are Standard and Poor's and Moody's. Corporate bonds are rated AAA, AA, A, BBB, BB, B, CCC, CC, C, DDD, DD, or D. Municipal bonds are rated AAA, AA, A, BBB, BB, B, or D. The ratings are based on the safety of investment. Since the market for bonds generally reflects this safety, an investor can usually tell how safe a bond is by looking at its interest rate. If the interest rate is much higher than that of other bonds, there is probably a reason traceable to the company's ability to pay the stated interest.

Bonds are usually issued in denominations of $1,000, and the interest rate is stated as a percent of the face and maturity value. An 8-percent bond pays $80 interest a year, or $40 every six months. In the financial quotations, bonds are listed at 10 percent of their total value. A bond selling for $1,000 is listed as "100." A bond selling for $950 is listed as "95." Regardless of the price at which the bond is selling, the holder of a $1,000 bond will receive $1,000 for it at maturity. Some bonds are issued in denominations as low as $500 and as high as $100,000.

Corporations usually back up the payment of interest during the term of the bond and its repayment at maturity with some form of security. In the case of mortgage bonds, the corporation puts up as security a mortgage or mortgages on some or all of the company's property. If the corporation fails to pay interest or principal, the bondholders may foreclose the mortgage and sell the property to recover what is owed to them.

Bonds that do not have any property or security behind them

are called *debenture bonds.* The only security they have is the reputation and credit of the borrowing corporation. Naturally, only the top-flight and largest companies and governmental bodies can float debenture bond issues. Their very high credit rating in the financial community is usually enough to sell out any bond issue as soon as it is announced.

Bonds, like stock, may be callable or convertible. Like callable preferred stocks, callable bonds can be paid off by the corporation at its option. A corporation will call in a certain bond issue when it is to its advantage to do so. Usually the corporation pays a small premium in addition to the maturity value of the called bonds. Convertible bonds, on the other hand, are convertible to common stock at the option of the bondholder.

Bond Aftermarket

Bonds, like stocks, are traded from investor to investor. Because bonds are a long-term agreement between a corporation or government and an investor, the original investor may want to sell them to another investor without waiting until the bonds mature. The price the individual will get will depend on the interest rate stated on the bond and on the prevailing interest rates for new bonds or other long-term investments. A 1970-issue bond with a stated rate of 6 percent and a maturity date of 1995 will surely not sell today for its $1,000 value if current interest rates on comparable bonds are 10 percent. The difference between the 6-percent rate and the 10-percent rate will be reflected by an offer that will compensate the second buyer for the loss in rate until maturity.

Figure 10-4 is a report on the aftermarket trading for E Corporation bonds. E Corporation bonds have a stated rate of 8½ percent, and they mature in 1995. If an individual purchased one of the bonds in the aftermarket at 94 ($940), the actual rate of return at maturity in 1995 would be 9 percent, as shown in the column "sales yield." The net change from the previous day's trading is 1 ($10). A long-term investment in bonds does not allow for guaranteed liquidity; rather, the emphasis is on safety.

		Yield	Sales ($1000)	High	Low	Close	Net Change
E Corp 8½	95	9.0	30	94	94	94	+1

FIGURE 10-4. A Corporation Bond

Choosing Bonds

Bonds, if bought at the right time, can be an excellent hedge against falling interest rates. The goal of many investors is to strike when the interest rate is high, hold the bonds as the rates fall, and then sell them for a profit. Others like bonds for the long-range security they give.

Lately the average investor is hearing a lot more about the tax-exempt interest on municipal bonds. However, municipal bonds do not benefit everyone. First, although the interest on municipal bonds is exempt from federal taxes, some states do tax it. Second, an investor who is not in a high tax bracket may actually lose money by choosing the tax-exempt bonds. For example, suppose Art, who pays in the 20-percent tax bracket on his last $1,000, buys a municipal bond that pays 5 percent. The 5 percent is his yield, since he pays no tax. However, he could have purchased a corporation bond with a yield of 10 percent, paid the 20-percent tax on the interest, and still have had 8 percent left over.

INVESTMENT COMPANIES

Many investors simply do not have the money necessary to invest in individual stocks or bonds. The sales commissions are high for small amounts, the small amounts of money do not allow for much diversification, and the individual often lacks the time or expertise to invest without help. For many of these investors, an investment company is the answer.

A consumer can buy an interest in many different corporations by purchasing shares in an investment company. The investment company accumulates money from many individuals and then invests its savings in a diversified securities portfolio. The portfolios of investment companies include many more common stocks than are usually found in the portfolios of savings institutions or life insurance companies.

There is a wide range of investment companies. Some specialize in new and highly speculative enterprises. Others concentrate variously on high-quality common stock, preferred stock, high-quality bonds, speculative bonds, or a balanced combination of stocks and bonds. Some are mainly concerned with high income, others with capital growth or the safety of principal. Whatever the basic objectives of investment companies may be, their policies must be clearly stated. This safeguard was provided in the Investment Companies Act of 1940.

There are two main types of investment companies, closed-end and open-end companies.

Closed-End Investment Companies

The closed-end investment company is a regular corporation whose major purpose is to reinvest its stockholders' money in other securities. A closed-end company does not redeem its shares, so a stockholder can get his or her money back only through the sale of the investment company's stock.

The closed-end corporation can only invest the amount of capital received from the sale of its shares. In a rising market, the fact that the company has only a limited amount of money to invest is a disadvantage. On the other hand, there is a strong advantage in not having to worry about many stockholders clamoring to redeem their shares when the market goes down.

The price of closed-end shares depends wholly on the demand for the shares of a particular closed-end fund. The shares of most closed-end funds are listed on the various stock exchanges. Regular brokerage fees are paid when the shares are bought and sold through brokers on the various exchanges or through the over-the-counter market.

All closed-end funds issue common stocks. Some also have preferred stock, bonds, and/or bank loans.

Before World War II the closed-end companies were very popular with the investing public, but after the war they lost out to some of the more aggressively promoted open-end companies. A relatively recent development in closed-end funds that may help restore their popularity is the *dual-purpose fund.* A dual-purpose corporation issues two entirely different kinds of stock—income shares and capital shares. Holders of the capital shares receive all the gains from the increase in the capital of the corporation but none of the income. The income shareholders receive all the income from all the shares purchased by the fund but none of the increase in capital. A prospective closed-end-fund investor has the choice of buying one or both types of shares. Investors in the dual-purpose fund must remember, however, that the life of the dual-purpose fund has a predetermined termination date. When the fund is dissolved, the capital gains shareholders receive all of the capital gains. The income shareholders have already received all the income earned through the years, so they recieve only a stated redemption price.

Open-End Investment Companies

An open-end investment company is popularly called a mutual fund. Like a closed-end company, a mutual fund sells its shares to various small investors and then invests the proceeds in shares of other corporations, the profits or losses from which are shared by the shareholders of the mutual fund. However, mutual funds can sell all the shares that investors will buy.

This is why they are called open-end in contrast to the closed-end corporations discussed previously. A mutual fund issues its shares continually as it sells them. This leads, of course, to very aggressive selling practices and to higher commissions for brokerage firms.

Mutual funds will buy shares back from their investors at any time at a price calculated twice a day. The price is determined by dividing the total number of shares outstanding into the market value of the stocks held by the fund. The product of this computation is called the *net asset value*.

Mutual Fund Objectives. The largest group of mutual funds handle diversified common stocks, but some specialize in balanced funds (common stock, preferred stock, and bonds), special industry funds, or income funds. Still others are classified, by objectives, such as short-term capital gain or long-term growth.

Mutual funds have a number of advantages over individual investments:

- The funds can invest in a number of different industries, and thus spread the risk.
- The funds can afford to engage management and investment experts, and to provide the continual supervision that the average investor cannot afford.
- Automatic investment plans enable a small investor to build up share investments on a regular basis.
- An investor in mutual funds can arrange to withdraw a certain amount on a monthly, quarterly, or annual basis as a retirement plan.

The main disadvantage of investing in mutual funds is the purchase or loading fee. The loading fee is used to cover the expenses of advertising and selling mutual funds. Fortunately, however, there are now many successful no-load funds which are doing as well as the load funds. But since they do not advertise extensively and do not employ salespeople, it is more difficult to obtain information about them.

New Types of Mutual Funds. Recently many mutual funds have become financial service institutions rather than just common stock specialists. By dropping loading charges and developing new types of funds, such as the following, they have attracted billions of dollars of investment money.

Municipal Bond Funds. A recent change in the federal income tax law opened up a huge market in tax-exempt municipal bonds. These bonds are issued by city, state, and federal agencies. Although they usually yield only about 5-percent interest, the fact that they are exempt from federal income tax means that for a taxpayer in the 28-percent federal tax bracket, the 5-percent yield is equivalent to almost 7 percent; in the 36-percent bracket, it is equivalent to 8 percent; in the 50-percent bracket, it is equivalent to 10 percent. Naturally, the municipal bond mutual funds have attracted a large amount of money that was formerly deposited in savings-bank time certificates.

Money-Market Funds.   Since 1974, many of the large funds have been taking advantage of the phenomenal increase in short-term interest rates to move into the money-market business. These funds invest in short-term U.S. government securities, bank money instruments, and commercial debt instruments, whose yields move up quickly when short-term rates go up. During 1979, when interest rates were high, these funds were paying a return of from 8 to 13 percent after commissions.

Some money-market funds have set up checking privileges, which enable the investor to transfer money from the fund by writing a check. Interest continues to increase in the investor's account until the check is cleared through the bank on which it was drawn. This flexibility has real appeal to many alert consumers.

Table 10-1 lists the addresses of some of the larger money-market mutual funds.

Mutual Funds Market.   The trading in mutual fund shares is reported in the financial and business sections of most urban newspapers, as well as in the *Wall Street Journal* and other financial publications. Figure 10-5 shows the standard format of a mutual fund report. The NAV column gives the net asset value of a mutual fund's shares, which each mutual fund calculates twice a day. This column is called the bid price in some newspapers.

The third column gives the buying price. In some papers, it is called the asked price. A buyer of fund A has to pay $5.40 for each share; apparently this fund has a load charge (sales fee) of 8 percent.

In the no-load funds the net asset value is the price of a share. Therefore, the buy or asked column shows the letters NL for no load. This is true of fund B. The figure in the change column is the difference between the sell or bid price yesterday and the sell or bid price today. The first quotation for fund C shows $10.00 as the sell or bid price today. Since the CHG column shows −.05 since yesterday, the bid price for fund C must have been $10.05.

The money-market and municipal bond funds are not often listed in daily newspapers. Since their return is computed monthly rather than daily, investors generally receive the latest returns directly from the com-

TABLE 10-1. The Ten Largest Money-Market Funds

	Minimum opening investment
Merrill Lynch Ready Assets Trust 165 Broadway, New York, NY 10080	$5,000
Dreyfus Liquid Assets 600 Madison Ave., New York, NY 10022	$2,500
Fidelity Daily Income Trust 82 Devonshire St., Boston, MA 02109	$5,000
Reserve Fund 810 Seventh Ave., New York, NY 10019	$1,000
InterCapital Liquid Asset Fund 130 Liberty St., New York, NY 10006	$5,000
Cash Reserve Management 1 Battery Park Plaza, New York, NY 10004	$10,000
Paine Webber CashFund	$5,000
Scudder Managed Reserves 175 Federal St., Boston, MA 02110	$1,000
Moneymart Assets 100 Gold Street, New York, NY 10038	$1,000
Rowe Price Prime Reserve Fund 100 E. Pratt St., Baltimore, MD 21202	$2,000

	NAV	Buy	Chg
Fund A	5	5.40	. . .
Fund B	5	NL	. . .
Fund C	10	10.80	− .05

FIGURE 10-5. Mutual Funds

pany. One periodical that does keep tabs on these funds is *Money* magazine's Fundwatch.

BUYING AND SELLING SECURITIES

Sources of Information

The first step in entering the investment market is to start reading about securities. Fortunately, this is a simple process.

Newspapers and Periodicals.   Most newspapers published in metropolitan areas and their suburbs contain daily reports on investment opportunities and processes. To name one or two of them may seem an injustice to the many others, but the *New York Times,* an excellent daily and Sunday paper, has a special section on business and financial news, and the *Wall Street Journal,* published Monday through Friday, is a newspaper specializing in financial and business news. Other outstanding specialized publications include *Barrons, Business Week,* and *Forbes.* Monthly, the U.S. government publishes the *Survey of Current Business* and *Business Conditions Digest.* These publications are available in some public libraries and in many college and university library reading rooms.

PROSPECTIVE INVESTORS

Put adequate emergency funds into low-risk savings first.
Study the market.
Hire a qualified broker.
Diversify.
Watch your investments closely.

In addition, there are many industry journals published either by trade organizations or by publishing companies. For example, there are specialized journals devoted to the fields of advertising, canning, chemicals, computers, construction, data processing, drugs and cosmetics, engineering, gas and oil, iron, paper, printing, and railways.

Stock Brokerage Firms. Most of the nationally known brokerage firms publish and distribute, free of charge, pamphlets and other publications dealing with financial securities of all kinds. In addition, a telephone call or a postcard to any reputable brokerage firm will assure you a personal interview with a broker's representative, called an account executive. Be sure to select a brokerage firm and an account executive by recommendation and reputation rather than by chance.

Stock Exchanges. The two largest stock exchanges, the New York Stock Exchange, called the Big Board or NYSE, and the American Stock Exchange, called the AMEX or ASE, publish pamphlets and materials relating to financial securities and their operations.

Using high-speed computers, the New York Stock Exchange re-

FIGURE 10-6. Investment Publications

cently compiled an index bearing its name. The index shows the average prices and net changes of all the stocks traded on the NYSE day by day. The exchange also publishes other indexes including a composite common stock index, an industrial stock index, a transportation stock index, a financial stock index, and a utility stock index. It is also well known for its bond rating service.

In addition to educational materials dealing with its operation and investments, the American Stock Exchange publishes an index of the stocks traded on the ASE.

Both the New York and American Stock Exchanges encourage visits to their facilities in New York City. Other major stock exchanges you might visit include the Pacific Coast Stock Exchange (PCSE), with trading floors in Los Angeles and San Francisco, and the Midwest Stock Exchange in Chicago. There are other regional and local stock exchanges serving Philadelphia-Baltimore-Washington (PBW), Boston, Montreal, Toronto, Detroit, Pittsburgh, and other cities.

Financial Services. Many organizations publish and sell financial advice. Some of the same organizations also compile and publish various securities averages that indicate price trends.

Among the best known is the Dow Jones Company, which also publishes the *Wall Street Journal.* It compiles the Dow Jones Averages, price indexes for thirty industrial stocks, twenty transportation stocks, fifteen utility stocks, and a composite of the sixty-five stocks. The stocks in each group are shown in Table 10-2. They have been selected to show a cross-section of the market leaders at a given time. Many of them are high-quality blue chips. The sixty-five are listed every Monday in the *Wall Street Journal.* The Educational Services Bureau of Dow Jones also publishes many information bulletins about investments and compiles commodity indexes. One of their important free publications is a *List of Free Materials Available to Educators.*

Standard and Poor's Corporation also publishes a large variety of financial and investment information. Among the best known publications is their *Stock Guide,* published monthly in a pocket-sized handbook. It contains important facts about many common and preferred stocks and a bulletin service on all the leading corporations. Standard and Poor's is also the compiler of the Standard and Poor's Averages, indexes for 425 industrial stocks, 50 utilities, 24 railroads, and a composite of all those stocks. Since this is a broader compilation than the DJA, it is considered a very good indicator of the overall trend of the stock market. It appears daily in the *Wall Street Journal,* the *New York Times,* and many other newspapers. Information about many industries can also be obtained from the annual revisions of *Industry Surveys,* published by Standard and

TABLE 10-2. The Dow Jones, A Weekly Listing of 65 Stocks

Thirty stocks used in Dow Jones Industrial Average:

Allied Chemical	General Foods	Owens-Illinois
Aluminum Company	General Motors	Procter & Gamb
Amer Brands	Goodyear	Sears Roebuck
Amer Can	Inco	Std Oil of Calif
Amer Tel & Tel	IBM	Texaco
Bethlehem Steel	Inter Harvester	Union Carbide
DuPont	Inter Paper	United Technologies
Eastman Kodak	Johns-Manville	US Steel
Exxon	Merck	Westinghouse El
General Electric	Minnesota M&M	Woolworth

Twenty Transportation Stocks:

American Air	MoPac Corp	Southern Pacific
Burlington North	Norfolk & West'n	Southern Ralway
Canadian Pacific	Northwest Air	Transway Int'l
Chessie System	Pan Am World Air	Trans World
Consolid Freight	St. Louis–San Fran	UAL Inc
Eastern Air Lines	Santa Fe Indus	Union Pac Corp
McLean Trucking	Seaboard Coast	

Fifteen Utility Stocks:

Am Elec Power	Consol Nat Gas	Panhandle EPL
Cleveland E Ill	Detroit Edison	Peoples Gas
Colum-Gas Sys	Houston Indust	Phila Elec
Comwlth Edison	Niag Mohawk P	Pub Serv E&G
Consol Edison	Pacific Gas & El	Sou Cal Edison

Poor's. The surveys are brief, comprehensive reports on a long list of selected industries.

Moody's Investors Service publishes *Moody's Manuals,* comprehensive annual reports on thousands of corporations and government agencies in various fields. The reports include each organization's history and complete financial details for a period of years. Moody's also publishes a weekly *Bond Survey* and a bimonthly *Bond Record,* as well as one-page summaries of individual bond issues. In addition, it has a highly recognized bond rating service.

The Value Line is a publisher of charts that show the performance of leading stocks. Each chart carries an opinion of how that stock is likely to perform over the next twelve months and the next three to five years. The company also supplies reports on special situations and market observations and advice, as well as a report on the Value Line Fund.

Wiesenberger Services publishes *Investment Companies,* an annual evaluation of the performance and rating of the various mutual funds, arranged by fund objectives into growth funds, growth income funds, income funds, and balanced funds. Wiesenberger also computes and publishes *Wiesenberger Mutual Fund Indexes.*

Corporations Themselves. The Securities and Exchange Commission (SEC) requires the preparation of a prospectus before a securities issue is approved. Written for potential investors, the prospectus includes a financial statement and a full description of the corporation, the company's business, the company's financial status, the proposed issue and where listed, and other outstanding security issues.

In addition, public corporations usually prepare at least one annual report to stockholders. The yearly report includes a letter from the president, information about the corporation's present and future prospects, and financial statements.

It is quite obvious from all the sources mentioned in this section that the prospective investor can learn much by investigating *before* investing!

Making Security Purchases and Sales

Once you have obtained a considerable volume of information about the stocks, bonds, or mutual funds you are interested in purchasing, the next step is to visit the broker you have selected. The following definitions of stock market terminology may help you with this encounter.

Bear or Bull: A bear is an investor who believes that the market is *going down.* On the other hand, a bull feels that the market will be *going up.*

Quotes: The broker will ask the computer terminal for a quote (quotation) on the stock desired. The answer may be "ask, 9½; bid, 9¼." This means that the last offer to sell was at $9.50, and the last potential buyer offered to pay $9.25. Quotes are given in eighths of a dollar.

Buy or Sell at Market: The buyer or seller is willing to transact a deal at the same rate as the last market sale.

Round or Odd Lot: A round lot of stock is 100 shares, or a unit of 100. An odd lot is any amount less than 100 shares.

Good-Till-Canceled Order (GTC): An order to buy or sell that remains in force until it is canceled.

Limit Order: An order to sell a stock at no less than a certain price. The limit order becomes a "sell at market" order when the stock reaches that price.

Dollar Cost Averaging: An investor may order that a specified amount of money be invested in the same long-term growth stock at regular intervals (monthly, quarterly, etc.) over a long period of time. When the price is high, fewer shares will be bought. When prices go down, more shares will be obtained. Many consumers find this a convenient way to make investing a habit.

Ex-Dividend or Record Date: The owner of a stock on a specified date after a dividend has been declared will receive the dividend. Anyone who buys after the ex-dividend date will not receive a dividend until the next dividend payment. Theoretically, the price of a stock should dip on the ex-dividend date by the amount of the dividend.

Street Name: If an investor prefers to let the brokerage firm hold the securities purchased, the stocks are held in the name of the broker rather than in the owner's name. The securities are then said to be in a street name.

Confirmation and Commission

Once a purchase or sale of securities has been completed, a notification of the transaction is sent to the investor. The investor is told how much the stock cost, plus how much commission is due to the broker for services performed. Brokerage firms no longer are allowed to fix commissions on an industrywide basis. As a result, more flexibility can be found from firm to firm. Another result of the abolishment of fixed fees was the emergence of discount brokerage firms. These firms do not give investment advice—they only buy and sell on the investor's instructions. Savings on commissions can only be realized on orders exceeding $1,200, however, as most firms, including the discount firms, have a minimum commission of $25 to $30 for each transaction.

Investing in securities is not a one-time transaction. You should constantly watch your investment, selling or switching when you have determined that it is in your best interest to do so. Consult your broker regularly for advice.

KEOGHS AND IRAS

While most of you will participate in a pension fund that is managed for you, some of you will have to manage your own pension plan. Two federal laws, the Employment Retirement Income Security Act and the Keogh Act, now allow qualified persons to form their own pension accounts using, among other vehicles, the popular savings account. The two retirement laws were created to aid two groups who formerly were without formal incentives to save for retirement.

The Keogh plan allows the self-employed to set up a tax-deferred retirement plan. An individual setting up such a plan may set aside 15 percent of income up to $7,500. This "nest egg" will not be taxed until it is actually used as retirement income after age seventy and a half. A person who is covered by a retirement plan in a regular job may set aside up to $750 earned by moonlighting. The 15-percent limitation does not apply in such a situation.

The Individual Retirement Plan (IRA) covers persons who work for an employer but who do not participate in any employer-sponsored retirement plan. The employer may not have a pension, profit-sharing, or stock-bonus retirement plan, or the employee may not choose to participate in such a plan. The IRA cannot be used in addition to an employer-sponsored retirement program. The employee who qualifies may contribute 15 percent of earnings up to $1,500 for an individual account and $1,750 for a joint account with a nonworking spouse.

Both the Keogh and the IRA plans offer a great deal of flexibility to the prospective user who studies their provisions carefully. Money may be placed in banks, in savings and loans, in mutual funds, in U.S. retirement bonds (available from the Federal Reserve), or in insurance companies (in the form of annuities).

Both plans have rather rigid early withdrawal rules and penalties. If the money is withdrawn before age fifty-nine and a half, except in the case of death or disablement, a 10-percent penalty must be paid, plus income taxes on the full amount. Therefore, this is a commitment that should be well planned and carefully selected. Since the number of institutions offering such plans has proliferated, and the various plans differ substantially in quality and in focus, it is most important that you analyze your investment goals. If your target is an 8- to 10-percent rate of growth, the time certificates offered by financial institutions may be your best course. If you are looking for a 12-percent rate of growth, more risk must be added, in which case you might want some bonds and money-market mutual funds for safety, as well as real estate or securities to provide a higher return. If your investment goal requires an even higher return more risk must be added; to supplement a base of safe investments, one might introduce more speculative stock, more real estate, or even investment in precious metals.

ANNUITIES

Purchase of an annuity is another way to provide for a regular retirement income. Although the word annuity is derived from the Latin word meaning year, annuity payments can cover any specified period of time —a month, a quarter, a year. An annuity is a contract in which the insurance company agrees to pay certain benefits to the individual at specified times for life in return for specific payments at certain intervals.

The amount the annuitant pays and the benefits he or she receives are determined from the same mortality tables that are used in life insurance calculations. The size of the benefit payments increases with the age at which the payout begins. Why? The older an individual is when payout begins, the fewer will be the periods in which benefits will be received. Thus an annuity is especially advantageous to a person who, because of heredity, seems to have good prospects for a long life. Since women have a longer life expectancy, they have to pay slightly more than a man of the same age to receive the same benefits.

An annuity has two periods. In the first period, the purchaser pays premiums of a fixed amount, on which interest accumulates until the predetermined payout date. On that date, the contract matures and the cash value is converted to a lifetime income payable to the annuitant.

Types of Annuities

An annuity may be purchased either with a lump-sum payment or in installments. An annuity purchased with a lump-sum payment is called a *single-premium annuity.* A single premium of $1,000 might buy a man of sixty-five a lifetime monthly income of about $8.00. When annuities are purchased on an installment plan of monthly, quarterly, semiannual, or annual payments, the funds paid in accumulate and earn interest until the payout period starts. An annuity paid for in yearly installments is called an *annual-premium annuity.*

Depending on when the payout period starts, an annuity is either immediate or deferred. An *immediate annuity* provides an income starting one month, three months, six months, or one year after the purchase date. This type requires the payment of a large premium in a short time, so very often the immediate annuity is a single-premium annuity. When payment to the annuitant begins some years after the company has been paid in full, the contract is called a *deferred annuity.*

Annuities have several different types of payment provisions, described below.

Straight Life Annuity.   The income in a straight life annuity terminates with the death of the annuitant. The straight life annuity has no cash value at any time after the income payments to the annuitant start.

Installment-Refund Annuity.   The installment-refund annuity provides that if the annuitant dies before the total amount of annuity income equals or exceeds the purchase price, the difference will be paid to a named beneficiary or the estate in installments of the same amount. The income payments from an installment-refund annuity are smaller than from a comparable straight life annuity.

Cash-Refund Annuity.   A cash-refund annuity resembles an installment-refund annuity, except that the balance of the purchase price is paid to the named beneficiary or the estate in one lump sum. The yield of a cash-refund annuity is slightly lower than the yield of an installment-refund annuity.

Life Annuity with Stipulated Payments.   In the life annuity with stipulated payments, the annuitant is guaranteed a specified lifetime income. If death occurs before a stated number of years, the payments will be continued to a designated beneficiary until the end of that period. If no beneficiary survives, a lump-sum payment of the unpaid balance will be made to the estate.

Joint-Life-and-Survivorship Annuity.   In a joint-life-and-survivorship annuity there are several annuitants, and income payments continue as long as any of the annuitants remain alive. The contract may be purchased on either a single-premium or annual-premium basis and may be either an immediate or a deferred annuity.

Advantages of Annuities

One reason annuities have become popular in recent years is because income tax need not be paid until the annuitant has withdrawn more than the original investment plus interest. Another reason is that the interest rates, which are guaranteed for one to seven years, depending on state laws, have risen to about 7 percent. Also, insurance companies are now selling annuity plans through investment brokers, who often understand the viewpoint of investors better than insurance salespeople do.

Annuities are of major interest to people who have accumulated or are in the process of accumulating a sizable sum of money that they want to invest for future income at the lowest possible income tax rate. Young people are usually more interested in savings accounts, home ownership, or stocks and bonds.

A NOTE ABOUT OTHER INVESTMENTS

Real Estate

The family home has been the most reliable of all investments in combating expected and unexpected inflation. Return on investment averaged nearly 15 percent annually during the 1970s, and it looks as though the 80s may bring more of the same. Many people do especially well buying homes that look shabby but require no major renovation—new owners will redecorate the dwelling and then sell it at a handsome profit.

Others invest in property such as apartment houses, raw land, and office buildings. A traditional investment for many is to buy a two-flat dwelling and then to live in one half and rent the other. Some caution is advised in the area of apartment rental, however, as rent control is beginning to spread to various parts of the country. Rent control has made it difficult for many landlords to profit, especially during periods of inflation.

Collectibles

Many investors enjoy making their investments hobbies as well. The hobbyist must remember, however, that he or she is competing against professionals, so investments may be risky and expensive. As the investments become riskier, they move into a realm of speculation.

The United Buying Service of Boston offers the following advice about investing in collectibles:

1. Deal only with reputable dealers.
2. Put no more than 20 percent of your investment capital into "hard" assets.
3. Plan how you will get rid of them.
4. Insure them.
5. Invest for a long term.[4]

---

[4]"The Bull Market for 'Collectibles,'" *U.S. News & World Report,* August 13, 1979, p. 88.

Before you move into a particular field of collectibles, be sure to read up on it.

Whether you are planning a Keogh or IRA or accumulating an investment portfolio from your savings, investigate before you invest. Don't rely on the fast promise of a big return, or the promise that an investment is tax-exempt when it is really only tax-deferred, or promises that the stated rate is the legal maximum when it is not. Investing can be rewarding, but it is definitely not a task to be taken lightly.

QUESTIONS FOR DISCUSSION

1. How do corporations choose whether to sell stocks or bonds to the public?
2. When one chooses an investment, dividend income and growth of capital must be considered. What circumstances would lead an investor to value one over another?
3. Many people are considered to be indirect investors in spite of the fact that they have never purchased securities. How is this possible?
4. What is the disadvantage of buying a small number of low-value shares? How can an individual avoid this problem?
5. Define yield on investment.
6. What is the difference between interest and dividends?
7. Distinguish between a cash dividend and a stock dividend.
8. Define market value and book value. Is it possible for book value to be higher than market value? If so, give an example of when this might occur.
9. Is a high dividend yield important in the selection of a common stock?
10. Define growth company and blue-chip company.
11. Is a cumulative preferred stock a guaranteed investment?
12. What should a bond investor check before purchasing a bond?
13. Define a closed-end fund and an open-end mutual fund.
14. What is the advantage of a no-load fund?
15. Compare the purpose of an annual report and that of a company prospectus.
16. Is a municipal bond fund a good investment for someone who wants to avoid income tax payments?

PERSONAL EXPERIENCE PROJECTS

1. Prepare a report or chart comparing various investments (savings account, savings certificate, stocks, bonds, mutual funds, real estate, gold, antiques, etc.). Evaluate each on the basis of safety, yield, inflation resistance, liquidity, and expenses involved.
2. Obtain copies of the annual reports of several companies. Evaluate the financial status of the organizations and their potential as investment prospects.
3. Read various articles in the *Wall Street Journal* regarding stock prices, company profits, dividend reports, and other business news. Determine which information could be helpful in making investment decisions.
4. Talk to a stock broker about the various investment plans available to consumers. Obtain suggestions as to the best investments for consumers of various ages and income levels.
5. Evaluate three stocks by researching the prices and dividends for the past five years, following current stock prices and earnings reports, and obtaining a copy of each company's prospectus from a stock broker.
6. Research the prices and yields of three companies' bonds and various municipal bonds over the past few years. Make suggestions for wise investments in the bond market.
7. Talk to a mutual fund salesperson and people who own mutual funds. Obtain information on the different types of funds, current prices, past earnings, and prospects for future growth.
8. Talk to someone who owns his or her own business. Discuss the advantages and disadvantages of self-employment as a financial investment.
9. Survey people who have invested in real estate, gold, antiques, stamps, or rare coins. Evaluate the financial and psychological benefits of these investment items.

11

PURSUING
CONSUMER
COMPLAINTS

A 1977 poll by Louis Harris for Sentry Insurance Company revealed widespread disenchantment with the marketplace. Almost two out of three consumers felt that they were getting a worse deal in the marketplace than they had received ten years earlier. According to the survey, people are "gravely concerned" about consumer problems such as

· poor product quality
· dangerous products
· misleading advertising and labeling
· soaring prices
· inadequate service and repair
· lack of sufficient redress of complaints
· confusing warranties
· lack of justice in the marketplace.

The best way for consumers to avoid these problems is to use all the information available to them in making buying decisions. However, when problems do arise, it is important that consumers make their dissatisfaction known. The general rate of complaining about consumer problems is extremely low. Ralph Nader's Center for the Study of Responsive Law completed a three-year study on consumer complaints in

1976. The survey involved 2,419 telephone interviews conducted in thirty-four cities. The results showed that more than one out of four purchases resulted in a real or imagined buyer problem. However, only about a third of these problems resulted in a complaint, in spite of the fact that consumers who did complain received satisfaction from business 56.4 percent of the time. Even more surprising is the fact that only 1.2 percent of the problems identified by consumers became known to a Better Business Bureau, consumer office, or other third party. And of those handled by the complaint-handling agencies, only about a third were resolved. Court action was used as a remedy in less than one in every thousand cases. The obvious conclusions are that the majority of people don't complain, that hardly anyone uses consumer complaint-handling agencies, and that the results are mixed even for those who do complain.

Why don't more consumers complain? Many do not consider the problem important enough for the amount of time, money, and energy a complaint would involve. Others probably feel that it would not do much good to complain. Still others simply do not know where or how to complain. The first reason is a consumer value judgment. The second reason is a combination of an individual consumer value judgment and a statement about the condition of the complaint-handling mechanisms in many business organizations. The third reason is the one we will tackle in this chapter, which will discuss the how and where of settling consumer complaints.

The chapter is organized around the following game plan for complaining:

1. First return to the point of sale. If necessary, go to the top (hot-line number, president, consumer affairs specialist).
2. Seek third-party help. Try locally first; then try state and national groups, private or governmental.
3. Take legal action.

RETURNING TO THE POINT OF SALE

When a problem is turned over to a third party, the organization will ask what action the individual has taken. Therefore, the first step in pursuing a complaint is to follow self-help procedures.

The following "famous last words" summarize some common problems:

"This is only the second day of the sale—you mean to tell me you're out of the merchandise?"

"It doesn't work—what do you mean it's not covered in the warranty?"

"I don't want a credit—I want my cash back!"

Sounds frustrating, doesn't it? At least in each of these instances the individual is taking the first important step—complaining! It isn't enough to stay at home and howl in exasperation or to rant and rave to your friends. Do something about it! The initial complaint may be oral or written, depending on the situation.

Face-to-Face Complaints

It does not take a grizzled fighter to complain. An ordinary person can be just as effective. In order to initiate a complaint, you must go not only to the original source but to the right person on the receiving line. Rather than deliver your problem to the first salesperson, ask for someone who has the power to resolve the complaint.

When you have found the right person—and that sometimes takes some firmness on your part—begin with the solution to your problem. If you want a refund, begin with "I want a refund on these shoes" and not "I am unhappy with these shoes—what can you do about it?" The problem with the second approach is that the solution suggested may be just the one you do not want. You say that sounds too "pushy"? Pushy is not the word for it—the word these days is *assertive*. In their book *Your Perfect Right,* Robert Alberti and Michael Emmons list the components of assertive behavior:

> Increasingly systematic observations of assertive behavior have led many behavioral scientists to conclude that there are a number of elements which constitute an assertive act. In our work helping others to develop greater assertiveness, we have given particular attention to these components:
>
> Eye contact: Looking directly at another person when you are speaking to him is an effective way of declaring that you are sincere about what you are saying, and that it is directed to him or her.
>
> Body posture: The "weight" of your messages to others will be increased if you face the person, stand or sit appropriately close to him, lean toward him, hold your head erect.
>
> Gestures: A message accented with appropriate gestures takes on an added emphasis (overenthusiastic gesturing can be a distraction!).
>
> Facial expression: Ever see someone trying to express anger while smiling or laughing? It just doesn't come across. Effective assertions require an expression that agrees with the message.
>
> Voice tone, inflection, volume: A whispering monotone will seldom

convince another person that you mean business, while a shouted epithet will bring his defenses into the path of communication. A level, well-modulated conversational statement is convincing without being intimidating.

Timing: Spontaneous expression will generally be your goal, since hesitation may diminish the effect of an assertion. Judgment is necessary, however, to select an appropriate occasion.

Content: We save this obvious dimension of assertiveness for last to emphasize that, although what you say is clearly important, it is often less important than most of us generally believe. We encourage a fundamental honesty in interpersonal communication, and spontaneity of expression. In our view, that means saying forcefully, "I'm damn mad about what you just did!" rather than "You're an S.O.B.!" People who have for years hesitated because they "didn't know what to say" have found the practice of saying something, to express their feelings at the time, to be a valuable step toward greater spontaneous assertiveness.[1]

Telephone Complaints

Although telephone complaints require a somewhat different technique, voice tone, timing, and content are still important. Before you take action, make sure that you have paper handy for notetaking. You might even list points you wish to discuss.

Remember to be clear about the purpose of your phone call, the nature of your problem, and your demand. Above all, be fair but firm. Most businesses will try very hard to accommodate you, but there are some situations where it will take all of the firmness you can muster to obtain a satisfactory resolution of your complaint.

Letter Writing

In certain cases you will need to embark on a letter-writing campaign to get satisfaction. Such a process takes time, but it can be rewarding.

It is best to address the letter to a specific person within a firm. Many individual corporations, especially those dealing with retail goods, have established a consumer relations office managed by a consumer affairs professional. If the organization you are dealing with has such a position, address your letter to the director of consumer relations. The 1977 Harris

---

[1]From Alberti, Robert E., Ph.D., and Emmons, Michael L., Ph.D., *Your Perfect Right: A Guide to Assertive Behavior* (Second Edition). Copyright © 1974. Impact Publishers, Inc., San Luis Obispo, California. Reprinted by permission of the publisher.

poll for Sentry Insurance Company revealed that these consumer professionals are hardly consumer advocates in the traditional Ralph Nader sense. They may, however, have a good deal of influence on functions ranging from product development to advertising. Their professional organization, Society of Consumer Affairs Professionals (SOCAP), now numbers 750 members. If your target organization does not have such an executive, address your letter to the president.

To get the name of the appropriate individual within a firm, you might consult the following sources:

- City or town directory
- *Standard and Poor's Register of Corporation Directors and Executives*
- Business directories
- Government offices where names and addresses of company officers must be recorded.

The three reference works can probably be found in your public or university library. If you can't locate a name, address your letter to the appropriate position and not to "To whom it may concern."

If you mail a letter to corporation headquarters, it is best to send the letter by certified mail, with return receipt requested. If you are showing evidence of having paid by check, photocopy both sides of the check. The letter itself should fit easily on one (photocopied) page.

The first paragraph should include the background of the source of your complaint. It should cover a description of the product or service, the date on which the purchase took place, promises made at the time of the purchase, an explanation of the situation that has given rise to your complaint, and steps you have taken to resolve the problem up to this point.

The second paragraph should contain a solution that would satisfy you. Don't make your demand in a nasty tone, because this will only make the reader unsympathetic to your problem. It is a good idea to stress long-time patronage and satisfaction.

The third paragraph should include some good reason why the firm should answer your letter. You should always ask questions that require answers, such as "When will you do this for me?" or "Will you tell me when I may expect my refund?"

The purpose of a return to the point of sale is to give the company a chance to restore your good will. If this does not happen, your next step is to seek third-party assistance.

THIRD-PARTY ASSISTANCE

Better Business Bureau

Probably the best known consumer-complaint organization is the Better Business Bureau. The headquarters of this business-sponsored organization is at 1150 17th Street, N.W., Washington, DC 20036. Your local Better Business Bureau has the authority to provide you with information about local firms, including how long the companies have been in business and their record of reliability. Although the BBB handles complaints, it cannot give legal advice or bring legal action. The quality of service by BBBs differs significantly from one to another of its more than 140 local offices.

Better Business Bureau figures for 1976 show that the two primary targets of complaints were mail-order companies (number one) and auto dealers (number two). The Better Business Bureau also released figures on the percentages of complaints resolved by their organization in 1976 (see Table 11-1).

The BBB generally applies an arbitration approach to the handling of consumer complaints. The steps in the arbitration process are as follows:[2]

1. The Complaint. Customer takes complaint to businessman— only if this fails does he go to the Better Business Bureau.
2. Better Business Bureau. BBB tries to resolve case informally— if not, arbitration is offered.
3. Agreement to Arbitrate. Parties sign binding agreement to arbitrate agreed issues in dispute and submit to the BBB arbitration program.
4. Choosing an Arbitrator. Depending on the amount and location of the dispute and the program, the parties will either: select a single arbitrator from the pool of volunteers, or each select a person of his choice and the two so chosen pick a third arbitrator from the pool to serve as panel chairman.
5. Inspection. If necessary, an inspection of the product, repair job, or construction site is conducted with the BBB furnishing technical expertise as needed.
6. The Proceedings. Informal proceedings are before an arbitrator. Both parties may be represented, have witnesses, and give supporting evidence.

[2]"This Is How Arbitration Works," *Roanoke* (VA) *Times & World-News*, June 5, 1977.

7. The Award. The decision may resolve all issues in favor of one party or it may be "split" between the parties. In most states, a court of law will enforce an award without rehearing the case.

This procedure is strictly voluntary. The number of hearings held by BBBs in 1977 was over 4,600. In that year 104 of the 143 existing bureaus were involved in the arbitration process.

Industry Groups

Several industry groups have established consumer action panels to provide a direct means of solving complaints.

The oldest of the industry consumer action groups is MACAP

TABLE 11-1. Rate of Complaints Settled by Better Business Bureau

Highest Settlement		Lowest Settlement	
Category	Percent Settled	Category	Percent Settled
Department Stores	88.3	Legal Services	44.0
Credit Card Companies	88.3	Work-at-Home Companies	46.4
Hospitals/Clinics	86.0	Business Opportunity Companies	54.5
Banks	85.6	Reupholstering Shops	57.7
Magazines by Mail	85.1	Vacation Certificate Companies	58.2
Savings & Loans	84.4	Paving Contractors	59.0
Insurance Companies	84.3	Roofing Contractors	60.7
Hearing Aid Companies	84.2	Miscl. Home Maintenance	61.9
Chain Food Stores	83.9	Waterproofing Companies	63.9
Drug Stores	83.8	Auto Repair—Excluding Transmission	64.9
Music/Record Stores	83.5	Market Research Companies	65.1
Utility Companies	83.5	Home Remodeling Contractors	65.4
Manufacturers/Producers	83.2	Miscl. Automotive	66.3
Mail-Order Companies	83.1	Gasoline Service Stations	66.5
Wholesalers/Distributors	82.5	Hair Product Companies	66.8

Additionally, these categories scored in excess of 80-percent settlement: Consumer Finance/Loan Companies (82.0); Telephone Companies (81.5); Security Brokers/Dealers (81.0); Encyclopedia—Direct Sales (80.9).
Source: Council of Better Business Bureaus.

(Major Appliance Consumer Action Panel). The panel always includes from seven to ten members, none of whom are connected with the appliance industry. Independent studies on the success of this organization have been very positive. If you have a complaint involving a major appliance, after attempting to resolve it with the manufacturer, write to:

> MACAP
> 20 N. Wacker Drive
> Chicago, Il 60606
> (Call collect 312-236-3165)

Another large industry group which we have already mentioned is AUTOCAP. Automotive Consumer Action Panels are available in thirty-two areas of the country. Among their objectives is establishing channels at the state and local levels for automotive customers to voice their complaints and obtain action. To obtain the address of the nearest AUTOCAP, write to:

> National Automobile Dealers Association
> 8400 West Park Drive
> McLean, VA 22101
> (703-821-7000)

Two other industry groups are FICAP (Furniture Industry Consumer Action Panel), P.O. Box 951, High Point, NC 27261, and CRI-CAP (Carpet and Rug Institute Consumer Action Panel), P.O. Box 1568, Dalton, GA 30702.

Public libraries and consumer education departments in high schools, colleges, and universities are good sources of information for names and addresses of other industry panels.

Private Consumer Organizations

To secure information about the location of private consumer groups in your area, you might contact the Consumer Federation of America, Suite 406, 1012 14th Street, N.W., Washington, DC. Hundreds of local consumer groups belong to this powerful voice for the consumer. Another organization that coordinates the work of many local consumer agencies is the National Consumers League, 1522 K Street, N.W., Suite 406, Washington, DC 20005. And finally, action lines of newspapers, radios, and television stations are good sources of information as well as assistance.

Governmental Complaint Agencies

Following are descriptions of some organizations set up on the federal level to help consumers in specific areas.

CPSC

> U.S. Consumer Product Safety Commission
> Washington, DC 20207
> (Toll-free hotline: 800-638-2666; Maryland only: 800-492-2937)

CPSC's primary goal is to substantially reduce injuries associated with consumer products in or around the home, schools, and recreational areas. Congress directed the Commission to protect the public against unreasonable risks of injury associated with consumer products; to assist consumers in evaluating the comparative safety of consumer products; to develop uniform safety standards for consumer products and minimize conflicting state and local regulations; and to promote research and investigation into the causes and prevention of product-related deaths, illnesses, and injuries. The Commission sets and enforces mandatory safety standards for consumer products and in certain instances bans hazardous products. The Commission also conducts information and education programs to raise consumer awareness and to change behavior concerning product safety. The Commission operates the National Electronic Injury Surveillance System, which monitors 119 hospital emergency rooms nationwide for injuries associated with consumer products. The Commission deals with over 10,000 consumer products—from architectural glass, stairs, and power tools to stoves, ladders, and lawn mowers. The Commission was established by the Consumer Product Safety Act of 1972 and also has the authority under the Federal Hazardous Substances Act, Flammable Fabrics Act, Poison Prevention Packaging Act, and Refrigerator Safety Act. The following products generally are exempted from the Commission's authority under the CPSA: foods, drugs, cosmetics, medical devices, motor vehicles, boats, airplanes, tobacco, firearms, alcohol, and pesticides.

FDA

> Food and Drug Administration
> Department of Health, Education and Welfare
> 5600 Fishers Lane
> Rockville, MD 20852
> (301-443-3170)

FDA enforces the federal Food, Drug and Cosmetic Act and related laws to ensure the purity and safety of foods, drugs, and cosmetics, the safety of therapeutic devices, and the truthful, informative labeling of such products. Food additives, color additives, antibiotic drugs, insulin, and most prescription drugs are subject to pre-marketing approval by the Agency. Veterinary drugs are regulated to ensure that they are safe, effective, and properly labeled. FDA licenses the production of vaccines, serums, and other biologic drugs and regulates blood banks. The Agency administers the Fair Packaging and Labeling Act as it applies to products covered by the Food, Drug and Cosmetic Act. FDA also enforces radiation safety standards for products such as X-ray equipment, color televisions, lasers, sunlamps, and microwave ovens.

NHTSA

National Highway Traffic Safety Administration
Department of Transportation
400 7th Street, S.W.
Washington, DC 20590
(202-426-9550)

NHTSA writes and enforces safety standards which set minimum performance levels for certain parts of motor vehicles and for the vehicle as a unit. Its jurisdiction includes automobiles, trucks, buses, recreational vehicles, motorcycles, bicycles, mopeds, and all related accessory equipment. The Agency pursues allegations of vehicle defects both to assure manufacturer compliance with federal standards and to identify all vehicle defects that may lie outside the applicability of the standards. NHTSA regularly publishes public advisories and protection bulletins, fact sheets on current automotive problems, and a complete monthly report of its investigative activity and conclusions.

FTC

Federal Trade Commission
Pennsylvania Avenue at Sixth Street, N.W.
Washington, DC 20580
(202-962-0151)

The FTC was created by Congress in 1914 to eliminate unfair competition in business and to protect the public from abusive or deceptive advertising and business practices by sellers of goods or services. The Agency administers numerous federal laws designed to further these purposes.

TABLE 11-2. FTC Regional Offices

Atlanta	Los Angeles
Federal Trade Commission	Federal Trade Commission
Room 1000	Room 13209
1718 Peachtree Street, N.W.	Federal Building
Atlanta, GA 30309	11000 Wilshire Boulevard
(404) 881-4836	Los Angeles, CA 90024
Boston	(213) 824-7575
Federal Trade Commission	New York
Room 1301	Federal Trade Commission
150 Causeway Street	2243-EB, Federal Building
Boston, MA 02114	26 Federal Plaza
Chicago	New York, NY 10007
Federal Trade Commission	San Francisco
Suite 1437	Federal Trade Commission
55 East Monroe Street	450 Golden Gate Avenue
Chicago, IL 60603	Box 36005
Cleveland	San Francisco, CA 94102
Federal Trade Commission	(415) 556-1270
Room 1339	Field Station
Anthony J. Celebrezze	Federal Trade Commission
Federal Office Building	Room 605, Melim Building
1240 East 9th Street	333 Queen Street
Cleveland, OH 44199	Honolulu, HI 98613
(216) 522-4207	(808) 546-5685
Dallas	Seattle
Federal Trade Commission	Federal Trade Commission
Suite 2665	28th Floor, Federal Building
2001 Bryan Street	915 Second Avenue
Dallas, TX 75201	Seattle, WA 98174
(214) 749-3056	(206) 442-4655
Denver	Washington, D.C.
Federal Trade Commission	Federal Trade Commission
Suite 2900	6th Floor, Gelman Building
1405 Curtis Street	2120 L Street, N.W.
Denver, CO 80202	Washington, DC 20037
(303) 837-2271	(202) 254-7700

The FTC is headed by five commissioners and is divided into several bureaus, each composed of smaller divisions. Most directly affecting the public are the Bureau of Competition and the Bureau of Consumer Protection.

The Bureau of Competition carries out the Commission's principal antitrust functions, regulating practices that tend to restrain free competition or promote monopoly in interstate commerce.

The Bureau of Consumer Protection implements and enforces laws under the FTC's jurisdiction that are designed to protect consumers.

Headquartered in Washington, D.C., the FTC also has eleven regional offices and one smaller field station, enabling citizens to contact and deal with the agency in their own geographical areas (Table 11-2). Through these regional offices, the Commission conducts investigations and maintains an awareness of businesses' activities and their effects on consumers throughout the country.

Agriculture Department

Animal and Plant Health Inspection Service (202-447-8293)
Agricultural Marketing Service (202-447-6766)
Food and Nutrition Service
Extension Service
Independence Avenue between 12th and 14th Streets, N.W.
Washington, DC 20250

The Agriculture Department, through its subdivisions, inspects and grades meats, poultry, fruits, and vegetables; provides some nutrition information to consumers through labels required on meat, poultry, fruits, and vegetables; provides food to poor families through programs such as food stamps; carries out studies on human nutrition, home economics, and farm-oriented science; and works with adult and youth education programs in the fifty states.

General Agencies. If you are not sure which agency to consult, contact the Office of Consumer Affairs, the General Services Administration Consumer Information Center, or your Senator or Congressional representative.

The Office of Consumer Affairs, under the Department of Health, Education and Welfare, serves as a coordinator for inquiries and complaints on subjects such as high prices, poor quality, and the safety of products.

Table 11-3 lists the types of complaints the agency received in 1976. Their address is

Office of Consumer Affairs
Executive Office Building
17th Street and Pennsylvania Avenue, N.W.
Washington, DC 20201
(202-245-6093)

The U.S. General Services Administration Consumer Information Center was established expressly to advise individuals on the correct government office to contact for help with a particular problem. Write:

General Services Administration
Consumer Information Center
7th and D Streets, S.W.
Washington, DC 20407
(202-343-6171)

TABLE 11-3. Top Complaint Categories of 1977 at the Office of Consumer Affairs

---

Automobiles
Mail Orders
Business Practices
Credit
Appliances
Housing/Real Estate
Insurance
Food
Travel
Automobile Tires
Magazines
Television/Radio
Advertising
Watches/Clocks
Mobile Homes/Recreational Vehicles
Utilities
Home Repairs
Household Movers
Medical/Dental

Source: Arthur E. Rowse, ed., *HELP: The Useful Almanac, 1977–1978* (Washington: Consumer News, Inc., 1978), p. 91.

In addition, to inform consumer of the information available from the federal government, the Consumer Information Center publishes a free quarterly listing of approximately 250 free or low-cost publications of consumer interest. This *Consumer Information Index,* as well as the publications, is available from Consumer Information, Pueblo, CO 81009.

Attorney Generals.   Some cities and counties also have consumer offices; if yours does not, you can probably get help from the attorney general's office. In recent years many attorney generals have become the champions of people. Some of their actions have involved large numbers of people, as in the case of Oldsmobile owners whose cars had Chevrolet engines (General Motors was obliged to make financial and/or warranty adjustments). More often, however, they have involved cases where an individual was wronged. In order to utilize the powers of the attorney general's office you must be the victim of a fraud rather than a mere witness. The process for filing your complaint with the attorney general is very painless —usually you simply fill out a one-page form such as the one found in Figure 11-1. If your problem involves a legal angle, you might want to consider making the attorney general's office your first stop, for the attorney general's staff has the right to prosecute, whereas newspaper action lines, the BBB, and some local agencies do not have that important power. In fact, many of these organizations ask the aid of the attorney general's office in situations where they suspect fraud.

THE COURTS

Initiating lawsuits seems to be rapidly becoming a favorite American pastime. Between 1967 and 1978, the number of civil cases filed in federal courts nearly doubled (see Figure 11-2), and the number of cases in state courts has kept pace with the federal increases. Correspondingly, a record number of about 470,000 lawyers were practicing in 1978. This works out to about 1 lawyer for every 468 people, according to the American Bar Association.

Why are there so many lawsuits? In recent years Congress has passed many laws increasing government regulation of corporate and individual behavior, and these laws placed new avenues of litigation into the court system (see Table 11-4).

Another reason for the sharp increase in litigation is that American citizens are becoming more aggressive. They have begun to sue when once they would have resigned themselves to loss, either out of a feeling of helplessness or out of inability or lack of desire to pay the high costs of

Set 1

FRANK J. KELLEY
Attorney General
State of Michigan

CONSUMER PROTECTION DIVISION
Room 670, 525 West Ottawa
Lansing, Michigan 48913

CONSUMER COMPLAINT

(Please type or use black ink)
NOTE: Please separate Set 1 & 2 before filling out.

Complainant: _____

Complaint No.: _____

V.C. _____ S.I.C. _____

Received: _____

Investigation No.: _____

Closed: _____ Value: _____

DO NOT WRITE ABOVE THIS LINE

Company complaining against

Street address of company

City and state   Zip Code

Company's telephone   County

Date of transaction? _____

Did you sign a contract? _____
(please attach a copy)
  Where? _____

Name of salesperson? _____

If advertised, when? _____
  Where? _____

Date you complained to company? _____
  How? _____ To whom? _____

Is there a court action pending? _____
  Where? _____
  Your Attorney _____

1. Type or Print FIRMLY.

2. Use Additional Sheets if Needed.

3. REMEMBER: If we can't read your complaint we can't act.

Referred by: _____

_____

Walk in ☐

Mail ☐

COMPLAINT DETAILS

_____

_____

_____

_____

_____

_____

_____

_____

_____

_____

_____

_____

_____

_____

_____

PRINT YOUR NAME   BUSINESS PHONE:

STREET NO.   HOME PHONE:

CITY   COUNTY   STATE   ZIP CODE   YOUR SIGNATURE

FIGURE 11-1. The Attorney General's Consumer Complaint Form

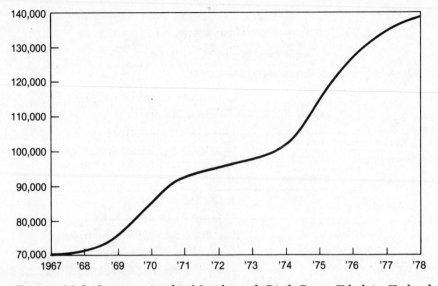

FIGURE 11-2. Increase in the Number of Civil Cases Filed in Federal Court. (Administration Office, U.S. Courts.)

legal action. This is not to say that cost is not still a problem. According to Tom Goldstein, "The cost of litigating has become so high that a day in court may cost as much as $2,000 for a lawyer and $1,000 for a transcript."[3] And according to an American Bar Association survey, about two-thirds of all adult Americans do not hire lawyers even when they seem to be needed. But a series of new developments in the legal field, such as the advent of do-it-yourself lawsuits, prepaid legal services, legal clinics, class action suits, and legal aid organizations, are helping consumers to either cope with or avoid the high price of a lawsuit.

Do-It-Yourself Lawsuits

In spite of the old maxim that "anyone who tries self-representation has a fool for a client," many people are now refraining from hiring attorneys for divorce and other standard legal matters such as small claims, wills, probate, bankruptcy, business incorporation, name changes, and real estate purchases. By completing his or her own legal forms, a participant in an uncontested divorce in a no-fault state can save a typical legal fee of $300 to $400 or more. Some divorce counselors tell their clients to avoid lawyers. And by filing a suit in small claims court, a consumer can

[3]"A Dramatic Rise in Lawsuits and Costs Concerns Bar," *New York Times,* May 18, 1977.

TABLE 11-4. Some New Regulations
That Have Increased Litigation in
Federal Courts

1970	Clean Air Amendments
	Consumer Credit Protection Amendments
	Fair Credit Reporting
	Occupational Safety and Health Act
1972	Black Lung Benefits
	Consumer Product Safety
	Equal Employment Opportunity
	Federal Election Campaign
	Water Pollution Control Amendments
1974	Antitrust Procedures and Penalties
	Employment Retirement Income Security
	Freedom of Information Amendments
	Speedy Trial
1975	Age Discrimination
	Consumer Goods Pricing
	Energy Policy & Conservation
1976	Consumer Leasing
	Equal Credit Opportunity Amendments
	Hart-Scott-Rodina Antitrust Improvements
	Toxic Substances Control
1977	Fair Debt Collection Practices Act

pursue a problem even though the amount in dispute is too small to be worth an attorney's time.

The attitude of many knowledgeable counselors seems to be that you should not get a lawyer unless you really need one. For a *Money* magazine article entitled "When to Take the Law into Your Own Hands," the magazine staff interviewed fifteen attorneys, including law professors, private practitioners, public interest lawyers, government lawyers, and staff members of the American Bar Association. The results of the survey are shown in Table 11-5.

Small Claims Courts.   If you wish to pursue a consumer problem involving a relatively small sum of money, your best course of action is to file a claim with your local small claims court. Small claims courts are found in every state. The maximum amount that may be sued for in one of these courts varies from $150 to $5,000, depending on the state (see Table 11-6). There are two major advantages of small claims courts. First, you don't need a lawyer. In some places lawyers are not even allowed. Hence legal costs are relatively low. Second, cases are dealt with swiftly. In most states cases are settled in a matter of a few weeks.

Small claims courts do, of course, have disadvantages, however. First, even if you win, it is not always easy to collect your money. Unless you are willing to invest further time exploring collection procedures, you may end up hiring a lawyer to collect your judgment. An out-of-court settlement is often a better way to collect damages, even if the settlement is for a smaller amount than you feel you deserve. Second, in some areas judges do not welcome *pro se* (without counsel) cases. Finally, it should also be mentioned that it is always possible for an individual to do himself or herself damage through ignorance of a point of law or precedent that should be mentioned in court.

But particularly if you have as evidence good records of the transaction in question, the small claims court may provide an effective solution to your consumer complaint. The small claims process is quite easy. The forms are not difficult to complete, and if you have any questions the court clerk is usually helpful in answering them. The complaint is filed in the county of the person being sued (the defendant). On most forms (see sample in Figure 11-3) all that is required is the following:

1. the plaintiff's name, residence address, and phone number
2. the defendant's name and place of residence, place of business or regular employment
3. the nature and amount of the plaintiff's claim, along with dates and other relevant information

TABLE 11-5. Fifteen Lawyers' Opinions about Hiring a Lawyer

The Legal Problem	Do You Need Counsel?		
	Yes	Maybe	No
Suing in a small claims court	0	0	15
Changing your name	0	1	14
Getting an uncontested divorce when there are no children or property complications	2	3	10
Adopting a child	7	2	6
Fighting a traffic ticket that could lead to a license suspension	7	6	2
Prodding an insurer to pay a claim	7	8	0
Incorporating a small business	8	3	4
Probating a will	8	3	4
Buying or selling a house	8	3	4
Defending your spouse and yourself against charges of disturbing the peace after a marital tiff	9	4	2
Writing a simple will	11	1	3
Defending your young son against a trespassing charge	11	1	3
Adding a bequest to a will	11	2	2
Defending your teenage daughter against a marijuana smoking charge	13	0	2
Suing in civil court	13	2	0
Defending a member of your family against a shoplifting charge	15	0	0
Getting a contested divorce	15	0	0

Source: Reprinted from the March 1975 issue of *Money* magazine by special permission; © 1975, Time Inc.

The accuracy with which you answer the questions is important, because service of the summons (the document notifying the defendant that he or she is being sued) may be difficult or even impossible if the address is incorrect. The fee for filing a complaint ranges from about $3 to $15, depending on the state and sometimes on the amount of the lawsuit. Some time before the court date, check to see that the papers have been delivered (or mailed) to the defendant. If the papers have not been served, you must appear but the trial will be postponed.

TABLE 11-6. Small Claims Court Dollar Limits

State	Maximum Amount of Suit	State	Maximum Amount of Suit
Alabama	$500	Nebraska	$500
Alaska	$1000	Nevada	$300
Arizona	$1000	New Hampshire	$500
Arkansas	$300	New Jersey	$500
California	$750	New Mexico	$2000
	($1500 in some counties)	New York	$1000
			$500 (justice court)
Colorado	$500		
Connecticut	$750	North Carolina	$500
Delaware	$1500	North Dakota	$1000
District of Columbia	$750	Ohio	$300
Florida	$1500	Oklahoma	$600
Georgia	$200	Oregon	$500
Hawaii	$300	Pennsylvania	$1000
	(no limit on security-deposit cases)	Rhode Island	$500
		South Carolina	$500
		South Dakota	$1000
Idaho	$1000	Tennessee	$5000
Illinois	$1000	Texas	$150
Indiana	$1500		$200 (employment contracts)
Iowa	$1000		
Kansas	$300		
Kentucky	$500	Utah	$400
Louisiana	$300	Vermont	$500
Maine	$800	Virginia	$5000
Maryland	$1000	Washington	$200
Massachusetts	$400		$300 (in some larger counties)
Michigan	$300		
Minnesota	$1000 (municipal court)	West Virginia	$1500
		Wisconsin	$1000
	$550 (county court)	Wyoming	$200 (informal procedure)
Mississippi	$500		$100 (formal procedure)
Missouri	$500		
Montana	$1500 (district court)		
	$750 (justice's court)		

When the trial takes place, be yourself. Have your evidence ready, and bring witnesses who have direct knowledge about the case. After the case is heard, some time may pass before a decision is rendered—most often the decision will be mailed to you. If you win and collect, you will feel gratified. If you lose, at least you will have had your speedy day in court. If you win and have a hard time collecting, you might go to an attorney or a collection agency for help, or else write the whole thing off as a learning experience.

Other Courts. Although the procedure is somewhat more complicated, it is not overly difficult to file a *pro se* complaint in the larger courts. In many states do-it-yourselfers and self-help groups have been successful in winning legal battles allowing them to sell self-help kits or books describing the process. These kits include all the legal papers necessary for filing divorces and other types of cases in various states.

Prepaid Legal Services

A prepaid legal service plan is becoming a fringe benefit of membership in many groups, particularly unions. The group makes regular payments to a fund, which is used to pay for legal services rendered to members. According to the Department of Labor, at least three million people are covered by 3,500 such plans.

Prepaid legal service plans resemble group insurance plans. They typically cover wills, divorce or annulment, and real estate proceedings. The prepaid legal plans have been designed to help the middle- to lower-income people who do not already have lawyers.

One group in the forefront of the prepaid-legal-service movement is the Illinois Public Action Council, a group of forty-seven consumer and community organizations from throughout the state of Illinois. A local legal firm provides legal services to the members of the plan. Two options are offered:

1. For $125 annually, the plan offers comprehensive noncriminal legal services for matters such as wills, real estate closings, property tax assessment appeals, divorces, adoptions, and landlord-tenant problems. Also included in the annual fee is unlimited consultation on any legal matter.
2. For $50, one receives two hours of consultation on any of the prepaid subjects, plus below-market fees for any further legal action needed.

IN THE CIRCUIT COURT OF THE NINETEENTH JUDICIAL CIRCUIT
LAKE COUNTY, ILLINOIS

Complaint _____ Case No. _____

_____

_____   vs.   _____

_____

_____

Plaintiffs   Defendants

SMALL CLAIM COMPLAINT

I, the undersigned, claim that the defendant is indebted to the plaintiff in the sum of $ _____

_____ for _____

and that the plaintiff has demanded payment of said sum: that the defendant refused to pay the same and no part thereof has been paid; that the defendant resides at _____

_____ Phone No. _____ ; that

the plaintiff resides at _____

_____ Phone No. _____ ; in the State of Illinois.

_____ 19 ___

Name
Attorney for
Address   _____
City   (Signature of Plaintiff)
Telephone

AFFIDAVIT

_____ on oath states that the allegations in

this complaint are true.

_____

Signed and sworn to before me _____ , 19 ___ .

_____

Notary Public

SMALL CLAIM DOCKET

Complaint filed on _____ by _____ Clerk

Date Set _____

Date Reset _____

FEES		
CLERK'S		
Certified Mail		
Sheriff		
Execution		

Plaintiff ___ in Court.

Defendant ___ in Court.

Judgment for _____

$ _____ Cost $ _____

Stay _____ days

Against _____

_____

Dismissed as to _____

_____

_____

_____

Magistrate

COURT'S NOTATIONS

_____

_____

FIGURE 11-3. A Small Claim Complaint

The legal community has provided a good portion of any resistance to prepaid legal plans, mostly from fear of losing business. Only about half of the states allow group legal plans to be funded as an item of insurance. The prepaid legal plan will most likely emerge eventually as a fringe benefit for employees or as a share of the "insurance dollar" for the public.

Legal Clinics

A 1976 advertisement by the law firm of Bates and O'Steen in the *Arizona Republic* began a series of events that paved the way for advertising by lawyers. Eventually the U.S. Supreme Court upheld the law firm's First Amendment right to advertise. Thus the consumer can now benefit from advertising that often includes a lawyer's professional concentration, as well as his or her fees.

This advertising has spawned a new concept called the legal clinic. Legal clinics, which are springing up around the country, generally charge low fees for standardized services, such as uncontested divorces, bankruptcy, simple wills, and business incorporations. The low fees, made possible by the large volume of work and the extensive use of paralegals, are attracting many clients who had never before used a lawyer.

Class Action

Another legal development that has opened up a vast new area of consumer litigation is the introduction of the class action suit. In a class action suit a small group of owners of car XY 1975 model can bring a suit against Company X in behalf of a large group of owners. The total expense of bringing the class action suit is much lower than if each individual car owner sued the company.

Class (group) action suits have been described as a "disaster for American business" or a "boon to consumers," depending on who is asked. Mark Green of Congress Watch says that because it is easier to take 5¢ from many people than it is to take $50,000 from one person, the class action has made it possible for those who would "bilk in bulk" to be sued in bulk. Unfortunately, there are two roadblocks to such suits. One is the minimum $10,000 claim that is required to get into federal court. The other is a U.S. Supreme Court ruling that prohibits consumers from bringing class action suits in price-fixing cases if they did not deal directly with the price-fixing organization. In the test case, the state of Illinois could not recover the extra cost paid for public buildings because the state did not actually purchase the concrete blocks.

Legal Aid and Legal Services

If you cannot afford to pay a lawyer or even premiums on a prepaid plan, one of the nation's Legal Aid Society or Legal Service offices may be for you. These organizations are funded by foundations and public funds and provide free services for people who cannot afford legal services or court costs. Your local office may be located by looking in the telephone book. These agencies are generally staffed by attorneys who specialize in poverty law. In criminal matters, you may be assisted by a public defender if you lack funds to pay for a private attorney; one will be assigned to you if you so request.

Selecting a Private Attorney

If you cannot obtain legal assistance under a prepaid plan or from legal services and your case is not suitable for self-filing or for class action through a consumer group, you are faced with the task of selecting a private attorney. Locating the best attorney for your needs may take some research, especially if you are not familiar with the city or state. Following are some guidelines for persons seeking legal help:

- Talk to an expert in the field in which you plan to take legal action. This might be a marital counselor or a member of the clergy in the case of a divorce, or a physician or a labor union officer if the case involves personal injury.
- If there is a law school in your community, ask a law professor to refer you to a competent lawyer.
- Talk to people who have had problems similar to yours. They will tell you whether to hire or avoid the lawyer they hired.

Individual lawyers or small firms tend to be more general in the types of personal cases they accept, while large firms may concentrate on serving commercial clients rather than personal clients. In addition, smaller firms or individual lawyers will often give more personal attention to a client. However, a large firm is more likely to have on its staff specialists able to handle complex cases. The consumer has to decide which type of firm to select on the basis of the particular situation.

Whatever you decide, when you meet with the attorney you are thinking of engaging, there are several questions you might want to ask, such as, "Do you handle many cases like mine?" "Are paralegals employed to complete routine forms, and if so, will the savings in cost be passed along to me?" "How much personal attention will I get from your firm?"

"Will you be doing my legal work personally?" "How are your fees computed?"

There are several methods of computing legal fees:

- An attorney may take a case on a contingent fee basis. In this case fees are paid only if the lawyer is able to get results. This method is used primarily in personal injury suits, where the contingent fee may range from 25 to 60 percent.
- An attorney may charge by the hour for work performed.
- An attorney may charge a flat fee, such as $400 for a divorce or $200 for a bankruptcy.
- If a client requires an attorney's services on a regular basis, the attorney may ask for a retainer. A retainer is a payment in advance based on an estimate of services to be performed. If the work done by the lawyer exceeds the amount of the retainer, there will be an additional charge for the difference.

Where routine legal services are involved, the best method of payment seems to be to arrange a flat fee in advance. In personal injury cases, the contingent fee is often the most satisfactory arrangement. In any case, the purchase of legal services should entail the same careful shopping you devote to the purchase of any other consumer good or service.

Few people enjoy complaining, through the courts or otherwise, but the alternatives of personal frustration and a sloppy marketplace are even worse. If all consumers voiced their dissatisfaction and frustration when they were not treated well, more retailers would become better business-people.

QUESTIONS FOR DISCUSSION

1. Why do many people fail to complain about unsatisfactory products and services?
2. Has assertive behavior ever "won the day" for you in a complaint situation? If so, how?
3. What are the possible advantages and disadvantages of consulting a consumer affairs person employed by a business firm?
4. What are the strengths and weaknesses of the Better Business Bureau?
5. Is arbitration a good substitute for court action? Defend your position.
6. Why have formal lawsuits dramatically increased in number over the past decade?

7. What are the advantages and disadvantages of *pro se* law?
8. Some experts state that the best small claim settlement is the one where the plaintiff collects before the trial. Explain why this may be true.
9. Define class action suit.
10. What types of information would you like to see in lawyers' advertisements?
11. What factors should an individual consider in selecting a law firm?
12. What are the advantages and disadvantages of the contingent fee system of compensation for legal services?

PERSONAL EXPERIENCE PROJECTS

1. Contact your state or local consumer protection office or local action line to obtain information on the most common consumer complaints. By talking to various consumers, determine whether they have the same complaints.
2. Conduct a survey of various stores' refund/return policies. For different types of stores, determine which products and circumstances merit a cash refund and which rate only an exchange for other merchandise.
3. Interview consumers who have had a complaint about a product or service. Find out what course of action was taken to solve the problem and how much satisfaction was received.
4. Prepare a local consumer complaint guide to assist consumers with questions and problems. Organize a committee to channel complaints to the appropriate consumer organization or government agency.
5. Visit your local small claims court to observe the various cases that are presented. Evaluate the effectiveness of this course of action for consumers.
6. Talk to a private or legal aid lawyer about class action suits, arbitration, and do-it-yourself law. Determine the value of these alternatives to consumers.
7. Contact your local legal aid organization to determine services provided and qualifications for assistance. Evaluate the effectiveness of this group in assisting low-income consumers.
8. Compare the costs of the following basic services at various firms and legal clinics—adoption, property purchase, bankruptcy, divorce, basic will.
9. Examine various lawyers' advertisements in newspapers and in the

telephone book. Indicate which advertisements would appeal to you (and why) if you needed a lawyer.

10. Contact a lawyer referral service or a public interest law center to obtain information on prepaid legal service and cooperative legal service. Determine the availability, benefits, and costs of these methods. (Information on legal cooperatives may be obtained from the Cooperative League of the USA, 1828 L Street, N.W., Washington, DC 20036.)

11. Study the consumer information on telephone and utility bills. Then contact your state public utility commission to obtain information on rate setting procedures, hearings, and opportunities for consumer representation. (For further information, refer to the "Utility Performance Ratings" in *HELP The Useful Almanac*, published by Consumers News, Inc., Washington, D.C.)

12. Contact the National Consumers League, 1522 K Street, N.W., Suite 406, Washington, DC 20005, and Public Citizen, Inc., 1346 Connecticut Avenue, N.W., Washington, DC 20086, for information on proposed laws to protect consumers. Also request information on the voting records of your Congressional representatives on consumer litigation.

12
TAXATION

In a 1975 study, the Conference Board, a business-oriented research organization, examined the tax situation in twelve industrial nations—the United States, West Germany, France, Britain, Sweden, Canada, Denmark, Austria, Belgium, Holland, Italy, and Switzerland. The researchers found that Americans spent only 11 percent of household income on personal federal income taxes and 8 percent on Social Security payments. This placed the United States in tenth place in income tax and ninth in Social Security payments. In another measure of global taxes by the Organization for Economic Cooperation and Development, the United States ranked seventeenth out of the twenty noncommunist and industrialized nations studied, with 29.6 percent of total output of goods and services devoted to all forms of taxes. In spite of the fact that these figures hardly put American taxpayers ahead in the global tax race, Americans continue to question the increased involvement of government and its related cost.

There is little question about the need for our federal, state, and local governments to receive some tax revenue. Taxes pay for the organization and operation of all governmental services, legislative, executive, and judicial, as well as many public services, such as police, fire, health, education, and welfare.

Taxes are also an important component of the federal government's plan for economic health—they are a primary means by which the government influences total spending, income, output, and employment in the economy. If consumers and businesses fail to put their money into the spending flow of the economy, the government will first increase its spending. If increased government spending should fail, a tax cut to business or consumers may put more money into the taxpayers' pockets for the stimulation of the economy.

The opposite is also true. Increasing taxes on consumers or business profits and using the new tax dollars to pay off past debts will take money out of the economy and it will also decrease government spending.

This policy may sound simple, but it is actually a very complicated economic problem, for the government must avoid both too much spending, which will overheat the economy and may result in inflation, and too little spending, which may cause a recession.

HOW MUCH TAX?

Given that taxes must be collected, how much can taxpayers afford to pay? This is a very controversial issue.

Economist Arthur Laffer constructed what has become known as the Laffer Curve. Simply stated, it plots the question "At what point will higher taxes actually discourage production and investment and in turn decrease revenue to the government through taxes?" He suggests that the peace-time equilibrium point at which people will maximize their output and still be able to pay their taxes is somewhere around 25 percent. Since we have slightly exceeded that amount in some states, a group of politicians and economists see the need for dramatic cuts in taxes.

On the other hand, others point to the comparative studies cited earlier, which show that in relation to the European countries, the United States already has very low taxes and spends very little on social programs (Social Security, aid to the handicapped and the poor).

Do Americans really want to slash government programs dramatically in order to reduce taxes? According to surveys, the public is ambivalent on this issue. Both a Roper poll conducted for H & R Block and an ABC News–Louis Harris poll show that although Americans are clamoring for tax cuts, they are not for reducing services. The ABC News–Louis Harris poll found that while people favored tax cuts (62 percent), they were opposed to cuts in aid to the elderly, disabled, and poor (71 percent); fire protection (66 percent); education (66 percent); police protection (62 percent); and hospital and health care services (62 percent). The only thing most Americans do agree on is the need for some kind of reform of our tax system. A majority in the Roper poll (64 percent), for example, thought that the income tax system was unfair.

Income Tax Reform

Numerous critics of our graduated income tax system are involved in a drive to eliminate or decrease the effect of inflation on income taxes. Currently, inflation automatically forces people who have not received any real gain in spendable income into higher tax brackets.

Other income tax critics favor a plan to reduce federal income taxes by 30 percent. They believe that this reduction would create more jobs and thus reduce inflation.

Yet another group of tax reformers advocate a personal spending tax instead of an income tax. They feel that since savings and investments by individuals are not a part of their in-pocket personal spending money, they should not be taxed. They feel that taxes should be based on the formula:

income − savings + withdrawals from savings = taxable income

In other words, these personal spending tax advocates believe that the individual who makes $20,000 but puts aside $5,000 for retirement, savings, or investments really should only be taxed on $15,000—the amount available for personal spending. Under our present system, such an individual would pay taxes on $20,000, while another individual who made $15,000 and saved nothing would also have $15,000 to spend but would pay less in taxes.

The Internal Revenue Service, on the other hand, is looking for ways to raise more income taxes, for a multitude of exclusions eroded $120 billion from federal income tax collections in 1977. Deductions responsible for this erosion included those for Social Security income, mortgage interest, property taxes, and accumulated interest on whole life insurance policies. The primary culprit, however, was the capital gains exclusion.

A *capital gain* is a profit made on the sale of property or stocks or other securities. Historically, individuals have been taxed on half the value of their capital gains. Business would like to see a large reduction in this taxation of capital gains, while the government would prefer the full taxation of capital gains at whatever rate has been set for a given taxable year.

Critics of the capital gains exclusion argue that the exclusion of over half the profits made from the sale of stocks, real estate, or other property held for more than a year only benefits high-income people. This is a situation that runs against the basic principle of the federal income tax system—to tax according to one's ability to pay.

Advocates of the capital gains exclusion reason that few people would be willing to invest in businesses if no exclusion were provided. Dropping the exclusion, they state, would be a real blow to the economy.

State and Local Tax Reform

State and local taxes have also been under serious attack, partly because of the extent to which they vary from state to state (see Table 12-1). A study by Dr. Stephen E. Lile, an economist at Western Kentucky University, showed that whereas a particular breadwinner in a family of four in

TABLE 12-1. Average State Taxes in 1976

Adjusted Gross Income	$10,000 –$15,000	$20,000 –25,000	$50,000 –100,000
Alabama	$ 817	$1,342	$ 3,381
Alaska	$1,069	$1,693	$ 4,685
Arizona	$ 950	$1,589	$ 4,214
Arkansas	$ 782	$1,326	$ 4,393
California	$1,232	$2,090	$ 7,432
Colorado	$1,111	$1,938	$ 4,726
Connecticut	$1,321	$1,699	$ 4,993
Delaware	$ 974	$1,777	$ 6,778
D.C.	$1,085	$1,751	$ 6,023
Florida	$ 715	$ 991	$ 2,502
Georgia	$ 804	$1,488	$ 4,692
Hawaii	$1,192	$2,022	$ 5,835
Idaho	$ 972	$1,736	$ 4,533
Illinois	$1,137	$1,719	$ 3,891
Indiana	$ 900	$1,350	$ 3,068
Iowa	$ 961	$1,695	$ 4,645
Kansas	$ 911	$1,564	$ 3,961
Kentucky	$1,034	$1,769	$ 4,287
Louisiana	$ 557	$ 913	$ 2,234
Maine	$1,096	$1,723	$ 4,816
Maryland	$1,468	$2,212	$ 6,072
Massachusetts	$1,636	$2,549	$ 7,047
Michigan	$1,366	$2,075	$ 5,152
Minnesota	$1,317	$2,397	$ 7,708
Mississippi	$ 835	$1,308	$ 3,540
Missouri	$ 947	$1,557	$ 3,771

New York City would pay $7,875 in state and local taxes (15.75 percent of gross annual income), a taxpayer in a similar set of circumstances in Jacksonville, Florida, would pay $1,236, or 2.47 percent of income. (See *Changing Times*, November 1978, p. 25.) Variations in local and state taxes have a direct bearing on where people choose to live, shop, and work. These taxes also influence business plant locations, employment levels, and, as a result, income levels.

California has been the leader in a widespread movement to reduce property taxes, currently the largest source of income for local governments. As home prices in California skyrocketed, homeowners saw their

Adjusted Gross Income	$10,000 –$15,000	$20,000 –25,000	$50,000 –100,000
Montana	$1,000	$1,665	$ 4,987
Nebraska	$ 922	$1,769	$ 4,400
Nevada	$ 843	$1,016	$ 2,419
New Hampshire	$1,320	$1,679	$ 3,434
New Jersey	$1,400	$2,055	$ 5,464
New Mexico	$ 788	$1,297	$ 4,396
New York	$1,574	$2,742	$10,135
North Carolina	$ 938	$1,694	$ 5,536
North Dakota	$ 792	$1,388	$ 3,813
Ohio	$ 829	$1,402	$ 3,971
Oklahoma	$ 692	$1,181	$ 3,996
Oregon	$1,099	$2,085	$ 6,357
Pennsylvania	$1,252	$1,847	$ 4,210
Rhode Island	$1,450	$2,121	$ 5,924
South Carolina	$ 813	$1,511	$ 5,064
South Dakota	$ 865	$1,152	$ 2,353
Tennessee	$ 682	$ 970	$ 1,972
Texas	$ 646	$ 916	$ 1,944
Utah	$1,023	$1,716	$ 4,198
Vermont	$1,235	$2,022	$ 6,665
Virginia	$1,079	$1,835	$ 4,616
Washington	$ 866	$1,325	$ 2,562
West Virginia	$ 702	$1,045	$ 3,323
Wisconsin	$1,461	$2,373	$ 7,829
Wyoming	$ 691	$ 969	$ 1,433

Source: U.S. Department of the Treasury.

property tax bills rise as much as 200 percent in a single year. California's Proposition 13 and others that have followed limit the level and/or growth of property taxes. The property tax has several drawbacks. First, the tax fails to respond to growth in prices or in demands for public services. Second, the tax is not even in its effect—taxpayers pay different amounts in spite of being in the same financial situation, or the same tax in spite of differing financial situations. Third, the property tax has proven to be a disincentive for rehabilitation of urban areas; high inner-city taxes have pushed people farther out from the central cities.

New sources of tax revenue and fairer methods of assessment are being discussed in nearly every state and municipality. Many mayors are calling for reductions in the property tax and substitution of revenues generated by liquor levies and license fees paid by businesses. Another alternative is to attempt to pry more money out of state and federal governments in order to operate the local governments. However, this form of funding would increase state and federal control of local government.

One tax-exempt group that is coming under intense scrutiny is the nonprofit organization. Two of the nation's largest nonprofit organizations, the American Association of Retired Persons and the National Teachers Association, are being charged with being front organizations for the Colonial Penn Insurance Company, one of the nation's most profitable insurance companies. Business investments by churches, colleges, and fraternal organizations are also being challenged. Such organizations pay lower postal rates for mass mailings of magazines and member solicitations, are exempt from most property taxes, and in many cases are paying large salaries to employees who work in tax-exempt offices.

Since state and local tax problems vary considerably from region to region, the remainder of this chapter will focus on the federal income tax. The federal income tax will be analyzed in its relationship to government spending and in its effect on the individual taxpayer.

THE MECHANISM OF TAXATION

In 1909, Congress passed the Sixteenth Amendment, which provides that "The Congress shall have the power to lay and collect taxes on incomes, from whatever source derived, without apportionment among the several states and without regard to any census or enumeration." The Amendment further provides that "all bills for raising revenue shall originate in the House of Representatives." Therefore all tax bills are introduced in the House, where they are referred to the Ways and Means Committee. They then follow the same route as other bills through Congress. Public hearings are a part of the process in both the House and the Senate. Thus consumers who are interested in tax reform on the federal level should keep in touch with their Congressional representative.

The task of collecting the income tax was assigned to the Bureau of Internal Revenue, which in 1952 became the IRS—the Internal Revenue Service. In 1977–78 the IRS had over 71,000 employees and about 900 local offices. Fortunately, Americans are for the most part extremely responsible taxpayers, so in collecting tax revenues the government can rely on voluntary compliance with the law and every individual's self-assessment of the tax owed.

As was pointed out previously, the basic principle underlying an income tax is to tax according to the ability to pay. The income tax is therefore based on graduated (increasing gradually) or progressive rates. The lowest income bracket is now taxed at 14 percent and the highest at 70 percent, with various percentages in between.

It is often said that a taxpayer is in "the 25-percent tax bracket" or "the 36-percent tax bracket" or some other bracket. Many people believe that such a taxpayer pays 25 or 36 percent of all income in federal income taxes. This is not true. An individual who earned $14,000 in taxable income (taxable income is income subject to taxes; it is not the same as net income) would pay no tax on the first $3,400; 14 percent on the amount between $3,400 and $5,500; 16 percent on the amount between $5,500 and $7,600; 18 percent on the amount between $7,600 and $11,-900; and 21 percent on the amount between $11,900 and $16,000 (see Table 12-2).

Tax bracket considerations are an important factor in assessing investments, expenditures, and retirement plans. The question is always "What should I do with the thousand dollars or so that would be taxed in the highest bracket in order to avoid paying a full tax on it?"

FILING INDIVIDUAL INCOME TAX RETURNS

A Roper survey revealed that, in a recent year, only 23 percent of all taxpayers prepared their own income tax returns. A startling 54 percent used an outside accountant or tax consulting firm, and the remaining 23 percent sought help from family members or from other nonprofessionals. In spite of the fact that the IRS has simplified the income tax instruction booklets, reducing the reading level from that of a college student to that of a high school sophomore or junior, Americans spend at least $1 billion for tax help to prepare their tax forms.

Is this outlay really necessary? Most taxpayers lead rather uncomplicated economic lives in terms of paying income taxes. Unless real estate

TABLE 12-2. 1979 Tax Rate Applied to
Portion of Income to $55,200

Taxable Income	Percent Tax on Income at This Level
0–$3,400	0
$3,400–$5,500	14
$5,500–$7,600	16
$7,600–$11,900	18
$11,900–$16,000	21
$16,000–$20,200	24
$20,200–$24,600	28
$24,600–$29,900	32
$29,900–$35,200	37
$35,200–$45,800	43
$45,800–$55,200	49

investments or other complex types of other income are involved, a calculator and a good set of personal records are really the only help most people need. In fact, if you have an income of $20,000 or less ($40,000 or less if filing a joint return) consisting only of wages, salaries, and tips and you do not itemize expenses, the IRS will actually compute your tax for you. To have the government figure your tax, you need only fill in the basic information and the income information on the form you use and mail it to the IRS on or before the April deadline.

It is difficult to establish permanent guidelines to follow in preparing a federal tax return, for yearly changes in the tax laws make it impossible to avoid restudying the instructions each year before preparing a return. However, the basic principles remain the same. If you study the 1979 forms that appear throughout this section, you will have little difficulty understanding the minor modifications introduced each year.

Personal Records

The first step in preparing to file an income tax return is to keep complete personal records. You should have a home file containing copies of old tax forms, receipts, bank statements, current canceled checks, records of employment, health-benefit papers, educational information (transcripts and resumés), credit-card information, insurance policies, copies of wills, warranties, and appliance manuals.

A safe-deposit box should be used to keep any record or document that cannot be replaced without considerable cost or inconvenience. Items in a safe-deposit box might include birth, death, and marriage certificates; divorce decrees; car titles; a list or photos of items in the home; veteran's papers, and stock and bond certificates. A list of what is in the safe-deposit box should be kept in the home file for easy reference. It does not take long for most of us to forget what assets we have.

For income tax purposes, a taxpayer's records are normally subject to audit by the IRS for three years after the date a return is filed. Certain tax records, however, such as those of gains on the sale of capital assets, should be kept longer. The IRS can go back six years in the event of a failure to report more than 25 percent of earnings, or indefinitely if an individual neglects to file a return or if the IRS suspects fraud. The older files can, of course, be stored in an out-of-the-way place to provide enough space to keep records for current taxes.

Form W-4

Income taxes are a pay-as-you-go proposition that starts with the W-4 form a wage earner completes before beginning a job. The more dependents an individual declares, the less is withheld from his or her gross salary. A taxpayer may decide to take less than his or her actual number of deductible dependents, but never more. Figure 12-1 shows a W-4 form with four allowances—some employees declare none so that more money will be withheld from their paychecks and they have a better chance of receiving a refund at the end of the year. The only problem with this system is that the taxpayer is losing the interest he or she could have earned by investing the money.

Form W-2

The next form in the taxation process is Form W-2. Every year before January 31, every wage earner receives a Form W-2 (Figure 12-2). This is a summary of the wages, tips, and other compensation received by the wage earner during the year. A copy of each W-2 must be attached in the space indicated on the income tax form.

Form 1040A or Form 1040

The final step in the tax process is to fill out either Form 1040A or Form 1040 sometime before April 15.

Form 1040A is a simpler form that may be used if all income (with the exception of not more than $400 in dividends or interest)

Form **W-4**
(Rev. May 1977)
Department of the Treasury
Internal Revenue Service

Employee's Withholding Allowance Certificate
(Use for Wages Paid After May 31, 1977)

This certificate is for income tax withholding purposes only. It will remain in effect until you change it. If you claim exemption from withholding, you will have to file a new certificate on or before April 30 of next year.

Type or print your full name
William Blank

Your social security number
_000-00-0000_

Home address (number and street or rural route)
98 Y Street

City or town, State, and ZIP code
Anytown, NJ 07042

Marital Status
☐ Single ☒ Married
☐ Married, but withhold at higher Single rate
Note: If married, but legally separated, or spouse is a nonresident alien, check the single block.

1 Total number of allowances you are claiming **4**
2 Additional amount, if any, you want deducted from each pay (if your employer agrees) **$25**
3 I claim exemption from withholding (see instructions). Enter "Exempt" . . . .

Under the penalties of perjury, I certify that the number of withholding exemptions and allowances claimed on this certificate does not exceed the number to which I am entitled. If claiming exemption from withholding, I certify that I incurred no liability for Federal income tax for last year and that I anticipate that I will incur no liability for Federal income tax for this year.

Signature ▶ _William Blank_ Date ▶ _January 5_ , 19 _80_

-------------------------------- Detach along this line --------------------------------

▲ Give the top part of this form to your employer; keep the lower part for your records and information ▲

Instructions

The explanatory material below will help you determine your correct number of withholding allowances, and will assist you in completing the Form W-4 at the top of this page.

Avoid Overwithholding or Underwithholding

By claiming the number of withholding allowances you are entitled to, you can fit the amount of tax withheld from your wages to your tax liability. In addition to the allowances for personal exemptions to be claimed in item (a), be sure to claim any additional allowances you are entitled to in item (b), "Special withholding allowance," and item (c), "Allowance(s) for credit(s) and/or deduction(s)." While you may claim these allowances on Form W-4 for withholding purposes, you may not claim them under "Exemptions" on your tax return Form 1040 or 1040A.

You may claim the special withholding allowance if you are single with only one employer, or married with only one employer and your spouse is not employed. If you have unusually large itemized deductions, an alimony deduction, or credit(s) for child care expenses, earned income, or credit for the elderly, you may claim additional allowances to avoid having too much income tax withheld from your wages. Please note that alimony is no longer an itemized deduction, but rather is an adjustment to gross income. It may be to your benefit to take the standard deduction in lieu of itemizing deductions because of this change.

If you and your spouse are both employed or you have more than one employer, you should make sure that enough has been withheld. If you find that you need more withholding, claim fewer exemptions or ask for additional withholding or request to be withheld at the higher "Single" status. If you are currently claiming additional withholding allowances based on itemized deductions, check the worksheet on the back to see that you are claiming the proper number of allowances.

How Many Withholding Allowances May You Claim?

Use the schedule below to determine the number of allowances you may claim for tax withholding purposes. In determining the number, keep in mind these points: if you are single and hold more than one job, you may not claim the same allowances with more than one employer at the same time; or, if you are married and both you and your spouse are employed, you may not both claim the same allowances with your employers at the same time. A nonresident alien, other than a resident of Canada, Mexico, or Puerto Rico, may claim only one personal allowance.

Completing Form W-4

If you find you are entitled to one or more allowances in addition to those you are now claiming, increase your number of allowances by completing the form above and filing it with your employer. If the number of allowances you previously claimed decreases, you must file a new Form W-4 within 10 days. (If you expect to owe more tax than will be withheld, you may increase your withholding by claiming fewer or "0" allowances on line 1, or by asking for additional withholding on line 2, or both.)

You may claim exemption from withholding of Federal income tax if you had no liability for income tax for last year, and you anticipate that you will incur no liability for income tax for this year. You may not claim exemption if your joint or separate return shows tax liability before the allowance of any credit for income tax withheld. If you are exempt, your employer will not withhold Federal income tax from your wages. However, social security tax will be withheld if you are covered by the Federal Insurance Contributions Act.

You must revoke this exemption (1) within 10 days from the time you anticipate you will incur income tax liability for the year or (2) on or before December 1 if you anticipate you will incur Federal income tax liability for the next year. If you want to stop or are required to revoke this exemption, you must file a new Form W-4 with your employer showing the number of withholding allowances you are entitled to claim. This certificate for exemption from withholding will expire on April 30 of next year unless a new Form W-4 is filed before that date.

The Following Information is Provided in Accordance with the Privacy Act of 1974

The Internal Revenue Code requires every employee to furnish his or her employer with a signed withholding allowance certificate showing the number of withholding allowances that the employee claims (section 3402(f)(2)(A) and the Regulations thereto). Individuals are required to provide their Social Security Number for proper identification and processing (section 6109 and the Regulations thereto).

The principal purpose for soliciting withholding allowance certificate information is to administer the Internal Revenue laws of the United States.

If an employee does not furnish a signed withholding allowance certificate, the employee is considered as claiming no withholding allowances (section 3402(e)) and shall be treated as a single person (section 3402(l)).

The routine uses of the withholding allowance certificate information include disclosure to the Department of Justice for actual or potential criminal prosecution or civil litigation.

Figure Your Total Withholding Allowances Below

(a) Allowance(s) for exemption(s)—Enter 1 for each personal exemption you can claim on your Federal income tax return* . . . **4**

(b) Special withholding allowance—Enter 1 if single with 1 employer, or married with 1 employer and spouse not employed** . . **0**

(c) Allowance(s) for credit(s) and/or deduction(s)—Enter number from line (k) on other side** **0**

(d) Total (add lines (a) through (c) above)—Enter here and on line 1, Form W-4, above **4**

*If you are in doubt as to whom you may claim as a dependent, see the instructions that came with your last Federal income tax return or call your local Internal Revenue Service office.
**This allowance is used solely for purposes of figuring your withholding tax, and cannot be claimed when you file your tax return.

FIGURE 12-1. A W-4 Form

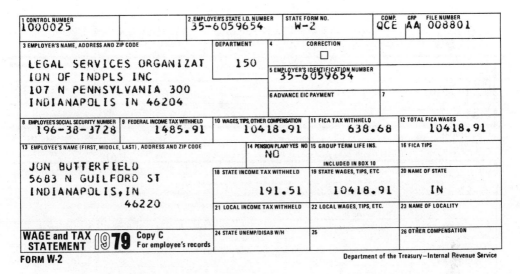

| 1 CONTROL NUMBER 1000025 | | 2 EMPLOYER'S STATE I.D. NUMBER 35-6059654 | STATE FORM NO. W-2 | | COMP. QCE | GRP AA | FILE NUMBER 008801 |

FIGURE 12-2. A W-2 Form

was from wages, salaries, tips, and other employee compensation; you have no income adjustments; and you do not itemize deductions. Many beginning employees qualify for the 1040A form, better known as the short form.

If you earned over $400 in dividends or interest, had income from special sources, are entitled to any income adjustments (see list below), or want to itemize, you must use Form 1040, the long form. However, the fact that you must use Form 1040 does not mean that you must itemize deductions.

Most married couples find that they pay less tax by filing their 1040 or 1040A form jointly, even if one of the partners did not have any income during the year. Married couples in the $15,000 to $30,000 combined income bracket with incomes at about the same level are victims of what is known as the marriage tax. At this tax level, the married couple, filing either jointly or separately, will pay more than if each were single and filing separately. Congress has begun work on this matter to see if a more equitable solution can be worked out. The marriage tax does not penalize all married couples filing joint returns: couples with only one taxable income or couples with a combined income of under $15,000 benefit from filing a joint return.

Interest and Dividend Income.   In addition to Form 1040, Schedule B must be used to report interest and dividend income if it exceeds $400. This income, which is recorded on the back side of the form used to

Form **1040A** Department of the Treasury—Internal Revenue Service
U.S. Individual Income Tax Return 1979

Use IRS label. Otherwise, please print or type.	Your first name and initial (if joint return, also give spouse's name and initial)	Last name	Your social security number
	Present home address (Number and street, including apartment number, or rural route)		Spouse's social security no.
	City, town or post office, State and ZIP code	Your occupation ▶	
		Spouse's occupation ▶	

Presidential Election Campaign Fund ▶
Do you want $1 to go to this fund? . . . . Yes / No
If joint return, does your spouse want $1 to go to this fund? Yes / No
Note: *Checking "Yes" will not increase your tax or reduce your refund.*

Filing Status
Check Only One Box.
For Privacy Act Notice, see page 14 of Instructions
1 Single
2 Married filing joint return (even if only one had income)
3 Married filing separate return. Enter spouse's social security number above and full name here ▶
4 Head of household. (See page 8 of Instructions.) If qualifying person is your unmarried child, enter child's name ▶

Exemptions
Always check the box labeled Yourself. Check other boxes if they apply.
5a Yourself — 65 or over — Blind } Enter number of boxes checked on 5a and b ▶
b Spouse — 65 or over — Blind }
c First names of your dependent children who lived with you ▶ . . . . Enter number of children listed ▶

d Other dependents:

(1) Name	(2) Relationship	(3) Number of months lived in your home.	(4) Did dependent have income of $1,000 or more?	(5) Did you provide more than one-half of dependent's support?	
					Enter number of other dependents ▶
					Add numbers entered in boxes above ▶

6 Total number of exemptions claimed . . . .

7 Wages, salaries, tips, etc. (Attach Forms W–2. If you do not have a W–2, see page 10 of Instructions) . . . . | 7 |
8 Interest income (See pages 4 and 10 of Instructions) . . . . | 8 |
9a Dividends _____ (See pages 4 and 10 of Instructions) 9b Exclusion _____ Subtract line 9b from 9a | 9c |
10a Unemployment compensation. Total amount received _____
b Taxable part, if any, from worksheet on page 11 of Instructions . . . . | 10b |
11 Adjusted gross income (add lines 7, 8, 9c, and 10b). If under $10,000, see page 2 of Instructions on "Earned Income Credit" . . . . | 11 |
12a Credit for contributions to candidates for public office. (See page 11 of Instructions) . . . . | 12a |
IF YOU WANT IRS TO FIGURE YOUR TAX, PLEASE STOP HERE AND SIGN BELOW.
b Total Federal income tax withheld (If line 7 is more than $22,900, see page 12 of Instructions) . . . . | 12b |
c Earned income credit (from page 2 of Instructions) . . . . | 12c |
13 Total (add lines 12a, b, and c) . . . . | 13 |
14a Tax on the amount on line 11. (See Instructions for line 14a on page 12; then find your tax in the Tax Tables on pages 15–26.) . . . . | 14a |
b Advance earned income credit payments received (from Form W–2) . . . . | 14b |
15 Total (add lines 14a and 14b) . . . . | 15 |
16 If line 13 is larger than line 15, enter amount to be **REFUNDED TO YOU** . . . . . . ▶ | 16 |
17 If line 15 is larger than line 13, enter **BALANCE DUE.** Attach check or money order for full amount payable to "Internal Revenue Service." Write your social security number on check or money order . ▶ | 17 |

Under penalties of perjury, I declare that I have examined this return, including accompanying schedules and statements, and to the best of my knowledge and belief it is true, correct, and complete. Declaration of preparer (other than taxpayer) is based on all information of which preparer has any knowledge.

Your signature   Date   Spouse's signature (if filing jointly, BOTH must sign even if only one had income)

Paid Preparer's Information	Preparer's signature and date ▶		Check if self-employed ▶ ☐	Preparer's social security no.
	Firm's name (or yours, if self-employed) and address ▶		E.I. No. ▶	
			ZIP code ▶	

✩U.S. GOVERNMENT PRINTING OFFICE: 1979–0–283-368   E.I. 52-107-4467   Form **1040A** (1979)

(side text: Please Attach Copy B of Forms W-2 Here Attach Payment Here Please Sign Here)

FIGURE 12-3. Form 1040A, the Short Form

Form **1040** Department of the Treasury—Internal Revenue Service **1979**
U.S. Individual Income Tax Return

| For Privacy Act Notice, see page 3 of Instructions | For the year January 1–December 31, 1979, or other tax year beginning , 1979, ending , 19 |

Use IRS label. Other- wise, please print or type.	Your first name and initial (if joint return, also give spouse's name and initial)	Last name	Your social security number
	Present home address (Number and street, including apartment number, or rural route)		Spouse's social security no.
	City, town or post office, State and ZIP code	Your occupation ▶	
		Spouse's occupation ▶	

Presidential Election Campaign Fund ▶

Do you want $1 to go to this fund? . . . . Yes ▨ No

If joint return, does your spouse want $1 to go to this fund? . . . Yes ▨ No

Note: *Checking "Yes" will not increase your tax or reduce your refund.*

Filing Status

Check only one box.

1 ☐ Single

2 ☐ Married filing joint return (even if only one had income)

3 ☐ Married filing separate return. Enter spouse's social security number above and full name here ▶ ....

4 ☐ Head of household. (See page 7 of Instructions.) If qualifying person is your unmarried child, enter child's name ▶ ....

5 ☐ Qualifying widow(er) with dependent child (Year spouse died ▶ 19). (See page 7 of Instructions.)

Exemptions

Always check the box labeled Yourself. Check other boxes if they apply.

6a ☐ Yourself ☐ 65 or over ☐ Blind

b ☐ Spouse ☐ 65 or over ☐ Blind

Enter number of boxes checked on 6a and b ▶

c First names of your dependent children who lived with you ▶ ....

Enter number of children listed ▶

| d Other dependents: (1) Name | (2) Relationship | (3) Number of months lived in your home | (4) Did dependent have income of $1,000 or more? | (5) Did you provide more than one-half of dependent's support? |
| | | | | |

Enter number of other dependents ▶

Add numbers entered in boxes above ▶

7 Total number of exemptions claimed . . . .

Income

Please attach Copy B of your Forms W–2 here.

If you do not have a W–2, see page 5 of Instructions.

8 Wages, salaries, tips, etc. **8**

9 Interest income (attach Schedule B if over $400) **9**

10a Dividends (attach Schedule B if over $400).............., 10b Exclusion...........

c Subtract line 10b from line 10a **10c**

11 State and local income tax refunds (does not apply unless refund is for year you itemized deductions—see page 10 of Instructions). **11**

12 Alimony received **12**

13 Business income or (loss) (attach Schedule C) **13**

14 Capital gain or (loss) (attach Schedule D) **14**

15 Taxable part of capital gain distributions not reported on Schedule D (see page 10 of Instructions) . . . . . : . . **15**

16 Supplemental gains or (losses) (attach Form 4797) **16**

17 Fully taxable pensions and annuities not reported on Schedule E **17**

18 Pensions, annuities, rents, royalties, partnerships, estates or trusts, etc. (attach Schedule E) **18**

19 Farm income or (loss) (attach Schedule F) **19**

20a Unemployment compensation. Total amount received.................

b Taxable part, if any, from worksheet on page 10 of Instructions **20b**

21 Other income (state nature and source—see page 10 of Instructions) ▶ **21**

Please attach check or money order here.

22 **Total income.** Add amounts in column for lines 8 through 21 . . . . ▶ **22**

Adjustments to Income

23 Moving expense (attach Form 3903 or 3903F) **23**

24 Employee business expenses (attach Form 2106) . . **24**

25 Payments to an IRA (see page 11 of Instructions) . . **25**

26 Payments to a Keogh (H.R. 10) retirement plan . . . **26**

27 Interest penalty on early withdrawal of savings . . . **27**

28 Alimony paid (see page 11 of Instructions) **28**

29 Disability income exclusion (attach Form 2440) . . . **29**

30 Total adjustments. Add lines 23 through 29 . . . . ▶ **30**

Adjusted Gross Income

31 Adjusted gross income. Subtract line 30 from line 22. If this line is less than $10,000, see page 2 of Instructions. If you want IRS to figure your tax, see page 4 of Instructions . . . . ▶ **31**

Form **1040** (1979)

FIGURE 12-4. Form 1040, the Long Form

Form 1040 (1979)
Page **2**

Tax Computation (See Instructions on page 12)	32	Amount from line 31 *(adjusted gross income)*	32	
	33	If you do not itemize deductions, enter zero . . . . } If you itemize, complete Schedule A (Form 1040) and enter the amount from Schedule A, line 41 . . . }	33	
		Caution: If you have unearned income and can be claimed as a dependent on your parent's return, check here ▶ ☐ and see page 12 of the Instructions. Also see page 12 of the Instructions if: • You are married filing a separate return and your spouse itemizes deductions, OR • You file Form 4563, OR • You are a dual-status alien.		
	34	Subtract line 33 from line 32. Use the amount on line 34 to find your tax from the Tax Tables, or to figure your tax on Schedule TC, Part I . . . . Use Schedule TC, Part I, and the Tax Rate Schedules ONLY if: • Line 34 is more than $20,000 ($40,000 if you checked Filing Status Box 2 or 5), OR • You have more exemptions than are shown in the Tax Table for your filing status, OR • You use Schedule G or Form 4726 to figure your tax. Otherwise, you MUST use the Tax Tables to find your tax.	34	
	35	Tax. Enter tax here and check if from ☐ Tax Tables or ☐ Schedule TC	35	
	36	Additional taxes. (See page 12 of Instructions.) Enter here and check if from ☐ Form 4970 } ☐ Form 4972, ☐ Form 5544, ☐ Form 5405, or ☐ Section 72(m)(5) penalty tax . . }	36	
	37	**Total.** Add lines 35 and 36 . . . . ▶	37	
Credits	38	Credit for contributions to candidates for public office . . .	38	
	39	Credit for the elderly *(attach Schedules R&RP)*	39	
	40	Credit for child and dependent care expenses (*attach* Form 2441) .	40	
	41	Investment credit *(attach Form 3468)*	41	
	42	Foreign tax credit *(attach Form 1116)*	42	
	43	Work incentive (WIN) credit *(attach Form 4874)*	43	
	44	Jobs credit *(attach Form 5884)*	44	
	45	Residential energy credits *(attach Form 5695)*	45	
	46	**Total credits.** Add lines 38 through 45	46	
	47	**Balance.** Subtract line 46 from line 37 and enter difference (but not less than zero) . ▶	47	
Other Taxes (Including Advance EIC Payments)	48	Self-employment tax *(attach Schedule SE)*	48	
	49a	Minimum tax. Attach Form 4625 and check here ▶ ☐	49a	
	49b	Alternative minimum tax. Attach Form 6251 and check here ▶ ☐	49b	
	50	Tax from recomputing prior-year investment credit *(attach Form 4255)*	50	
	51a	Social security (FICA) tax on tip income not reported to employer *(attach Form 4137)* . .	51a	
	51b	Uncollected employee FICA and RRTA tax on tips *(from Form W–2)*	51b	
	52	Tax on an IRA *(attach Form 5329)*	52	
	53	Advance earned income credit payments received *(from Form W–2)*	53	
	54	**Total.** Add lines 47 through 53 . . . . ▶	54	
Payments Attach Forms W–2, W–2G, and W–2P to front.	55	Total Federal income tax withheld	55	
	56	1979 estimated tax payments and credit from 1978 return	56	
	57	Earned income credit. If line 32 is under $10,000, see page 2 of Instructions	57	
	58	Amount paid with Form 4868	58	
	59	Excess FICA and RRTA tax withheld (two or more employers)	59	
	60	Credit for Federal tax on special fuels and oils *(attach Form 4136 or 4136–T)*	60	
	61	Regulated Investment Company credit *(attach Form 2439)*	61	
	62	**Total.** Add lines 55 through 61 . . . . ▶	62	
Refund or Balance Due	63	If line 62 is larger than line 54, enter amount **OVERPAID** . . . . ▶	63	
	64	Amount of line 63 to be **REFUNDED TO YOU** . . . . ▶	64	
	65	Amount of line 63 to be credited on 1980 estimated tax . . . . . ▶	65	
	66	If line 54 is larger than line 62, enter **BALANCE DUE.** Attach check or money order for full amount payable to "Internal Revenue Service." Write your social security number on check or money order . . ▶ (Check ▶ ☐ if Form 2210 (2210F) is attached. See page 15 of Instructions.) ▶ $	66	

Please Sign Here

Under penalties of perjury, I declare that I have examined this return, including accompanying schedules and statements, and to the best of my knowledge and belief, it is true, correct, and complete. Declaration of preparer (other than taxpayer) is based on all information of which preparer has any knowledge.

Your signature	Date	Spouse's signature (if filing jointly, BOTH must sign even if only one had income)

Paid Preparer's Information

Preparer's signature and date ▶		Check if self-employed ▶ ☐	Preparer's social security no.
Firm's name (or yours, if self-employed) and address ▶		E.I. No. ▶	
		ZIP code ▶	

itemize deductions (see Figure 12-5), must be computed regardless of whether deductions are itemized.

Other Income. The 1040 form expands the income section to include income such as alimony received, capital gains (profit made on capital assets held for at least one year), and pensions. For each type of special income, a supplemental form must also be completed.

Adjustments to Income. The following are examples of adjustments to income:

· Income received while totally and permanently disabled.
· Alimony or separate maintenance payments that you have paid under a court decree of divorce or separation (provided certain conditions prevail).
· Moving expenses incurred in moving in order to work as an employee at another job, or as a self-employed individual. There are, of course, certain limitations; for example, the new place of employment must be at least thirty-five miles farther from the old residence than the old residence was from the old place of work.
· Certain educational expenses that are either required by the employer or necessary to maintain or improve skills used in performing the duties of one's present employment, trade, or business.
· Expenses incurred in work-related travel and entertainment, provided the employee is not reimbursed by the employer. Automobile expenses for such travel were allowed in 1979 at 18.5¢ per mile by the IRS.
· Business expenses. A principal business expense for many traveling salespeople is the cost of depreciation (wear and tear) of the automobile.

Itemized Deductions. The IRS automatically allows every taxpayer two types of deductions from adjusted gross income:

· A personal exemption for each taxpayer and for each dependent the taxpayer supports. For 1979, the exemption was $1,000 per person.
· A zero bracket amount, which supposedly represents the amount needed to support the taxpayers during the tax year. This zero bracket amount was once called the standard deduction. For 1979, it was $2,300 for single persons and $3,400 for married couples filing joint returns. This minimum amount of income is not subject to taxation.

Schedules A&B (Form 1040) 1979   **Schedule B—Interest and Dividend Income**   Page **2**

Name(s) as shown on Form 1040 (Do not enter name and social security number if shown on other side) | Your social security number

Part I **Interest Income**

1 If you received more than $400 in interest, complete Part I and Part III. Please see page 9 of the instructions to find out what interest to report. Then answer the questions in Part III, below. If you received interest as a nominee for another, or you received or paid accrued interest on securities transferred between interest payment dates, please see page 18 of the instructions.

Name of payer	Amount

2 Total interest income. Enter here and on Form 1040, line 9 . . . .

Part II **Dividend Income**

3 If you received more than $400 in gross dividends (including capital gain distributions) and other distributions on stock, complete Part II and Part III. Please see page 9 of the instructions. Write (H), (W), or (J), for stock held by husband, wife, or jointly. Then answer the questions in Part III, below. If you received dividends as a nominee for another, please see page 19 of the instructions.

Name of payer	Amount

Part III **Foreign Accounts and Foreign Trusts**

If you are required to list interest in Part I or dividends in Part II, OR if you had a foreign account or were a grantor of or a transferor to a foreign trust, you must answer both questions in Part III. Please see page 19 of the instructions.

	Yes	No
A At any time during the tax year, did you have an interest in or a signature or other authority over a bank account, securities account, or other financial account in a foreign country (see page 19 of instructions)?		
B Were you the grantor of, or transferor to, a foreign trust which existed during the current tax year, whether or not you have any beneficial interest in it? If "Yes," you may have to file Forms 3520, 3520–A, or 926.		

4 Total of line 3 . . . .

5 Capital gain distributions. Enter here and on the appropriate line(s) on Schedule D. See Note below . . . . . .

6 Nontaxable distributions . . . . . .

7 Total (add lines 5 and 6) . . . . . .

8 Dividends before exclusion (subtract line 7 from line 4). Enter here and on Form 1040, line 10a . . . .

Note: If your capital gain distributions for the year do not include any gains before Nov. 1, 1978, and you do not need Schedule D to report any gains or losses, do not file that schedule. Instead, enter the taxable part of your capital gain distributions on Form 1040, line 15.

FIGURE 12-5. Schedule B, Interest and Dividend Income

However, if your actual deductible expenses exceed the zero bracket amount, it is to your advantage to itemize expenses. If you think you might have enough deductions, you should try filling out Schedule A, Itemized Deductions (Figure 12-6).

Following are the types of expenses that may be deducted:

Medical Expenses.   If the individual, rather than the employer, pays for health insurance, then half of the premiums up to $150 are deductible.

The rest of the premiums may be included in "other medical and dental expenses," which must be in excess of 3 percent of adjusted gross income before they can be deducted (Figure 12-6, line 33). For example, the Hills had an income of $12,125 and medical expenses of $350. They were not able to deduct them because 3 percent of $12,125 is $363.75. Only expenses beyond $363.75 would be deductible.

Another category of medical expenses is payment for medicine and drugs. Only amounts in excess of 1 percent of adjusted gross income are deductible in this classification.

Taxes.   Many state and local taxes are deductible, including property taxes, general sales taxes, and state income taxes. You need to know your yearly mileage to calculate gasoline taxes.

Interest.   Most interest payments are deductible, including those on mortgages, credit-card payments, and installment loans.

Charitable Contributions.   Contributions that are made to qualified organizations established and operated exclusively for charitable, religious, educational, scientific, or literary purposes are deductible. There is a limit of 50 percent of the taxpayer's adjusted gross income that may be claimed as contributions.

Casualty or Theft Losses.   Losses resulting from sudden and unexpected or unusual causes or the unlawful taking and removing of money or property are considered casualties or thefts. The amount of each provable loss must be reduced by both $100 *and* the amount collected on insurance policies.

Assume that a home was broken into and items worth $1,400 were stolen. Suppose the homeowner was covered for such losses through a homeowner's policy to the extent of $600. For income tax purposes, the amount deductible for casualty loss would be $700—$1,400 less $600 less $100 (because the IRS deducts the first $100 from any allowable loss).

Miscellaneous Deductions.   This category includes dues to professional organizations, home office expenses, union-related expenses, certain employment-related educational expenses, and items related to one's occupation, such as uniforms or employment agency fees (assuming the person is not self-employed).

Schedules A&B—Itemized Deductions AND
(Form 1040)
Department of the Treasury
Internal Revenue Service
Interest and Dividend Income

▶ Attach to Form 1040. ▶ See Instructions for Schedules A and B (Form 1040).

1979

08

Name(s) as shown on Form 1040

Your social security number

Schedule A—Itemized Deductions (Schedule B is on back)

Medical and Dental Expenses (not paid or reimbursed by insurance or otherwise) (See page 16 of Instructions.)

1 One-half (but not more than $150) of insurance premiums you paid for medical care. (Be sure to include in line 10 below.) ▶

2 Medicine and drugs . . . .

3 Enter 1% of Form 1040, line 31 . . .

4 Subtract line 3 from line 2. If line 3 is more than line 2, enter zero . . . .

5 Balance of insurance premiums for medical care not entered on line 1 . . . .

6 Other medical and dental expenses:

a Doctors, dentists, nurses, etc. . . .

b Hospitals . . . .

c Other (itemize—include hearing aids, dentures, eyeglasses, transportation, etc.) ▶

7 Total (add lines 4 through 6c) . . . .

8 Enter 3% of Form 1040, line 31 . . . .

9 Subtract line 8 from line 7. If line 8 is more than line 7, enter zero . . . .

10 Total medical and dental expenses (add lines 1 and 9). Enter here and on line 33 . ▶

Taxes (See page 16 of Instructions.)

Note: Gasoline taxes are no longer deductible.

11 State and local income . . . . . .

12 Real estate . . . .

13 General sales (see sales tax tables) . .

14 Personal property . . . .

15 Other (itemize) ▶

16 Total taxes (add lines 11 through 15). Enter here and on line 34 . . . . ▶

Interest Expense (See page 17 of Instructions.)

17 Home mortgage . . . .

18 Credit and charge cards . . . . . .

19 Other (itemize) ▶

20 Total interest expense (add lines 17 through 19). Enter here and on line 35 ▶

Contributions (See page 17 of Instructions.)

21 a Cash contributions for which you have receipts, cancelled checks, or other written evidence . . . .

b Other cash contributions (show to whom you gave and how much you gave) ▶

22 Other than cash (see page 17 of instructions for required statement) . . . .

23 Carryover from prior years . . . .

24 Total contributions (add lines 21a through 23). Enter here and on line 36 . ▶

Casualty or Theft Loss(es) (See page 18 of Instructions.)

25 Loss before insurance reimbursement .

26 Insurance reimbursement . . . . .

27 Subtract line 26 from line 25. If line 26 is more than line 25, enter zero . . .

28 Enter $100 or amount from line 27, whichever is smaller . . . . . .

29 Total casualty or theft loss(es) (subtract line 28 from line 27). Enter here and on line 37 . ▶

Miscellaneous Deductions (See page 18 of Instructions.)

30 Union dues . . . .

31 Other (itemize) ▶

32 Total miscellaneous deductions (add lines 30 and 31). Enter here and on line 38 ▶

Summary of Itemized Deductions (See page 18 of Instructions.)

A

33 Total medical and dental—from line 10 .

34 Total taxes—from line 16 . . . . .

35 Total interest—from line 20 . . . .

36 Total contributions—from line 24 . .

37 Total casualty or theft loss(es)—from line 29 .

38 Total miscellaneous—from line 32 . .

39 Add lines 33 through 38 . . . . .

40 If you checked Form 1040, Filing Status box:
2 or 5, enter $3,400 . . . . .}
1 or 4, enter $2,300 . . . . .} . . .
3, enter $1,700 . . . . . .}

41 Subtract line 40 from line 39. Enter here and on Form 1040, line 33. (If line 40 is more than line 39, see the instructions for line 41 on page 18.) . . . . . ▶

FIGURE 12-6. Schedule A, Itemized Deductions

To see how the "to itemize or not to itemize" decision works, let us look at the following example:

Helen Royle purchased a condominium early in the tax year. She added her allowable expenses on Schedule A and was delighted to find that largely because of her mortgage interest and property taxes, her deductibles exceeded by $1,200 the zero bracket amount of $2,300 allowed single persons. Thus she wrote $1,200 on line 33 of Form 1040. She is said to have itemized her allowable expenses. If her expenses had not exceeded $2,300, she would have entered $0. (The $2,300 deduction is automatically included on the tax table.)

Tax Tables

Whether you use Form 1040 or Form 1040A, you can find your tax from the tax tables if your adjusted gross income is under $40,000 for married couples filing jointly and under $20,000 for single persons.

Ann and Murray Williams, who file jointly on a 1040A tax form, will use the joint return section of Tax Table B to find the tax on their adjusted gross income, recorded on line 11 (see Figure 12-7). The table takes into consideration the zero bracket amount of $3,400. Sally and John Hill file on Form 1040, because they have incurred moving expenses. However, they are still able to utilize the same tax table (Table B) to compute the tax on their adjusted gross income, reported on line 31. Both couples have no dependents, so they read their tax from Column 1—two exemptions.

Special Credits

After computing your tax, you must determine whether you qualify for any of the special credits. Following are the three most common.

Energy Conservation Deduction. You may deduct 15 percent of the cost of such materials as insulation, storm windows and storm doors, caulking, weatherstripping, and clock thermostats, up to a maximum credit of $300. If you have installed an item of "renewable energy source equipment," such as a solar system, you may deduct 30 percent of the first $2,000 spent and 20 percent of the next $8,000 spent, up to a maximum credit of $2,200.

Child-Care Credit. Parents with one child may deduct up to $400, and parents with two or more children may deduct up to $800 from their tax for child-care expenditures.

Form **1040A**   *Williams*

11   Adjusted gross income *(add lines 7, 8, 9c, and 10b). If under $10,000, see page 2 of Instructions on "Earned Income Credit"*   11   *12,125*

If Form 1040, line 34, is—		And the total number of exemptions claimed on line 7 is—								
Over	But not over	2	3	4	5	6	7	8	9
					Your tax is—				
11,200	11,250	923	743	570	410	256	116	0	0
11,250	11,300	932	752	578	418	263	123	0	0
11,300	11,350	941	761	586	426	270	130	0	0
11,350	11,400	950	770	594	434	277	137	0	0
11,400	11,450	959	779	602	442	284	144	4	0
11,450	11,500	968	788	610	450	291	151	11	0
11,500	11,550	977	797	618	458	298	158	18	0
11,550	11,600	986	806	626	466	306	165	25	0
11,600	11,650	995	815	635	474	314	172	32	0
11,650	11,700	1,004	824	644	482	322	179	39	0
11,700	11,750	1,013	833	653	490	330	186	46	0
11,750	11,800	1,022	842	662	498	338	193	53	0
11,800	11,850	1,031	851	671	506	346	200	60	0
11,850	11,900	1,040	860	680	514	354	207	67	0
11,900	11,950	1,049	869	689	522	362	214	74	0
11,950	12,000	1,058	878	698	530	370	221	81	0
12,000	12,050	1,067	887	707	538	378	228	88	0
12,050	12,100	1,076	896	716	546	386	235	95	0
12,100	12,150	1,085	905	725	554	394	242	102	0
12,150	12,200	1,094	914	734	562	402	249	109	0

Form **1040**   *Hills*

Adjusted Gross Income   31   Adjusted gross income. Subtract line 30 from line 22. *If this line is less than $10,000, see page 2 of Instructions. If you want IRS to figure your tax, see page 4 of Instructions* . . . . ▶   31   *12,125*

FIGURE 12-7. Using the Tax Table

Political Contributions.   Up to $50 for a single person and up to $100 for taxpayers filing joint returns may be deducted for political contributions.

The Final Step

During the year your employer withheld part of your salary to be credited toward your tax bill. Compare the withheld figure as shown on your W-2 form to the tax you owe. If the withholding is greater than the tax, you get a refund. If your tax is greater than your withholding, you will have to pay. In any case, be sure to sign and date your return. Surprisingly, this is a step many people forget.

Income Averaging

If your income has changed drastically from one tax year to another, it may be to your advantage to compute your tax under the income averaging method. Under the income averaging method some of the income earned during a particularly good year is taxed at the lower rate of less bountiful years.

The form to be used (Schedule G) is relatively uncomplicated, but you must have your tax forms from the past four years. (Upon request, the IRS will send you copies of your old forms for a small fee.) Even if you have gotten married during the four-year period, you may still combine your incomes and income average.

Guides and Aids

Tax forms appear to be so complex because they must fit many situations. If your income consists of wages alone, you will find that you need very few of the blanks on the 1040 form. If, on the other hand, you have income from rentals and other investments, have sold property, have used child-care services, or have moved (to name but a few variations on the wage situation alone), you will need to fill in more blanks and to attach supporting schedules as needed.

To assist you in preparing your taxes, the IRS has prepared a comprehensive booklet of tax rules for individuals called *Publication 17 (Your Federal Income Tax)*. In addition to *Publication 17,* the IRS publishes booklets on special phases of income tax information, such as moving expenses and educational deductions. They can be obtained by calling the Internal Revenue Service office in your community or by circling the numbers of booklets you desire on the card provided in your tax booklet and mailing it to the IRS.

You can also obtain advice on the telephone or in person—consult the local telephone directory under "United States Government—Internal Revenue Service." You can obtain information from booklets sold on newsstands and in bookstores, but remember that much of what these printed materials contain is available free from the government.

Any college student who is willing to read carefully and can use a calculator can prepare the kind of income tax return filed by individuals whose incomes are derived from wages, salaries, or tips. If you are in doubt about the accuracy of the computation, you can always contact IRS office personnel for assistance. However, be sure that you understand their reasoning, for their employees do not guarantee their work—you are still on your own if you must defend your return. And in a 1976 IRS study reported by *Consumer Reports* magazine, it was found that taxpayer service representatives computed the wrong tax 72 percent of the time and the phone service gave the wrong answer about 20 to 25 percent of the time.[1]

Computing your own taxes can be an excellent method of summarizing your financial progress over the year. In addition, it often acts as an impetus for keeping better records in the future. Finally, it helps taxpayers become better informed about the United States income tax collection process.

Professional Assistance

If you do feel the need to seek professional assistance, there are several possibilities open to you.

Many special income tax services set up offices that are open from January through April. Some of them advertise their services on radio or television.

In some communities, the IRS examines individuals who have prepared themselves to assist the public in filling out federal income tax forms. These private individuals are listed by the IRS as enrolled agents. You can obtain a list of enrolled agents in your community by writing or calling the IRS office in your area. (This is the only way to find them.) Enrolled agents pass rigorous tests and are able to argue in the tax courts in your behalf.

Another possible source of assistance is to employ an accountant who has been recommended to you.

The most reliable and probably the most expensive kind of assistance can be obtained from the services of a certified public accountant. Businesspeople who employ accountants frequently use them to help with their individual personal income tax returns.

The California Department of Consumer Affairs suggests that you consider the following issues when choosing a commercial preparer.

1. Choose a preparer registered with the Tax Preparer Program. Ask to see the Certificate of Registration if it is not displayed.
2. Friends and acquaintances may recommend tax preparers with whose work they are satisfied.
3. Some preparers give written guarantees that they will pay any interest and penalty that is assessed as a result of their work.
4. Some preparers will accompany you and act as a witness if you are audited by the government.

[1]"Where to Go for Tax Help," *Consumer Reports*, March 1976, pp. 131–132.

5. The earlier in the tax season you have your return prepared, the less likely you are to suffer last-minute frustrations.
6. Commercial preparers are not tested for their competency or ability. You should review their work and question any item you do not understand.

QUESTIONS FOR DISCUSSION

1. How would a personal spending tax differ from our current income tax?
2. What is meant by a capital gain on investment?
3. What are the weaknesses of the property tax as a revenue-raising measure?
4. If a taxpayer is in the 50-percent tax bracket, does that mean that one-half of all income is paid in taxes? Explain.
5. What types of information should be kept in a home file?
6. What is meant by the zero bracket amount on federal income tax?
7. How does itemizing deductions differ from using the zero bracket amount in computing income tax?
8. What steps would a taxpayer go through in calculating his or her tax if itemizing is not advantageous?

PERSONAL EXPERIENCE PROJECTS

1. Obtain tax preparation booklets and information from your local IRS office. It is listed in your telephone directory under "United States Government—Internal Revenue Service." Determine whether this material provides people you know with enough background to prepare their own tax returns.
2. Contact a variety of income tax preparation services—a local tax service, a national tax service, a local accountant, an enrolled agent, and a certified public accountant. Compare the costs and amount of assistance. Then, for information on degree of accuracy, read "Where to Go for Tax Help," *Consumer Reports*, March 1976, p. 130.
3. Contact the National Association of Enrolled Federal Tax Accountants, 6108 N. Harding, Chicago, IL 60659, and the National Society of Public Accountants, 1717 Pennsylvania Avenue, N.W., Washington, DC 20006. Obtain information on the requirements for membership and a list of members in your area.
4. Contact your local Internal Revenue Service with a list of questions

on tax deductions, reportable income, and other questionable areas. Decide whether the information you receive is consistent with your interpretation of IRS material and with information you receive from tax preparation services.

5. Interview employees of various tax preparation services to obtain information on each preparer's college education (accounting and tax courses), tax-training courses, number of years of tax-preparation experience, full-time occupation. Also find out what assistance would be provided to you if you were audited by the IRS.

6. Talk to an investment counselor to obtain information on various tax-exempt investments. Evaluate the cost, benefits, restrictions, and availability of these investments.

7. Survey consumers to determine their opinions on inequities in our income tax system. Write your Congressional representative to express your opinions and to obtain information on proposed changes in tax laws.

8. Contact local government offices to obtain information on property tax rates and on services paid for by property taxes. Compare this information to that for other locations in nearby areas.

9. Compare the sales taxes in various states. Determine differences in rates and in tax-exempt items, such as food and prescription drugs.

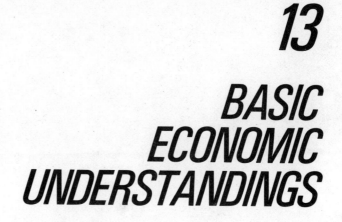

13

*BASIC
ECONOMIC
UNDERSTANDINGS*

Although economists have a reputation for disagreeing with one another, they generally agree with the definition of economics formulated by the British economist Alfred Marshall. He defined economics to be "the study of mankind in the ordinary business of life." Another economist, Dr. Leonard Silk, interpreted Marshall's definition to mean "pursuing the money gains, the profits, the higher wages and salaries, the bargains, and savings and pleasure that shrewd, rational economic choice confers."

Basic economic principles and concepts are very closely related, therefore, to the problems of consumer money management.

THE SITUATION: UNLIMITED WANTS AND LIMITED RESOURCES

A lawyer who earns $60,000 a year is turned down for credit, while a garage mechanic who earns $12,000 a year is granted credit. New York City, which collects billions of dollars in taxes, is in financial difficulty. The W. T. Grant Company declares bankruptcy in spite of an established reputation among consumers.

What do these situations have in common? Although many would blame "the economy," the problem in each case is actually money management.

317

A clearer picture of the lawyer's economic problem emerges when we learn that the lawyer, who is forty-five years old, recently purchased a $150,000 home; keeps poor records and thus forgets to pay bills on time; owns but has not paid for two cars and a boat; and has no savings. On the other hand, the twenty-five-year-old garage mechanic has $2,000 in savings; owes practically nothing; and has a secure job with a promising future.

Unlimited wants and limited resources is a basic economic fact. Every consumer, government, or business at some time has to say "no" to yet another spendable desire—or someone has to say it for him or her. In the case of New York City, the demands made on the tax dollars far exceeded the supply of revenue or credit available. Just as the credit agency felt obliged to turn down the lawyer, the state and national governments were forced to say "no" to further requests for aid to New York City.

In the case of the W. T. Grant Company, the company decided to use its scarce resources to compete with other mass merchandisers in the shopping center market. The decision was not a good one. The company's resources proved to be inadequate for effective competition, and the decision came too late to catch the consumers' fancy. Thus the result was economic disaster.

Three economic questions must be answered in order to solve the problem of unlimited wants vs. limited resources.

What Shall We Produce?   Unfortunately, the decision-making process sometimes stops with the first question, "What shall we produce?" A list of wants is informally drawn, and then wants are simply satisfied as they arise. Failure to look at the two subsequent steps in the economic decision-making process can be a bad mistake, as the lawyer and New York City discovered.

How Shall We Produce What We Want?   The second question in the economic decision-making process is "How shall we produce what we want?" Answers include such traditional resources as income (for consumers), taxes (for governments), and investors (for business). Another ingredient or extender of resources for production is credit.

How Shall We Share the Production?   The third question then arises: "How shall we share the production?" The consumer, government, or business must try to do as well as possible with what is available. It was impossible for the lawyer, New York City, and W. T. Grant Company to satisfy all of their wants. When economic decisions are being made, therefore, consideration must be given to the scarce resources available.

This is the basic problem of consumer money management: How can people and society employ, produce, and distribute scarce resources for maximum satisfaction?

MEASURES OF ECONOMIC HEALTH

Economic decision making is less complicated when the economic climate is positive. Several indicators signal a healthy economy: full employment, stable prices, and economic growth. Each of these economic indicators is regularly monitored by the federal government, and results are made public to help indicate the direction the economy is taking. The unemployment rate is a barometer of the full employment goal, the consumer price index measures economic stability, and the gross national product reflects economic growth.

Unemployment Rate

As an economic indicator, the unemployment rate has an influence on all economic planning. It is impossible for the unemployment rate to be zero. Workers will always quit their jobs, get fired, or move from one part of the country to another. It has been estimated that 4 to 5 percent of the working population will always be out of a job at any one time for reasons such as these. In recent years, however, this low rate has not been achieved. After reaching a high of 9 percent in May 1975 and then hovering around 8 percent, the rate of unemployment had finally dropped to slightly less than 6 percent in late 1978 (see Figure 13-1), only to rise to the double-digit level in 1979.

The unemployment rate will vary from area to area. For example, even when national unemployment is high, a great demand for oil may result in a low unemployment rate in an oil-producing area. When the automobile is selling well, the north central region enjoys prosperity, but when automobile sales are off, the local unemployment rate rises because of layoffs in the auto industry and related fields. Unemployment also differs among work groups within the work force. When the unemployment rate is 5.9 percent, adult males may really have a 4.1-percent rate while adult women may be unemployed at a 6.1-percent rate. A further breakdown in the Labor Department data may place the unemployment rate among married men at 2.8 percent. During the same period, black unemployment may be 11.7 percent, and unemployment among teenagers could hover around the 16 percent rate.

A figure secondary to the unemployment rate but equally important is the number who enter the work force. Even when the unemployment

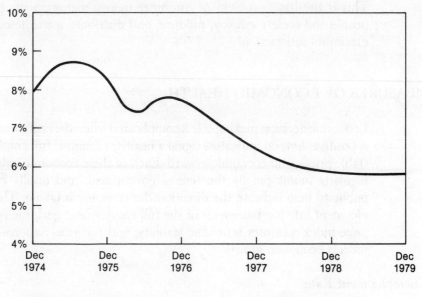

Seasonally Adjusted

FIGURE 13-1. Unemployment Rate. (Department of Labor.)

rate is rising, the total number of persons employed can still increase. Population growth and previously nonsalaried individuals entering the work force may account for this increase. Separate figures record the total number of persons employed, as well as the average work week and the average weekly and hourly wages. In spite of high unemployment during the mid 1970s, a record number of over 94 million United States citizens were employed in 1978.

Consumer Price Index

Price stability is reported by means of the consumer price index (CPI). There are actually two indexes. One measures the spending of urban clerical workers and wage earners. The second index, started in 1977, represents all the households in urban areas. The first one reflects the spending of 35 to 40 percent of the population. The second index reflects the spending habits of approximately 80 percent of the population.

The consumer price index measures the changes in a "market basket" of over 400 consumer items selected by the U.S. Department of Labor. The items in the index are weighted to reflect proportionate spending by the population for each item. Each month the same items are priced at the same locations. Prices are then compared, both to those for previous months and to those for the base year.

The base year used by the U.S. Department of Labor is 1967. If a 500 gram (1.1 pound) loaf of bread that cost 15¢ in 1967 (100-percent base) costs 30¢ now, the CPI would be $(30 \div 15) = 2 = 200$. This is a 100-percent increase in the cost of bread from the base-year price of 15¢.

At the time of writing, the consumer price index was hovering around the 225 level. This means that there had been more than a 100 percent increase in the prices of goods in the market basket.

What is the significance of the CPI? The consumer price index reflects the cost of living in the United States. A monthly rise in the consumer price index may indicate a broad rise in prices, or it may show a rise in prices of one or more classes of items, such as food or energy.

Table 13-1 illustrates both versions of the consumer price index for August 1978. Statistics for both urban consumers and the wage earners and clerical workers show increases in the cost of food, housing, apparel and upkeep, transportation, medical care, and entertainment. Highest increases over the previous year's figures are for fruits and vegetables (15.3), sugar and sweets (12.7), and home ownership (11.2). Lowest increases are in apparel and upkeep and nonalcoholic beverages.

Consumer price index figures for specific geographic areas are also kept by the U.S. Department of Labor's Bureau of Statistics. For example, during the August 1978 period, food and beverage cost increases for wage earners and clerical workers ranged from 9.1 in Denver to 12.2 in Kansas City.

When the cost of living varies by 1 or 2 percent a year, prices are considered stable. However, the increase in the cost of living has been much higher (6 to 12 percent a year) during the 1970s.

Gross National Product

The gross national product (GNP) is simply the total of all the economic goods and services produced in the nation during a period of time, usually one year. The GNP is measured by the U.S. Department of Commerce. In order to absorb new workers into the labor force, as well as to take care of workers displaced because of changes in technology, the economy must continually expand. Historically, we know that an annual gain in the GNP of less than 3 percent creates increased unemployment and a decrease in total national income. Through use of the GNP, we can tell how our economic progress compares not only to that of prior years, but also to that of other nations.

Gross national product is reported in two ways. The first measurement compares production in current dollars; the second measures GNP in real dollars, which take inflation into consideration. If the GNP ex-

TABLE 13-1. Consumer Price Index, August 1978

	All Urban Consumers			Wage Earners and Clerical Workers		
		Percent change from			Percent change from	
	Index 1967 = 100	1 month ago	1 year ago	Index 1967 = 100	1 month ago	1 year ago
All Items	197.8	0.6	7.9	197.7	0.5	7.9
Food and Beverages	210.1	0.2	10.1	210.0	0.2	10.1
Food	215.4	0.2	10.3	215.4	0.3	10.3
Food at home	214.5	−0.1	11.0	214.3	−0.1	10.9
Cereals & bakery products	203.1	0.9	11.2	203.9	0.9	11.6
Meats, poultry, fish & eggs	210.4	−0.2	16.5	210.5	0.0	16.6
Dairy products	186.1	0.4	6.3	186.3	0.5	6.4
Fruits & vegetables	221.4	−1.9	15.3	219.9	−2.4	14.5
Sugar & sweets	262.0	0.6	12.7	261.6	0.2	12.5
Fats & oils	214.5	0.5	6.7	214.5	0.2	6.7
Nonalcoholic beverages	340.7	−0.3	−1.9	340.0	−0.3	−2.1
Other prepared foods	192.0	0.9	10.2	191.8	0.9	10.0
Food away from home	221.7	0.8	9.2	221.9	1.1	9.3
Alcoholic beverages	161.0	0.6	6.6	161.3	0.5	6.8
Housing	205.2	0.7	9.0	204.8	0.6	8.8
Rent residential	165.1	0.5	6.9	165.1	0.5	6.9
Homeownership	230.6	1.0	11.2	230.4	0.9	11.1
Fuel & other utilities	218.1	0.0	6.7	218.2	0.0	6.7
Household furnishings & oper.	178.9	0.4	6.2	177.8	0.3	5.6
Apparel & Upkeep	159.6	1.0	3.1	159.7	0.9	3.2
Men's & boys' apparel	156.7	0.3	1.6	157.0	0.1	1.7
Women's & girls' apparel	149.1	1.8	1.4	149.2	2.0	1.5
Infants' & toddlers' apparel	219.3	1.3	3.6	217.7	1.1	2.8
Footwear	163.5	0.9	3.9	163.0	0.7	3.6
Transportation	188.1	0.5	5.2	188.7	0.5	5.5
Private transportation	187.7	0.5	5.3	188.2	0.5	5.6
Public transportation	187.6	−0.1	2.2	187.9	0.0	2.4
Medical Care	221.4	0.9	8.1	221.3	0.8	8.0
Medical care commodities	144.5	0.3	7.0	145.0	0.3	7.3
Medical care services	237.7	1.0	8.2	237.5	0.9	8.2
Entertainment	177.4	0.2	5.2	176.5	0.2	4.7
Other Goods and Services	184.0	0.5	6.9	184.3	0.3	7.0
All Items (1957–59 = 100)	230.0	—	—	230.0	—	—

Source: Department of Labor, Bureau of Statistics.

pressed in current dollars is rising more rapidly than the GNP in real dollars, inflation is occurring. If the real GNP is rising more rapidly than the increase in general population, incomes will increase because of the rise in real spending power.

Although it is not completely accurate, the GNP is based on a large mass of data and is the best measure we have of our economic growth.

THE FREE ENTERPRISE SYSTEM

Americans are often called capitalists. This is more than a simple label—it is a description of our economic system. Under this system, machinery, buildings, and the money to buy them, instead of being government-owned, are all privately owned and operated for profit.

The United States is further described as having a free enterprise system. This means that decisions about how much to produce and how services and goods are to be allocated are made by private industry rather than the government. Dollars spent by consumers are their economic votes and are most often the real determiners of what and how much will be produced.

Strictly speaking, our economy is a mixed economy rather than a purely capitalistic system. This is because all industry is not completely free to do whatever it wishes however it wishes. Many industries are tightly regulated by the government, such as those engaged in banking, agriculture, freight hauling, and public service. And all commercial concerns are subject to government intervention in the areas of safety, environmental effect, employment practices, and competition.

Central Premises

Our economy rests on three central premises: private property, profit, and competition.

Private property refers to the private ownership of real estate, as well as the right of the individual to spend earnings as desired.

Profit is the incentive that encourages individuals to produce, work, or invest in the free enterprise system. Realizing that our economy is based on this profit incentive, the consumer should look with suspicion on the lure of winning free prizes, such as sewing machines or dance lessons. The business that really gave its merchandise away would not remain in business long. Our economic system is based on the assumption that profit is ordinarily a good guide as to what should be produced. When profits are high in an industry, output will usually be expanded. If losses are being incurred, output will usually be cut or eliminated.

The key element in the free enterprise system is competition. Competition exists because resources are scarce. Businesses must share the consumer dollars; individuals must seek the same employment opportunities. Without competition, the free enterprise system would become mired in waste in the form of high prices, poor products, and low efficiency.

The Free Market

The free enterprise system exists in a setting called a free market. A market consists of transactions between buyers and sellers. The grocery store is sometimes referred to as a market—it is really a collection of markets for products offered by sellers.

A market is not necessarily based in a fixed geographical area. Buyers and sellers may be far apart, as long as a method of communication exists. Where distances are great or situations complex, middlepeople may be necessary to arrange transactions between buyers and sellers. Insurance agents and stockbrokers are examples of middlepeople.

The free market is a reconciler of interests that are sometimes conflicting. For example, when buying a lawn mower the consumer must decide how much money to sacrifice for safety considerations. Is the consumer willing to pay 20 to 30 percent more for features that protect feet and hands from injury? The market can tell manufacturers whether these features are important, based on sales to consumers. Consumers can also influence the addition of safety features through government agencies. In the past, when faced with higher costs, some manufacturers chose to modify or ignore the standards imposed by government agencies, but today the government safety regulations are enforced more stringently.

Laws of Supply and Demand

The forces of supply and demand are determiners of price in a free enterprise system.

The law of demand states that the higher the price of a product, the less willing people are to buy that product. The lower the price, the more willing people are to buy it. Demand exists where there are buyers with money or credit in hand who want to purchase goods and services. Dreaming about owning a Porsche does not constitute demand for a Porsche. But when the desire for a Porsche is backed with purchasing power, then there is demand for a Porsche. Demand is measured in terms of the number of people who want the same item. And all of them have one idea in common—all want to buy the item at the lowest possible price.

The law of demand is related to the buyers' side of the market, while the law of supply is related to the sellers' side. The quantities of goods and services that are offered for sale at all different prices represent supply. Since suppliers and producers want to make as much money as possible, they will produce whatever promises to provide the most profit. Thus the law of supply states that the quantity supplied increases as price rises.

When buyers and sellers negotiate en masse, there is a certain amount of testing and bargaining going on. Some buyers will get a better deal than others, and some will put off their purchases altogether.

For example, a new automobile carries a sticker price listing the maximum cost of the car and the options. Some buyers will pay the sticker price without negotiation. Others, who negotiate, may buy at just above the dealer cost. Still others will find the price too high and will refuse to buy. Most of the buyers will pay a price that is close to what may be considered a common price.

In turn, some sellers will negotiate for higher prices, while some will stop producing an item because it is not economically profitable for them to do so.

The prices paid for a product tend to group around a central point called the *equilibrium price*. This is the price on which most of the buyers and sellers agree. At this price there will be enough automobiles of a certain type for all who want to buy them. At a higher sticker price, fewer buyers would purchase the car. This means that some of the sellers would have to either drop out of the marketplace or be stuck with unsold cars. On the other hand, at a lower sticker price, more cars would be demanded than could be supplied. When such a situation develops, price is forced up until supply matches demand or until production increases.

A change in price does not in itself change desire; it changes only the number of people who are prepared to buy. The same may be said about supply. As the potential for more profit becomes evident, more producers are willing to risk an investment. When potential profits diminish, fewer producers decide to enter the market.

Various other factors may also cause the demand or supply for a product to change. Alterations in tastes or preferences may change demand. The reduction in the number of people who cast votes for Chrysler products caused them to lose over $700 million in 1979. The demand for larger cars decreased when gasoline prices rose dramatically, and it may decrease even more if the government imposes a tax on the sale of larger cars.

Supply changes most often when high costs create unfavorable production conditions. Producer costs are classified as either fixed or variable. *Fixed costs* remain the same even if no goods are produced. *Variable costs* per item decrease as more items are produced. If variable costs, such as the cost of advertising, become too high, the prospective producer may decide not to produce a product at all.

Demand for some products is said to be *elastic*. This means that price changes will affect the quantity of a product purchased. Other products are considered *inelastic* in demand because demand is not affected to a great extent by changes in price. Demand for luxury items is generally elastic. On the other hand, demand for necessities, such as milk, is rather inelastic. Very often, the demand for items that require only a small portion of the total family budget, such as pepper or matches, tends to be inelastic. The demand for larger items, such as cars or houses, tends to be elastic. If consumers have the option of trying to repair the goods, as in the case of lamps or watches, demand for the products will be elastic. The demand for perishable or nonrepairable items, such as foods or light bulbs, is more inelastic. If it is possible for a consumer to substitute one item for another, the demand for that item is elastic—you can drink tea instead of coffee or drive instead of fly. The demand for goods that do not have ready substitutes, such as a muffler for the car or a fuse for the furnace, is considered to be inelastic. Like most other marketplace principles, the principle of elasticity of demand is based on common sense.

THE DECISION MAKING

The market economy is directed by the economic decisions of three groups of active participants—buyers, sellers, and government. Consumers seek the best value for their dollar, and businesspeople seek the highest price for what they offer in the marketplace, while the government is concerned with the best interests of all participants.

All of the groups—government, business, and consumer—make the same type of economic decisions. Whether a businessperson is hiring a new employee, a homeowner is painting the house, or a government is fighting poverty, a three-step decision-making process is taking place.

The first question is "What is the situation?" For the consumer, the situation may be that the paint on the south side of the house has begun to peel.

The second question is "What are the alternatives for solving the problem?" For each economic problem there is a list of alternatives. Some are plausible and others are quite unrealistic. The alternatives for the homeowner include painting just the south side of the house and painting the whole house. Either could be accomplished by: (1) hiring a painter to do the job; (2) painting the house on evenings and weekends or vacations; (3) taking time off from work to complete the job. Another possible course would be to put the job off for another year.

The third question is "What are the consequences of each alternative?" By painting just one side of the house, the consumer would save money this year, but would the paint fade by next year, causing a permanent variation in color? Also, the cost of paint might be higher next year. Hiring a painter would be quite costly. Painting the house on weekends would definitely take much longer, and the individual would have to give up several weekends. Taking time off from work would mean lost pay or sacrificed vacation time. Finally, putting the job off for another year is not a very desirable alternative, as the house would become even more unsightly in a year's time.

Several economic principles are then utilized in the actual decision making. The consumer may decide to hire a professional painter on the basis of absolute advantage. An *absolute advantage* is a real, unconditional, positive advantage. When the probable costs and hours are tallied, the consumer may find that the time needed to do the painting could be better spent. Perhaps the consumer is a rather slow and inexperienced painter. If so, by doing the job himself the consumer might actually wind up with an inferior paint job, in addition to having spent time and money.

If the consumer is a good painter and a well-paid worker, quality is not a factor, but time and energy utilization still are. The decision would then have to be based on a comparative advantage. A comparative advantage is a relative good; it is not positive or absolute. Decisions based on comparative advantage are, of course, harder to make.

An economic principle that is utilized in evaluating alternatives is opportunity cost. *Opportunity cost* is an estimate of the amount of money or other benefits you would give up if you decide on the first alternative rather than the second, or vice versa. It is best to calculate the probable cost in lost revenue of the "next best" alternative before making a final decision.

No attempt will be made here to select the most economical alternative in the house-painting example. This analysis merely shows that there are angles to consider before making choices. Snap decisions on the part of government, business, or consumers may be costly in terms of both money and satisfaction. Needless to say, each of the participants in the marketplace needs to make difficult economic choices. These choices can be made more readily and more accurately if the decision maker has an understanding of economic decision making. This brings us to a closer examination of the roles of government, business, and consumers in the marketplace.

THE ROLE OF GOVERNMENT

Is the government a meddler or a positive force in our economic system? The federal responsibility for influencing levels of growth, employment, and prices through its powers to spend, tax, and control money are widely recognized and accepted. State and local governments have equally accepted powers. The more controversial functions are those performed by what some refer to as the fourth branch of government—federal administrative agencies. Federal regulation through these agencies has come a long way from the first attempt to merely curb the power of monopolies. Since the establishment of the Interstate Commerce Commission in 1887 and the passage of the Sherman Antitrust Act in 1890, hundreds of other federal departments, agencies, divisions, and bureaus have been created to regulate various aspects of the nation's commerce.

Each of the many federal agencies was created by Congress. The agency administrators are appointed by the President, with confirmation by the Senate. The agencies write and enforce regulations. Here are some recent examples of regulations and their subsequent enforcement:

- The Consumer Product Safety Commission required all stores to remove children's nightwear treated with "Tris" from the shelves. This action was based on a report that the product might cause cancer. When the F. W. Woolworth Company refused, the Commission obtained a court order forcing the company to comply.
- The Federal Trade Commission directed CBS Inc. not to bill consumers for unordered copies of *Field and Stream* magazine sent out by the company. According to FTC regulations, merchandise may be considered a gift if it has not been ordered.
- The Food and Drug Administration seized about twelve tons of apricot kernels because they are the basic ingredient of the substance sold under the name Laetrile. Laetrile is considered by some doctors and cancer patients to provide effective relief from cancer, but many medical researchers in this country are positively convinced that it is not a cure for cancer sufferers.

Government's presence is welcomed by many consumers, who do not trust businesses to initiate social improvements. Government is also welcomed by many businesses, who depend on it for protection against the predatory practices of their competition.

Most economists agree that the size and complexity of the United States economic system necessitate some sort of governmental supervision. Business takes its cue from the marketplace, where demand is balanced against what it will cost to supply a product. But societal interests are not accurately assessed or readily measurable in the marketplace value system. The polluted stream, the unhired minorities, and the question of product safety are more equitably considered by a democratic government which responds to the verdicts of the ballot box and the appeals of all special-interest groups.

On the other hand, governmental regulation can and often does interfere with free enterprise. Federal, state, and local governments have passed laws that have a direct influence on the marketplace. For example, various states have laws that require hundreds of individuals to be licensed before they can practice their occupations—doctors, morticians, beauticians, auto mechanics, and television repairpeople are but a few examples. Do such laws protect the consumer, or do they actually restrain trade by regulating the numbers of persons allowed to enter these occupations?

Consumer groups and businesses are attempting to improve the quality of governmental regulation. Reforms are being pushed in virtually all areas.

Recently the old fair trade laws were abolished. The Justice Department estimated that this form of factory price-setting cost consumers 19 to 27 percent more than if the merchants had set their own prices. With the removal of fair trade laws, prices on products as diverse as component stereo systems and barbeque grills fell dramatically. They eventually reached their true market price based on supply and demand.

Moves are currently underway to deregulate both the airline and the trucking industries in order to allow the marketplace forces to determine prices.

The Senate Governmental Operations Committee, in hearings on ways to reform governmental regulation of the trucking industry, was startled to hear of the ICC's handling of the Yak Fat Case. The case involved a trucker named Leroy Hilt, who was so upset about the ICC's favoritism toward railroads that he decided to test how far the Agency would go. He concocted a fake tariff for a nonexistent commodity, yak fat, and proposed that the ICC set a truck rate of 45¢ per 100 pounds from Omaha to Chicago. The railroads, who had failed to do their homework, protested that everyone knows that yak fat can't be transported for less than 63¢ a pound. The ICC ruled against trucker Hilt, saying that he had "failed to sustain" his rate.

In the area of airline regulation, a Senate committee study has found that business-interest lobbying dominates the Civil Aeronautics Board.[1] In a recent year eleven of the major airlines spent $2.8 million to have lawyers represent them before the CAB. The only consumer organization that testified before the CAB, Aviation Consumer Action, spent $20,000.

The question of protection vs. restraint aside, many Americans are critical of the amount of money spent on governmental regulation. For-

[1]G. Carl Wiegand, ed., *The Menace of Inflation* (Old Greenwich, Conn.: Deven-Adair Company, 1977), p. 5.

TABLE 13-2. Federal Regulatory Agencies

Environmental Protection Agency	Created to protect and enhance the natural environment and to control and abate pollution in the areas of air, water, radiation, noise, and toxic substances. The Agency has an annual budget of $78 million and employs 2,312.
Food and Drug Administration	The FDA is housed in the Department of Health, Education and Welfare. Among its many functions, the FDA approves the licensing of manufacturers of biological products and regulates the distribution of their products in interstate commerce. It also scrutinizes the labeling, safety, and effectiveness of all drugs for human use; conducts research on and develops standards on the quality, composition, nutrition, and safety values of foods, cosmetics, and food additives; and develops standards for safe units of radiation exposure. The Administration has an annual budget of $289 million and employs 8,032.
National Highway Traffic Safety Administration	The NHTSA prescribes motor vehicle safety standards, develops miles-per-gallon fuel economy standards for cars, administers the 55-mph speed limit, and operates research and testing programs concerned with traffic safety. The Administration's annual budget is $54 million, and it employs 828.
Equal Employment Opportunity Commission	EEOC was created with the purpose of ending discrimination based on race, color, religion, sex, or national origin in hiring, promotion, wages, job testing, training, apprenticeships, and all other conditions of employment. It promotes voluntary action programs by business, unions, and communities to make equal employment a reality for everyone. The Commission operates on a budget of $77 million and employs 2,539.

Note: Budget data are for 1978.

Consumer Product Safety Commission	The CPSC was established to reduce deaths and injuries associated with more than 10,000 consumer products. Among the twenty-four most serious safety and health hazards are asbestos and benzene (the inhalation of which has been linked to cancer), skateboards, and public playground equipment. The Commission has an annual budget of $40 million and employs 900.
Securities and Exchange Commission	The SEC protects investors and the public against shady practices in the financial and securities markets by requiring the fullest possible disclosures to consumers about financial investment ventures. It also supervises brokerage firms and corporation bankruptcies. The Commission has a budget of $56 million and employs 2,000.
Interstate Commerce Commission	The ICC regulates all interstate surface transportation (trains, trucks, buses, inland waterway and coastal shipping, express companies, and freight forwarders). The Commission has a budget of $63 million and employs 2,301.
Occupational Safety and Health Administration	OSHA was set up to develop and promote safety and health standards in factories, shops, offices, and other workplaces. The Administration has an annual budget of $139 million and employs 2,847 agents to enforce the laws.
Federal Trade Commission	The FTC is charged with keeping competition free and fair. Its duties include preventing price-fixing agreements, boycotts, illegal mergers, and deceptive advertising. The Commission also regulates packaging and labeling of many commodities and proper disclosure of credit terms. The Commission has a budget of $62 million and employs 1,762.

mer President Ford estimated that in 1975 the average person spent as much as $2,000 in higher prices caused by governmental regulation. In addition to the cost in dollars, Americans pay in terms of time spent filling out government forms. For example, the U.S. Office of Management and Budget estimates that a 1040 tax return (the long form) takes 2 hours and 42 minutes to complete. In all, the Management and Budget Office estimates that Americans spent more than 785 million hours filling out federal forms in 1978. Although many of the dollars and hours have been well spent for such marketplace reforms as increasing product safety and cleaning the air, others have been wasted on boondoggles and on mounds of unnecessary paperwork.

The costs of various regulatory agencies, shown in Table 13-2, are unlikely to decrease in future years. Attempts have been made to legislate sunset laws and zero-based budgets, but such forms of control have drawbacks. (Zero-based budgets would force agencies to start their budgets from base zero each year, and sunset laws would set a date when each agency will go out of business unless it could justify continuing its existence.) Under a sunset law, an agency might spend most of its time justifying its existence. And the zero-based budget might force an agency to devote most of its time to preparing its case for a higher budget each year. President Carter is an advocate of zero-based budgeting to reduce spending and to trim bureaucracy. One suggestion that might improve the effectiveness of zero-based budgeting is to prepare budgets to cover a three- to five-year period.

THE ROLE OF BUSINESS

Entrepreneurship

Starting a business, especially a small business, is a high-risk proposition. The tasks of organizing the production and assuming the risk fall to the entrepreneur. The entrepreneur may use his or her own land, labor, and capital, or he or she may use the resources of others. The result may be a one-person business or farm, or it may be a very large corporation. Each year, thousands of persons risk their money setting up new businesses. Over a third of these businesses fail within the first three years. Within five years, over half of them fail. Nevertheless, the hope of earning a lot of money is a strong motivating factor that ensures the continuation of entrepreneurship.

For legal and practical purposes, businesses are formed as single (sole) ownerships, partnerships, corporations, or cooperatives.

The *single ownership,* as the name implies, is a business owned by one person. This form of legal ownership is by far the most common—most small retail and service establishments are single ownerships. The proprietor of a single ownership has unlimited liability to pay for all losses. If the losses are too great to be covered by the business alone, the owner must use personal possessions to repay debts. There are other disadvantages as well. First, it is often difficult for one person to raise the large amount of capital necessary to start or expand a business. Second, the long hours and numerous responsibilities of operating a business are often too much for one person. The incentives of profit and independence, however, are strong.

Few American businesses are organized as general *partnerships*, because this form of ownership has two serious drawbacks. First, the individuals who own a general partnership have unlimited liability both for their own and for each other's business debts. Second, there are legal limitations on the life of a partnership: if one partner dies or withdraws, the partnership is dissolved.

It is possible to add limited partners to a partnership to raise more capital. These limited partners are merely investors; they have little say in the operation of the business, and they have no legal liability to pay debts in excess of the capital they actually invest.

The *corporate form* of ownership is employed by 14 percent of American businesses. This form of business ownership is popular for several reasons. First, a great amount of initial capital can be generated through the sale of stock. A public corporation offers stock to public investors; a private or closed corporation makes its stock available to only a small number of persons. Second, the greater amount of capital generated through multiple ownership makes it possible to borrow greater amount of capital for expansion. Finally, the liability of the owners is limited to the amount each owner has invested in the corporation. In most states one or more persons may incorporate by obtaining a charter from the state.

Cooperatives resemble corporations in one essential way: liability of the members (rather than the stockholders) is limited to their investment. But the similarity ends there. A corporation strives to make a profit for its stockholders, who may or may not be buyers of the corporation's products or services. The cooperative is formed to provide products or services to its members, who band together to accomplish the purpose more economically. Any money generated from the sale, purchase, or manufacture of products and services is passed on to the members. Cooperatives may range from very small neighborhood buying clubs to grocery stores, service stations, credit unions, or even huge marketing co-ops such as Ocean Spray and Sunkist.

According to the Cooperative League of the USA, there are about

28,000 co-ops, 23,000 of which are credit unions. In 1978, the National Cooperative Bank was organized to provide loans to cooperatives. This new funding could double the number of co-ops by making possible the creation of new food, medical, and housing cooperatives. Co-ops can be organized around any product or service, as long as there are people who are willing to sacrifice time and energy to get lower prices.

Concentration

Most American businesses are quite small. According to economist John Kenneth Galbraith, there are from 10 to 12 million small firms in the United States.[2] But although there are relatively few large firms, the power of these firms is not in proportion to their number—the 2,000 largest firms now produce about half of all private products.

There are two basic types of concentration: market concentration and aggregate concentration.

Market concentration is considered heavy within an industry when the four largest firms produce at least 50 percent of all shipments. In his book *A Primer on Monopoly and Competition,* economist Willard Mueller cites market concentration figures that suggest that competition is quite intense in well over half of American manufacturing industries.[3]

Recent figures on aggregate concentration, however, are more alarming. A figure for *aggregate concentration* is derived by adding all manufacturing assets or sales accumulated by the largest corporations. The list resembles the *Fortune* magazine index of the 500 largest firms, except that any number of firms may be used (top 100, 200, or 2,000), depending on the researcher's goals. John Shenefield, Chief of the Antitrust Division at the Justice Department, recently noted with alarm that the share of manufacturing assets owned by the 200 largest companies rose from 46 percent in 1947 to 61 percent in 1972.[4]

The increase in aggregate concentration is occurring largely through mergers. Mergers may be of three types: horizontal, vertical, or conglomerate. In a *horizontal merger* two firms that produce the same product (Union Oil California and Pure Oil Company, 1965) get together. A *vertical merger* adds a new step to the production process of a manufactured item. A grocery chain that acquires farms would then have a vertical

[2]John Kenneth Galbraith, "Small Firms Victimized by 'Equality'," *Chicago Tribune,* September 21, 1978.
[3]New York: Random House, 1970, p. 36.
[4]A. F. Ehrbar, " 'Bigness' Becomes the Target of the Trust Busters," *Fortune,* March 26, 1979, p. 34.

organization capable of producing and selling its goods. Today most mergers are conglomerate in nature. A *conglomerate merger* involves the integrating of companies producing different products. The mergers of Kaiser Jeep Corporation (with American Motors), Libby, McNeil & Libby (with Nestlé Alimentana), Parke Davis & Company (with Warner Lambert), Green Giant (with Pillsbury), and Armour (with Greyhound Corporation) were all of a conglomerate nature. Antitrust laws are quite explicit about regulating vertical and horizontal mergers but unclear regarding conglomerate mergers.

The mere shuffling of assets accomplished through mergers is generally considered a poor substitute for a corporation's creation of new products and jobs. In the past it was felt that mergers were often desirable because a healthy firm would absorb one that was not very solvent. This is no longer true. Many healthy firms are now being purchased through takeover rather than through mutual agreement. This trend has even caused some firms to add amendments to their articles of incorporation to make it financially unprofitable for another corporation to force a takeover.

Is concentration dangerous? This depends on how the larger firms use their power. One justification for large size or even concentration is based on an economic principle called *economy of scale*. The principle states that the more a producer manufactures, the less the variable costs will amount to per unit and thus the less the manufacturer will have to charge.

However, if a firm uses its considerable size to squeeze out other firms in its new market, size can definitely be dangerous. The Federal Trade Commission is raising this accusation in its suit against the cereal companies. The FTC maintains that the three largest cereal companies (General Mills, Kellogg, General Foods) sell 86 percent of all ready-to-eat cereal on the market today. In itself, this is not necessarily bad. However, the FTC has charged that the firms have used heavy advertising and the proliferation of brands (eighty to date) to dominate shelf space in order to keep other companies from competing in the cereal market. The FTC argues that it would cost $150 million for a new company to enter into competition with just one of these many types of ready-to-eat cereals. And the FTC estimates that a lack of new-company competition has cost consumers $200 million per year in higher prices. This figure is based on the fact that return on investment for the five largest manufacturers of cereal averaged more than 15 percent between 1958 and 1970, almost twice the U.S. manufacturing average.

Public concern about competition has been focused recently on oil-company ownership of fuel pipelines and other energy-related businesses, such as coal and solar energy companies. Also in the news are antitrust suits filed by the Justice Department against IBM, AT&T, and others. Unfortunately, these cases will cost millions of tax dollars to conduct, and some question their effectiveness in improving competition.

There are other ways concentration can be dangerous. If a firm becomes so diversified that it no longer needs to buy many products from other firms, competition is seriously restrained. If firms make reciprocal agreements with each other, saying "You buy this from my firm and we will buy something else from yours," this too suppresses competition and thus hurts the consumer.

Another danger of concentration is that it is relatively easy to fix prices when an industry is dominated by a few companies. Some tough treatment by the Justice Department now awaits those who would fix prices. The four concerns involved in a recent price-fixing case concerning paper bags paid fines of $200,000, $500,000, $600,000, and $750,000, and two executives were sentenced to four months in jail. Total corporate fines rose to almost $11 million in the fiscal year 1978, up from $2.6 million in fiscal 1977. Unfortunately, however, in its zeal to regulate big business for the sake of competition, government always runs the risk of having a negative effect on small businesses, which must adhere to the same regulations and engage in time-consuming information-gathering efforts to measure competition.

THE ROLE OF THE CONSUMER

Knowledge of economic principles is as important a tool for the consumer as it is for government and business. When consumers shop, they consciously or unconsciously form a subjective scale of preference for goods and services, for they are continually applying scarce means—in this case money—to their unlimited wants. Each month the budget, whether formal or informal, is used to allocate funds for food, clothing, entertainment, and savings, after fixed expenses for shelter, insurance, and installment purchases have been paid.

Effective operation of the free enterprise system depends on informed decision making by consumers. Thus, to obtain maximum satisfaction in the market, consumers should engage in three decision-making steps before they allocate scarce resources.

First, consumers should carefully decide what they want. Consumers with short-term, intermediate, and long-term goals will be more effective than consumers who buy on impulse.

Second, consumers should determine the effectiveness of various purchases in meeting goals. In most cases, this takes some research of literature, advertising, and other resources.

Third, consumers should study prices. It would be very easy, but not too wise, to walk into an auto showroom and pay the sticker price for a new car. As a tool for price knowledge, comparison shopping is unequaled.

Consumers must also learn to become more assertive as well as better informed. Individual buyers can do little to rectify wrongs in the marketplace, but collective consumer pressure is beginning to give consumers a stronger position in relation to business.

Because of consumer pressure, business firms have made many changes in their own complaint structures. Many have hired consumer affairs specialists to deal with consumers. Also, as a result of the consumer movement, products have become safer and of better quality.

CONSUMER DECISION MAKERS

Establish goals.
Evaluate effectiveness of potential purchases in meeting goals.
Study prices.
Be assertive.

The government, too, has come under criticism from the consumer movement. It has been faulted both for its regulatory agencies' abuses of consumers and for its general lack of interest in consumer problems.

Many of the regulatory agencies are directed by people who came from the industries they are supposed to regulate. These agencies, under the threat of monitoring by a federal consumer protection agency, have begun to open more of their hearings to the public. Some are now paying for consumers to come to testify on proposed regulations that would affect them.

In addition, offices of consumer affairs are now available in many areas to funnel consumer problems where they will be heard. And new laws have been passed to place the consumer on a stronger footing with the door-to-door salesperson, the credit industry, and other potential consumer victimizers.

Consumers have begun to realize that consumer rights—the right to be heard, to be informed, to safety, and to consumer education—will only come into being if they are demanded. And by demanding them, the consumer movement is making the marketplace stronger.

Consumers, business, and government are all moving toward a recognition of their common goals within our economic system. A well-informed and well-monitored market system will work to the benefit of all.

QUESTIONS FOR DISCUSSION

1. How does the problem of unlimited wants and limited resources manifest itself on the personal, governmental, and business levels?
2. How do this year's indicators of employment, stable prices, and economic growth compare to last year's?
3. Why is it impossible to achieve full employment?
4. What is the effect of inflation on the economic growth rate and the consumer price index?
5. Could an individual construct a consumer price index? What steps would be involved in developing one?
6. In the United States, where is there evidence of central planning by the government?
7. Do you think competition is always healthy in all markets? If not, cite some areas where you feel it is not healthy.
8. Where do you see evidence of the principle of supply and demand driving prices up? Driving prices down?
9. Would you describe the demand for gasoline as elastic or inelastic? Why?
10. Cite some everyday examples of the principle of opportunity costs.
11. What are some benefits and some drawbacks of government regulation? Do you see the need for more or less regulation in the marketplace?
12. Give an example of entrepreneurship.
13. What would be the advantages and disadvantages of joining a neighborhood buying club?
14. Name some possible reasons why many industries have become more concentrated.
15. Name several areas where the consumer is supplied with greater quantities of buyer information. Do you see areas where there could be more buyer information?

PERSONAL EXPERIENCE PROJECTS

1. Discuss with relatives, friends, and other students their ideas of what constitutes a "healthy economy." Note how their responses differ from those of business leaders, labor leaders, and government officials.

2. Contact the Bureau of Labor Statistics, Consumer Information Department, U.S. Department of Labor, Washington, DC 20210, to obtain a copy of the consumer price index. Observe price changes reported for various products and services. Compare these changes to those you have observed.

3. Conduct a survey of common consumer products (breakfast cereals, soap, toothpaste, etc.) to determine how many manufacturers produce competing brands of the same product. Note the number of manufacturing companies represented and the amount of shelf space each gets in various stores.

4. Interview local owners of small businesses. Discuss their concerns regarding competition, inflation, government regulation, and unions.

5. Observe recent changes in consumer prices for various consumer products and services. Attempt to determine from business news reports how changes in supply and demand have influenced these prices.

6. List the government regulations that are imposed on various industries. Discuss the benefits and costs of these restrictions to consumers.

7. Observe influences that consumers, business, government, and labor have on one another. Discuss with others whether a healthy balance exists among these various sectors of our economy.

8. Survey the opinions of others regarding the effect of consumerism on our free enterprise economy.

14
INFLATION

The phrase "Buy now and pay later," a common expression of the 1960s, has now been expanded tó "Buy now and pay less later." Credit purchases in our economy have come to involve repaying loans of today's dollars with tomorrow's "worth-less" money. The phenomenon seems advantageous at first glance—it sounds like a reason for consumers to buy more. Indeed, eager salespeople invoke the principle to try to speed up consumers' buying decisions. But when the consumer turns around to buy food or clothing or to pay the rent, the advantage turns out to be a hollow one.

The villain is inflation. No one thought much about inflation until 1969. By 1974, however, the term had begun to send shivers of fear and disgust down American spines. That year the rate of inflation over the preceding year became "double digit"—11 percent. The following year was only slightly better, with a rate of 9.1 percent.

WHAT IS INFLATION?

Most economists define inflation as a situation where prices are increasing on a broad front because incomes are increasing faster than the available goods and services. In other words, too many dollars are chasing after too few goods.

The problem of inflation is tied to that of the multiple functions of money. Money has at least three separate functions. First,.it is a medium of exchange. Barter is still practiced occasionally in exchanging labor for food or goods, or in swapping one item for another, but money is the only widely accepted medium of exchange. The second function of money is that of an accounting unit. Money provides a way of keeping track of how much. In its third function, money is a store of value. This last function causes the confusion when inflation strikes. When money value is constantly being bombarded by inflation, its worth, especially future worth, is never certain. Each inflated dollar buys progressively fewer goods and services.

TYPES OF INFLATION

Economists refer to three different types of inflation.

Demand-Pull Inflation

Demand-pull inflation usually occurs during times of prosperity and low unemployment. The economy produces a limited amount of goods and services in a given year. If the demand for these goods exceeds the supply, the prices for the scarce goods rise. Even if more money is created by the government to pay for these scarce goods, or if incomes increase, supply will remain the same for the short term. But both demand and prices will increase, so even more money will be chasing the still scarce goods. Each new dollar will buy less because demand-pull inflation is operating in the market.

Cost-Push Inflation

There are various opinions about just what causes cost-push inflation. Cost refers to all the costs of producing goods and services, including labor costs.·

Labor unions are often blamed for cost-push inflation on the theory that it is their wage demands that cause a rise in the price of the finished product. However, labor leaders and some consumerists prefer to call this type of inflation price-pull inflation because they blame businesses for raising their prices to yield a set percentage of profit regardless of production costs. In any case, it is a vicious cycle, for laborers, since they are also consumers, must again ask for higher wages simply to pay the higher prices.

The argument over what starts the cycle—wage demands or profits —may never be resolved. But since labor is not the only element even in production costs, it really does not deserve all the blame.

Structural Inflation

The third type of inflation is called structural inflation. This type of inflation can occur in time of either high or lower unemployment. Demand for a certain product encourages increased production, and as a result the particular industry involved either agrees to pay more for labor or decides to charge more for the finished product. Price increases, if significant, may spill over into other industries even though their products do not experience any higher demand. In general, there is less resistance to higher prices than there is to lower prices.

THE INFLATIONARY SPIRAL

Whatever the type of inflation, there are many ways to recognize its presence. Creeping inflation (0 to 3 percent per year) may be a bit difficult for the consumer to detect at first, but the galloping inflation (3 percent and over) we have been experiencing since 1968 (see Figure 14-1) is quite obvious to the consumer.

Prices and Quality

Consumers first recognize the inflationary villain when shopping. They notice, for example, that the supermarket shelves hold cans with two or three or sometimes even more price stickers, and that prices at the college, toll gate, and shoe store are rising almost simultaneously. It is actually the latter trait that most clearly signals inflation—the fact that all prices rise in a virtually simultaneous fashion.

Where prices do remain the same, the quality or quantity of items tends to fall. Even products such as candy bars shrink in size if not in price. A survey by *U.S. News & World Report* revealed that nowadays very few industries and businesses are rated "excellent" or "good" by a majority of the respondents in giving the customer value for the money. The only industries listed as excellent or good by a majority of those surveyed were airlines, watch manufacturers, and color TV manufacturers. Those industries rated excellent or good by the fewest consumers were the auto insurance companies, automobile manufacturers, gasoline pro-

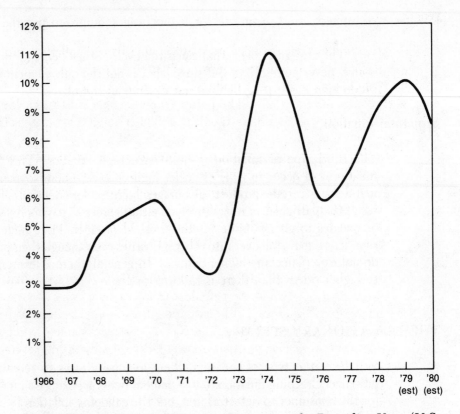

FIGURE 14-1. Increases in Consumer Prices over the Preceding Year. (U.S. Department of Labor Statistics.)

ducers, and automobile dealers.[1] It is no wonder that the consumer regards inflation as a treacherous disease!

Investments and Loans

Inflation also erodes the value of many types of investments, particularly those available to the small investor—life insurance, savings accounts, and savings bonds. An investment with a return that looked high at the time of purchase may actually provide a very low "real" return after prolonged inflation. To make matters worse, because new investors want higher returns on their investments and new savers want more interest on their savings, lenders must charge more for home mortgages and auto and business loans.

[1]"Getting Your Money's Worth," *U.S. News & World Report,* June 27, 1977, p. 28.

Wages

Inflation's effect on wage increases is obvious. An inflation rate of 6.8 percent has a disasterous effect on an 8-percent raise. For example, consider a person who made $15,000 in 1977 and was granted an 8-percent raise for 1978. The person's new income is $16,200. But since the additional $1,200 is taxed at a higher rate, the individual's new after-tax income is $14,421, as compared with $13,339 in 1977. (This average was derived from an actual return with typical deductions and exemptions.) Since an inflation rate of approximately 6.8 percent occurred during the year, however, the real value of the increased wage is decreased to $13,440. Thus the gross increase of $1,200 turns out to be a real wage increase of only $101. During the same year, an 8-percent increase on the $75,000 level would have amounted to a real gain of only $5!

To cope with this effect of inflation, workers then make new wage demands, which perpetuate the inflationary spiral. Interestingly, many people seem not to be aware of this cause and effect. When the psychological economist George Katona asked respondents in a survey why they were making more money than they had been several years ago,[2] they referred most often to their own efforts, to increased experience and ability, and to progress in their careers. They did not refer to inflation or to activities of the government or trade unions. These persons saw little or no connection between wage increases and price increases.

ECONOMIC INDEXES

There are a number of concrete statistics that economists use to gauge and to predict rates of inflation. Unfortunately these statistics do not appear on the financial pages in most newspapers. However, they do appear in the *Wall Street Journal*, and they are beginning to catch on with popular news magazines, radio announcers, and television newscasters. It is not unusual now to find reports of the most recent trend of the CPI, or of the rise or fall of leading indicators. This is a sign that business and the consumer are joining with government planners in an attempt to make planning a more exact science. Following is a look at the four basic indicators.

[2]George Katona, *Aspirations and Affluence: Comparative Studies in the U.S. and Western Europe* (New York: McGraw-Hill, 1971).

Consumer Price Index

The consumer price index can be a helpful indicator of inflation. Even though many items in the index market basket are outdated, the CPI gives the reader a good measure of how fast the general price level is rising. Some people multiply the monthly change in the CPI by twelve to determine an annual inflation rate, but this is a misleading test. By that test, a drop in the CPI in one month from 1 percent to ½ percent would make it appear that inflation had dropped from 12 percent to 6 percent in a one-month period.

Earnings versus Productivity

Another inflationary indicator actually involves two indexes. If the monthly index of adjusted hourly earnings is rising more rapidly than the average output per hour (productivity) index, there is underlying inflation in the economy. Inflation can only slow down if productivity increases faster than wages.

Money Supply

Money watchers pay close attention to money supply statistics as an inflationary signal. The Federal Reserve issues these figures in two parts: M1 is currency in circulation and in checking accounts; M2 is money in savings-type accounts in commercial banks.

The Federal Reserve has the power to change short-term interest rates, and it will do so if the combined M1, M2 money supply in the economy exceeds or falls below the amount needed for a healthy economy. The stock market has become particularly sensitive to the M1, M2 figures. Any hint that prevailing amounts may exceed Federal Reserve goals will send the stock market down, for investors know that the Federal Reserve will raise interest rates. Higher rates are definitely a poor sign for the investor, for they decrease the amount business will be able to borrow for expansion.

Composite Leading Indicator Index

The three sets of figures mentioned so far—CPI, output and wage rates, and money supply—are all based on past performance. Even though they have definite implications for the future, other indexes, such as the composite leading indicator index, are better forecasters of the shape of things to come.

The composite index of leading indicators (see Figure 14-2) comprises ten to twelve individual statistics with a good record of moving ahead of the economy as a whole. The U.S. Commerce Department usually reports its data using the following ten indexes:

1. *Sensitive Materials Prices.* Sensitive materials prices are wholesale prices of nonfood crude materials—a forecaster of future prices of retail items.

2. *Number of Companies Reporting Slower Deliveries.* Slower deliveries mean that companies are backlogged. This is a good sign.

3. *Inflation-Adjusted Money Supply.* The greater the supply of money, the greater the possible spending for scarce products. The result of oversupply is usually inflation.

4. *Liquid Assets Held by Businesses.* Like consumers, businesses can spend or refrain from spending available cash. Huge re-

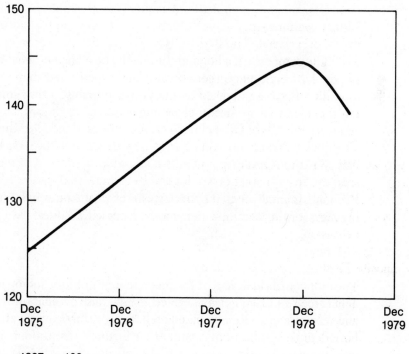

1967 = 100

FIGURE 14-2. Leading Indicators

serves show a caution on the part of business and impede expansion.

5. *Common Stock Prices.* Stock prices are a good indicator of the general feeling of investors.

6. *Length of the Average Work Week.* The longer the average work week, the more goods are being produced and the greater the employment possibilities.

7. *Layoff Rate.* Heavy layoffs are a bad sign.

8. *New Orders for Durable and Nondurable Consumer Goods.* More orders are a good sign.

9. *Building Permits.* An increase in the number of building permits signals good times for the building trades, as well as many other related work and financial areas.

10. *Contracts and Orders for Plants and Equipment.* The more plant and equipment orders there are, the more expansion may be foreseen.

The composite leading indicator is the best known signal of business trends. However, since the indicator has experienced many short-term monthly advances and declines, most economists use a three-month moving average to gauge future economic activity.

CAUSES OF INFLATION

Economists are divided in their opinions of what causes inflation. Following are a few of the most commonly accepted theories.

Too Much Money

The monetarists believe that too much money in the economy in the form of checking and savings accounts is the only cause of inflation. They would have the Federal Reserve Bank sell treasury obligations (notes, bills, bonds) to the public, banks, and other financial institutions, in order to take money out of the economy. If there were less money to spend or loan, the economy, the monetarists say, would "cool off."

If money became too hard to get, the Federal Reserve Board could always place more money into the economy by buying back treasury instruments. The money from the sale of the treasury instruments would then be used by business and consumers for loans and spending. Thus a recession could be avoided.

Other economists, however, feel that the monetarists overestimate the importance of the "too much money" situation.

Wartime Economy

Another explanation for inflation is that it is produced by a wartime economy. War brings low unemployment, because workers are needed to produce wartime tools just when the labor pool is smallest. When labor is short, wages increase and so does spending for scarce consumer goods.

Deficit Spending

The U.S. government has chosen to finance both wartime and peacetime programs through deficit spending. This means that the government must compete in the money market to sell its debt instruments. Such competition can drive up the cost of borrowed money for both business and government, thereby pushing up other costs as well.

Some business borrowers will actually be crowded out. This hampers the economic expansion necessary to produce new goods and services. The demand for goods and services, meanwhile, is pushed up by people who make money as a result of government spending. Hence there is inflationary pressure on the fewer goods available.

Lack of Competition

Many economists blame inflation on a lack of competition in industry. Economist John Kenneth Galbraith, a major spokesman for the group, states:

> In the United States a couple of hundred large industrial corporations now provide around 60 percent, not much less than two-thirds, of all manufacturing employment. Similarly the handful of big airlines, the two telephone companies, the three broadcasting networks, the separate power companies that are dominant in their respective industries and markets. Around fifty of the largest banks provide about half of all the banking services in the United States. The insurance business is yet more concentrated. Even retailing is dominated by a relatively small number of large chains. The overall result is that a couple of thousand big corporations now provide more than half of all private production of all goods and services.

An inescapable consequence of the development of the large corporation is that price-making ceases to be competitive and impersonal. Instead, the corporation gains the power to set its own prices.[3]

According to Senator William Proxmire, "there isn't any question that we have wage and price fixing, particularly in concentrated industries and with big labor unions."[4] And government may have actually fanned inflation in this wage and price area. The Interstate Commerce Commission and the Civil Aeronautics Board, for example, which were originally created to hold down prices in areas where there was little competition, have often served to hinder competition.

Energy Shortage

The energy shortage, with its subsequent effect on energy costs, has been another inflationary force. This shortage, which has directly affected the price of raw products such as gasoline and heating fuel, has indirectly affected the price of virtually everything else we buy. It has also had an adverse effect on our balance of payments (exports over imports). Money leaving the country for imports now exceeds money coming in from exports, mainly as a result of our huge purchases of energy.

If we choose to blame any one or any combination of the causes discussed above, we can find support from some economic corner. The public seems equally divided. In a recent study, household heads were asked to name the group that they thought was "most to blame" for higher prices. Thirty-six percent blamed labor unions. Thirty percent said that the government's deficit spending (payments exceed revenues) was to blame. Twenty-three percent thought that business was the major culprit.

REDISTRIBUTION OF WEALTH

Economically, inflation is feared mainly because it brings about unfair redistribution of wealth and income, as business, government, and various groups of consumers are affected to different extents.

[3]John Kenneth Galbraith and Nicole Salinger, *Almost Everyone's Guide to Economics* (Boston: Houghton Mifflin Company, 1978), p. 35.
[4]G. Carl Wiegand, ed., *The Menace of Inflation* (Old Greenwich, Conn.: Deven-Adair Company, 1977), p. 5.

Business

Businesses can usually protect their profits during times of inflation by writing clauses into contracts (especially long-term contracts) that enable them to pass on increased costs to buyers. It is not unusual, for example, for a contract for a new automobile to contain a clause stating that if the manufacturer raises the cost of the car before it is delivered, the customer must pay that increased cost in addition to the previously determined price. And it is no longer unusual for auto manufacturers to raise their prices in the middle of the year as well as at the beginning of a new model year.

Government

News headlines are always announcing government projects that have failed to meet original cost estimates. The Alaskan pipeline is an example of a project with a huge cost overrun. Original estimates of the cost were set at $900 million, but the final price of the project was closer to $10 billion, including interest on the debt. Much of this increase was due to the inflation that occurred during a four-year delay in the project.

Government, however, can protect itself from the pinch of inflation. Inflated prices are covered to some extent by the additional income taxes that are collected as taxpayers' cost-of-living increases force them into higher and higher tax brackets. If funds are still not sufficient, to protect itself the government will raise taxes.

The Consumer

Inflation has many day-to-day effects on all families, but certain groups are more adversely affected than others. Stanford University economist G. L. Bach believes that the kind of unpaid-for assets a family possesses does much to determine its vulnerability to inflation.[5] Those families that have considerable debt which is payable in cheaper future dollars are not very likely to be damaged by inflation. This is especially true if the debt was incurred to buy property or other assets with a high resale value.

Let us take a look at various consumer classes.

The Poor. The poor are adversely affected because they cannot obtain loans. What little help is available tends to be monetary rather than income-producing. On the other hand, however, welfare benefits and Social Security payments generally seem to increase at about the same rate as the general price level.

[5]*Money,* November 1973, p. 39.

Older People.   Older people are seriously hurt because they have comparatively large holdings in such low-interest assets as bank deposits, pensions, and insurance. Those on Social Security have some relief, though, as raises in these payments are now tied to the cost of living.

The Very Rich.   The very rich do not suffer much from inflation. First of all, many of these people rely on business profits for their income, and profits tend to keep pace with or exceed inflationary price increases. Second, even if their real incomes are reduced, this only affects their savings and reinvestments and not their standard of living. Third, those who are salaried seem to have enough clout to see that their salaries keep pace with inflation. A report filed with the Securities and Exchange Commission in 1978 showed that ITT Chairman Harold A. Geneen was paid $986,000, and International Harvester Chief Executive Archie R. McCardell made $460,000 (after receiving a bonus of $41.5 million for coming to IH).[6] These are representative of the high salaries paid to top executives of large corporations. Union leaders are no slouches at beating

Reprinted, courtesy of the *Chicago Tribune*.

[6]Bill Neikirk and R. C. Longworth, "Inflation Robs US of Ability to Create Wealth, Jobs," *Chicago Tribune*, November 15, 1978, p. 10.

inflation either. Teamster President Frank Fitzsimmons earned $169,000, and Chicagoan Edward T. Hanley of Hotel and Restaurant Employees got $126,000.[7]

In general, available figures showed a 19 percent raise for top officials in 1976. During the same period, the pay of wage earners rose by 7.3 percent.

The Middle Class. The middle-income group, which makes up the bulk of the population, bears the brunt of inflation. Nonunion employees, teachers, government employees, and other groups with limited bargaining power fare the worst. But even those employees whose contracts have cost-of-living escalator clauses have problems. Rarely are the escalator clauses built so that a 1-percent increase in inflation (CPI) is matched with a 1-percent increase in wages.

CAN INFLATION BE CURED?

Policymakers have few tools with which to work on the wage-price spiral, which feeds on itself. Complicating the situation further are psychological factors, such as the public's expectations about the future and their trust in the government's ability to control inflation. It will certainly be some years before inflation is brought under control. Some people say that it will never be under control and that Americans will just have to learn to live with it.

The traditional method for attacking inflation is to slow down economic growth by reducing government spending, raising taxes, or cutting back on the growth of the money supply. These possible approaches have one element in common—an unfortunate retardation of economic activity occurs. Thus traditional government measures will raise the unemployment rate. Use of these tools, therefore, involves a great deal of politics. In addition, many feel that even if the government applied its traditional tools, there is no guarantee that the inflation rate would be dampened permanently.

The government has two basic alternatives. The first is to gradually reduce spending and money creation. The goal in making such a move would be to affect prices without increasing unemployment or causing a recession. The second alternative is to adopt a policy that would hold down prices and wages without controls. Because of an unsuccessful attempt at controls made during the early 1970s, the idea of controls has very little support among the American public. Ben E. Laden of the

[7] *Ibid.*

investment-research firm of T. Rowe Price Associates suggests that "the government offer tax incentives to unions and businesses that make a special effort to hold down wages. For example, the government might offer a tax cut if unions would agree to hold their wage increases to a specified low level."[8] Ideas such as Laden's are still in the brainstorming stages. The fact remains, however, that new approaches to the problem must be tried if inflation is to be brought under control.

COPING WITH INFLATION

There is not much the ordinary citizen can do about inflation except to suffer. However, it is possible to adjust spending and investing plans somewhat to take some of the pressure of inflation off the family income.

Adjusting Spending Plans

How do families cope with inflation? Following are some methods commonly adopted by American families to deal with inflation.[9]

Leisure Time. For families seriously hurt by the economic downturn, the first step is to cut back on the "nice things of life":

- eating out in restaurants
- entertaining friends for dinner
- engaging in hobbies and sports.

Overall, many families report they have begun to spend most of their free time at home rather than "going out."

Vacations. Families are not necessarily giving up vacations, but they often regard them differently. Annual vacations today are considered a luxury by many families.

Use of Electricity. Most families are caught in a losing battle with their utility bills. Although they are cutting back on the use of electricity, they are paying more for utilities than they used to. The utility-bill component of American family expenditures increased 14.6 percent between 1972 and 1978.[10]

[8]*U.S. News & World Report,* August 22, 1977, p. 18.
[9]Inspiration for a number of these categories comes from a Yankelovitch, Skelly, and White study, "General Mills American Family Report for 1974–75." Copyright 1975 General Mills, Inc. 9200 Wayzata Blvd., Minneapolis, Minn. 55440.
[10]"Consumer Buying: The Party Is Over," *U.S. News & World Report,* August 6, 1979, p. 43.

Food Costs.   Family efforts to hold the line on food costs include trying to cut back on the use of prepared and frozen foods, regularly having meatless meals (for some meat is actually a luxury), eliminating "seconds," and spending less on sweets.

Shopping Patterns.   An integral part of the effort to beat inflation is bargain hunting. Since many consumers assume that inflation will get worse, not better, they believe it is smart to buy as soon as possible, especially when items are on sale. However, this presents a real conflict to families that are trying to cut back. The availability of credit and credit cards makes it especially tempting to go ahead and buy now. Consequently, statistics show that the volume of auto loans outstanding has doubled and that of revolving-credit-card debt has tripled from 1975 to 1978.[11]

Health Care.   Unfortunately, preventive health care is one area in which people try to save money. Many people are postponing regular medical and dental checkups.

Moonlighting.   Another method of coping with inflation that may have health implications is moonlighting. In many families, someone, usually the male head, is forced to supplement the family income with a second or even a third job.

Reading Habits.   Some families cut back on magazine and newspaper subscriptions in order to pare down their expenses. This may result in a public that is less well-informed and less exposed to badly needed money management help.

Making Do.   Families are learning that many objects in their homes are repairable, and that is possible to do with less. For example,

- wearing what clothes they have, rather than buying new ones
- repairing things that they would normally throw out.

Car Repairs.   Car maintenance presents a special problem to most people, for repair costs are increasing at a rapid rate. Most people meet these higher costs by trimming other expenses, but some put off repairs until it is too late and end up with either an accident or a permanently disabled car.

Smaller Cars.   In a 1979 study of auto purchases, the Transportation Department reported that imported cars had increased their market share from 17.9 percent in 1978 to 20.9 percent for the first four months of 1979. Purchases of American subcompacts increased from 10.9 percent to 17.6 percent for the same time period. Conversely,

[11]*Ibid.*, p. 42.

sales fell in both the compact and the intermediate classifications. Americans are clearly looking for a better bargain in miles per gallon. *Working Wives.* Having two incomes in the family is becoming more and more common as a way of dealing with the family's financal problems. Working, however, presents its own problems:

· Frustration rises as additional income does not produce major financial improvement.
· Working spouses lack time for bargain shopping, preparing meals, baking, preserving, canning, and getting things fixed.
· Anger and bitterness grow among those men and/or women who are opposed to having both spouses working.

As the discussion indicates, consumers utilize many avenues to cut spending, some of which are not advantageous in the long run. The postponed medical checkups are particularly damaging in terms of possible consequences. The best way to adjust your spending is to develop a concrete spending plan. During a period of inflation it is difficult to avoid debt if spending is not planned. With extensive use of credit, it takes but a short time to run up excessive bills, particularly now that even grocery stores accept credit cards in many cities.

You might incorporate the following savings tactics in your spending plan:

· Look for clothing bargains at seasonal clearance sales.
· Increase deductibles on insurance policies.
· Shop for a used car or a year-end model rather than a new-year model.
· Buy slightly used household items, tires, baby clothes, furniture, and other goods at yard sales and through classified advertisements in newspapers.
· Adjust thermostats, use appliances sparingly, and take other energy conservation steps.
· Engage in family activities at home instead of traveling.
· Repair your own car.
· Grow your own food.

Adjusting Investment Plans

What investments, if any, have kept pace with inflation? Eugene F. Fama, Professor of Finance at the University of Chicago Graduate School of Business, and G. William Schwert, Assistant Professor of Finance at the University of Rochester Graduate School of Management, investigated this problem. They reported their findings in a December 1977 article in the *Journal of Financial Economics*. [12] Using statistics for the period of 1953–71, they found that real estate was the only investment that offered capital gain increases in times of both anticipated and unanticipated inflation. Capital gains, however, take into consideration only the amount of gain on the sale and not the expenses of maintaining the property.

Although the researchers found that common stock was sometimes a good investment, gains or losses seemed to bear little relationship to inflation. Treasury bills (short-term government investments) were a good hedge against expected inflation but not against unexpected inflation. Unexpected inflation posed a particular problem when the instrument had to be held for a long period of time, as in the case of bonds, or had to be sold at a loss because inflation had forced up the rates on new instruments.

Now, however, because the small investor has become increasingly wary of the stock market (the number of individuals owning shares in public corporations dropped from 30.8 million in 1970 to 25.3 million in 1975), the securities industry is developing new funds to lure the consumer-saver. These funds collect investor money and invest it in instruments such as tax-free municipal bonds, corporation bonds, government treasury instruments, and large bank savings certificates. The investments range from ultraconservative to highly speculative.

Even the insurance industry is offering new types of savings vehicles in addition to the traditional whole life policy. A new type of variable policy, not widely accepted as yet, assures the insured of a certain minimum amount of insurance in return for a fixed annual premium. Most of the premium, though, is invested in a "separate account," which is essentially the company's own internal mutual fund. This fund consists mostly of stock, which one hopes will have increased in value by the time of the insured's death or the time of policy maturity.

A detailed spending plan and a good savings plan, along with a watchful eye on the economic statistics, are the basic elements of a sound financial structure, even in times of severe inflation.

[12]As reported in the *Chicago Tribune*, January 25, 1978, "Inflation Hedges: Some Work, Some Don't, Some Better," by Michael Edgerton.

QUESTIONS FOR DISCUSSION

1. Why do consumers save less during periods of inflation?
2. Explain the importance of the relationship between productivity and increases in salaries.
3. How does money supply affect inflation?
4. Why is inflation referred to as a hidden tax?
5. Contrast the implications of the consumer price index with the implications of the index of leading indicators.
6. Define monetarist. How would a monetarist remedy inflation?
7. How does the government contribute to inflation?
8. Why is it possible for some industries to maintain profits during periods of falling demand?
9. During periods of inflation, does government revenue decrease, increase, or stay the same in dollars? Defend your answer.
10. How has inflation changed the way Americans live?
11. What remedies could be applied to attempt to slow inflation? Which remedy do you think would be most effective?
12. What are some expenses the typical family cuts back on during periods of inflation? What are the possible effects of these cutbacks?

PERSONAL EXPERIENCE PROJECTS

1. Survey various consumers to determine the influence inflation has had on their buying habits and style of living.
2. Through the use of business news articles, find examples of products or services whose prices have increased due to either an increase in demand or a decrease in supply.
3. Analyze the evolution of a product from producer to consumer. Determine the various cost factors involved in the final retail price.
4. Select a variety of products and services commonly used by consumers. Prepare a chart to show changes in the prices of these items from month to month.
5. Ask friends, relatives, and other consumers who they believe to be the main cause of inflation—business, government, consumers, or labor. Obtain suggestions of ways inflation might be reduced.
6. Compare price changes in "competition-dominated" industries to price changes in "concentration-dominated" industries.
7. Propose revisions in governmental regulation of business that would create more competition in our economy.

INDEX